· MILET ·
BILINGUAL VISUAL
DICTIONARY
ENGLISH · CHINESE

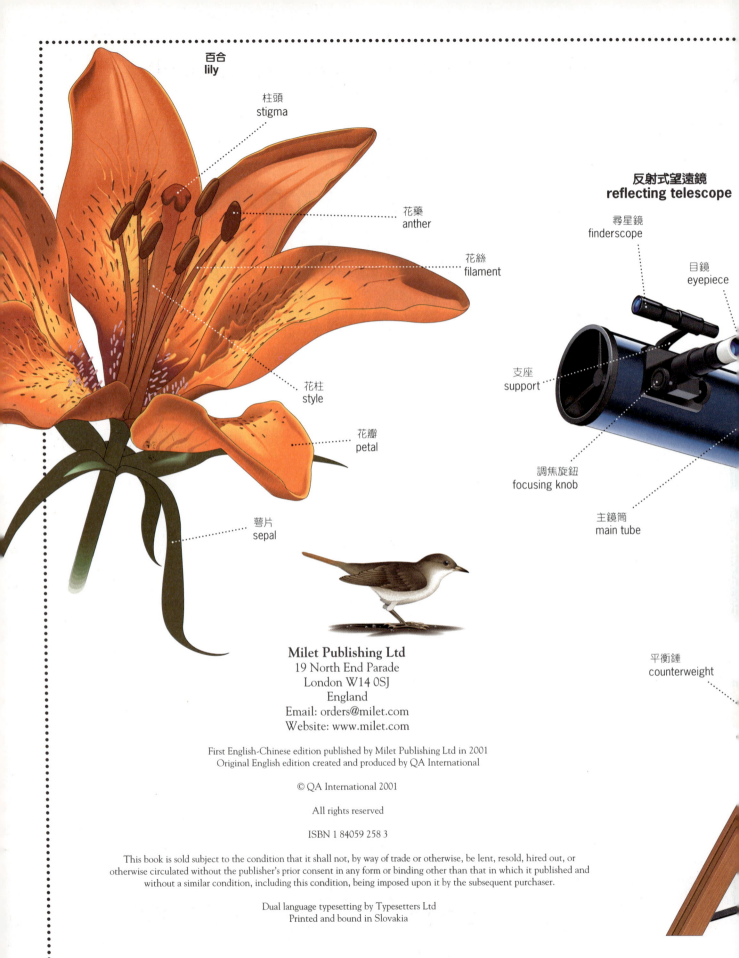

百合
lily

柱頭
stigma

花藥
anther

花絲
filament

花柱
style

花瓣
petal

蕚片
sepal

反射式望遠鏡
reflecting telescope

尋星鏡
finderscope

目鏡
eyepiece

支座
support

調焦旋鈕
focusing knob

主鏡筒
main tube

平衡錘
counterweight

Milet Publishing Ltd
19 North End Parade
London W14 0SJ
England
Email: orders@milet.com
Website: www.milet.com

First English-Chinese edition published by Milet Publishing Ltd in 2001
Original English edition created and produced by QA International

© QA International 2001

ISBN 1 84059 258 3

Dual language typesetting by Typesetters Ltd
Printed and bound in Slovakia

Jean-Claude Corbeil • Ariane Archambault

· MILET ·
BILINGUAL VISUAL
DICTIONARY
ENGLISH · CHINESE

Authors
Jean-Claude Corbeil, Ariane Archambault
Director of Computer Graphics
François Fortin
Art Directors
Jean-Louis Martin, François Fortin
Graphic Designer
Anne Tremblay
Computer Graphic Designers
Marc Lalumière, Jean-Yves Ahern,
Rielle Lévesque, Anne Tremblay, Jacques Perrault,
Jocelyn Gardner, Christiane Beauregard,
Michel Blais, Stéphane Roy, Alice Comtois,
Benoît Bourdeau
Computer Programming
Yves Ferland, Daniel Beaulieu
Data Capture
Serge D'Amico
Page Make-up
Lucie Mc Brearty, Pascal Goyette
Technical Support
Gilles Archambault
Production
Tony O'Riley

Chinese translation by Dai Hong and Wu Wei

Editorial Note: For objects whose English terms are
different in North America and Britain,
we have used both terms: the North American term
followed by the British term. In the
index, these dual terms are listed alphabetically
by the first term.

Translation Note: In cases where there is no direct
Chinese term for an object, the translator has
used an approximate term or a descriptive term.
In cases where the English term is commonly used in
Chinese, or where there is no Chinese term,
the translator has used a transliteration of
the English term.

THEMES AND SUBJECTS

SKY

EARTH

PLANT KINGDOM

FRUITS AND VEGETABLES

GARDENING

ANIMAL KINGDOM

HUMAN BODY

ARCHITECTURE

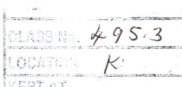

HOUSE

DO-IT-YOURSELF

CLOTHING

PERSONAL ARTICLES

COMMUNICATIONS

5

太陽系
SOLAR SYSTEM

行星與衛星
planets and moons

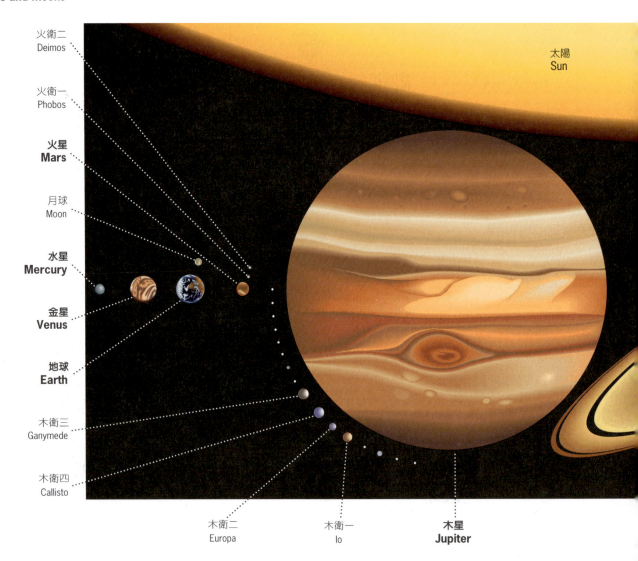

火衛二
Deimos

火衛一
Phobos

火星
Mars

月球
Moon

水星
Mercury

金星
Venus

地球
Earth

木衛三
Ganymede

木衛四
Callisto

太陽
Sun

木衛二
Europa

木衛一
Io

木星
Jupiter

行星軌道
orbits of the planets

小行星帶
asteroid belt

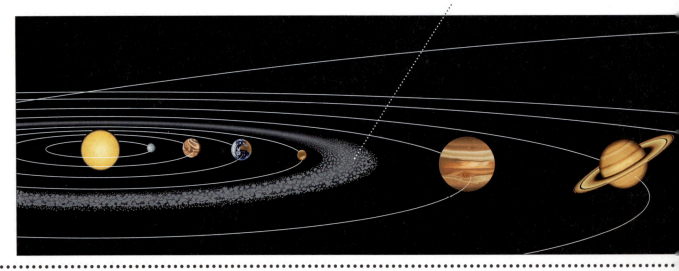

海王星
Neptune

冥王星
Pluto

卡戎（冥王星衛星）
Charon

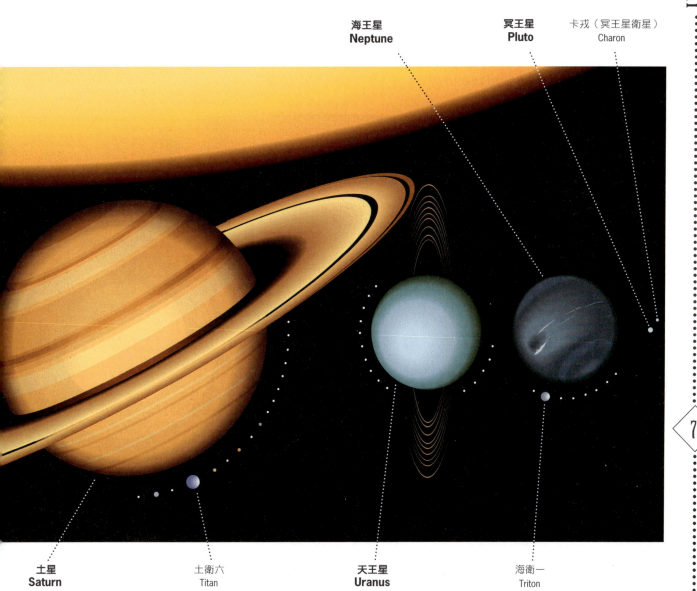

土星
Saturn

土衛六
Titan

天王星
Uranus

海衛一
Triton

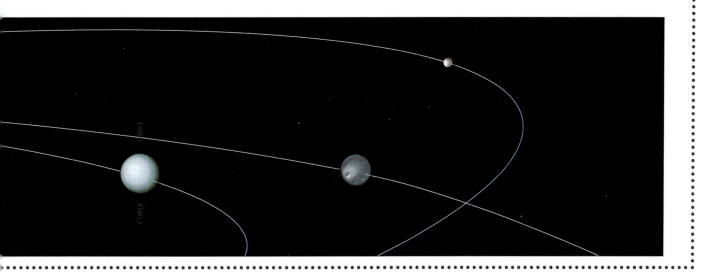

太陽
SUN

太陽的構造
structure of the Sun

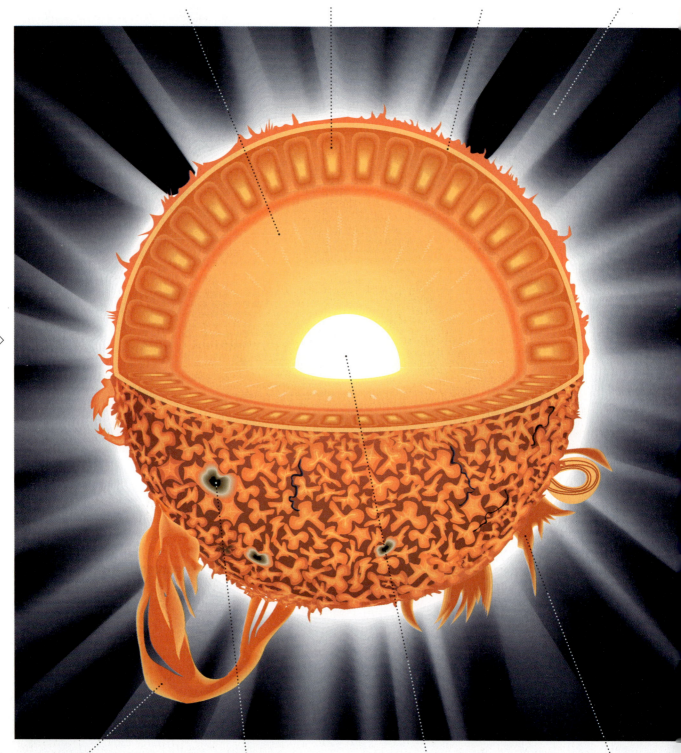

輻射區
radiation zone

對流層
convection zone

太陽表面
Sun's surface

日冕
corona

8

日珥
prominence

太陽黑子
sunspot

日核
core

太陽耀斑
flare

月球
MOON

月貌特征
lunar features

灣
bay

峭壁
cliff

洋
ocean

湖
lake

海
sea

山脈
mountain range

火山坑
crater

盆沿
wall

月球盆地
cirque

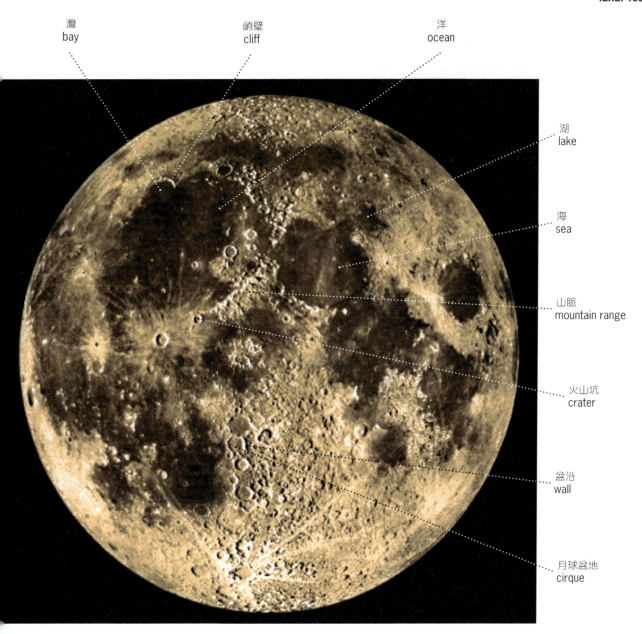

月相
PHASES OF THE MOON

盈蛾眉月
new crescent

盈凸月
waxing gibbous Moon

虧凸月
waning gibbous Moon

虧蛾眉月
old crescent

新月
new Moon

上弦月
first quarter

滿月
full Moon

下弦月
last quarter

彗星
COMET

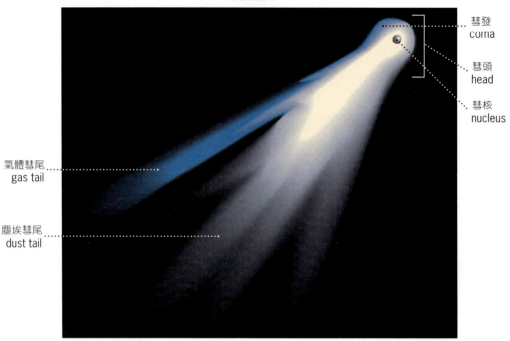

彗發
corna

彗頭
head

彗核
nucleus

氣體彗尾
gas tail

塵埃彗尾
dust tail

日食
SOLAR ECLIPSE

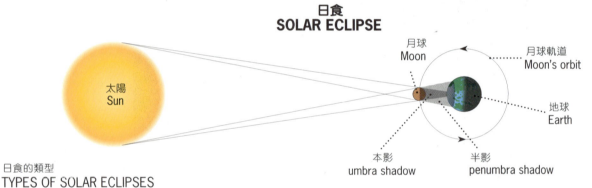

月球
Moon

月球軌道
Moon's orbit

太陽
Sun

地球
Earth

本影
umbra shadow

半影
penumbra shadow

日食的類型
TYPES OF SOLAR ECLIPSES

日全食
total eclipse

日環食
annular eclipse

日偏食
partial eclipse

月食
LUNAR ECLIPSE

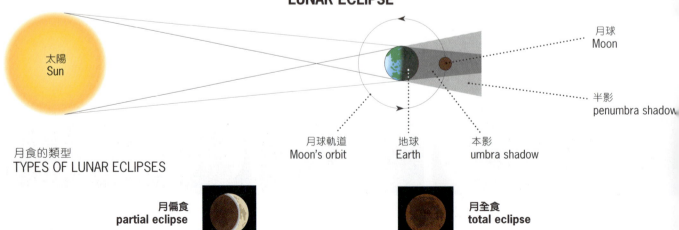

太陽
Sun

月球
Moon

半影
penumbra shadow

月球軌道
Moon's orbit

地球
Earth

本影
umbra shadow

月食的類型
TYPES OF LUNAR ECLIPSES

月偏食
partial eclipse

月全食
total eclipse

反射式望遠鏡
REFLECTING TELESCOPE

尋星鏡
finderscope

目鏡
eyepiece

主鏡筒
main tube

調焦旋鈕
focusing knob

赤緯標尺
declination setting scale

平經夾
azimuth clamp

赤經標尺
right ascension setting scale

平緯夾
altitude clamp

平經度微調
azimuth fine adjustment

平緯度微調
altitude fine adjustment

反射式望遠鏡橫斷面
cross section of a reflecting telescope

目鏡
eyepiece

主鏡筒
main tube

主鏡
main mirror

反射鏡
flat mirror

光線
light

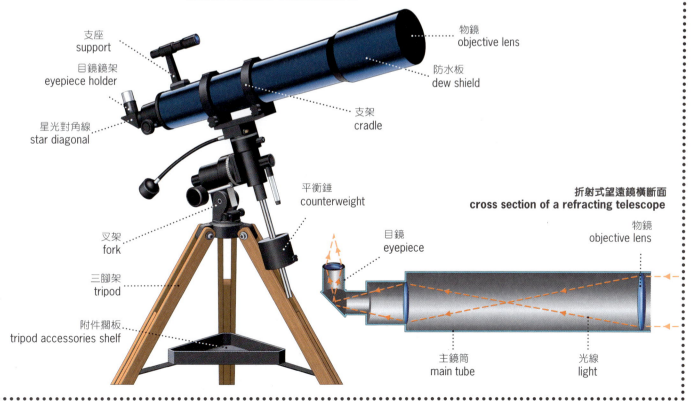

折射式望遠鏡
REFRACTING TELESCOPE

支座
support

目鏡鏡架
eyepiece holder

星光對角線
star diagonal

物鏡
objective lens

防水板
dew shield

支架
cradle

平衡錘
counterweight

叉架
fork

三腳架
tripod

附件擱板
tripod accessories shelf

折射式望遠鏡橫斷面
cross section of a refracting telescope

目鏡
eyepiece

物鏡
objective lens

主鏡筒
main tube

光線
light

地球坐標系
EARTH COORDINATE SYSTEM

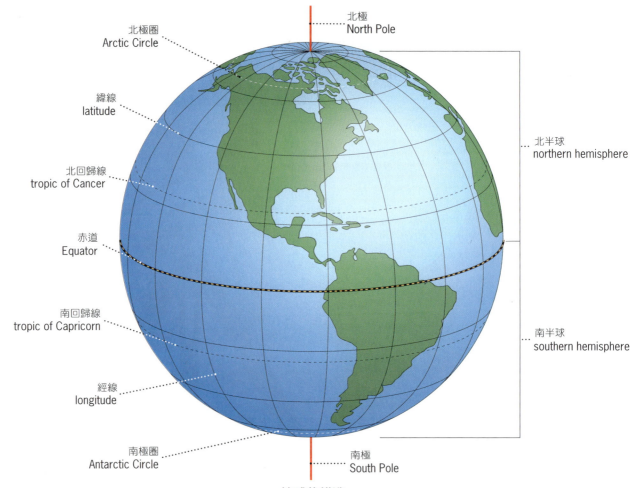

北極
North Pole

北極圈
Arctic Circle

緯線
latitude

北回歸線
tropic of Cancer

赤道
Equator

南回歸線
tropic of Capricorn

經線
longitude

南極圈
Antarctic Circle

南極
South Pole

北半球
northern hemisphere

南半球
southern hemisphere

地球的構造
STRUCTURE OF THE EARTH

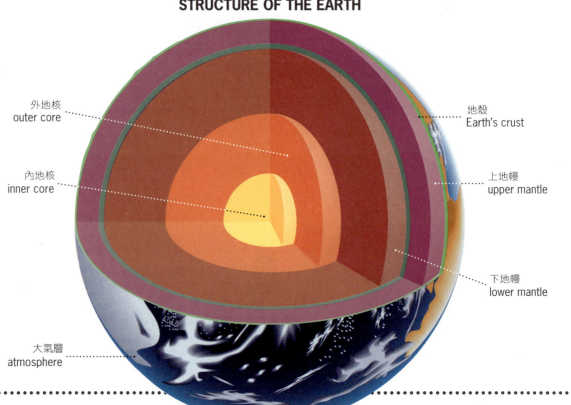

外地核
outer core

內地核
inner core

大氣層
atmosphere

地殼
Earth's crust

上地幔
upper mantle

下地幔
lower mantle

地震
EARTHQUAKE

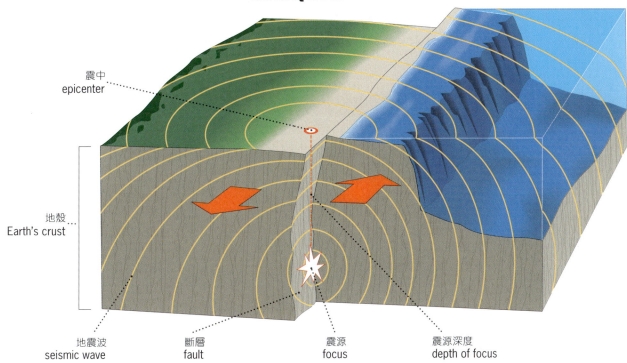

震中
epicenter

地殼
Earth's crust

地震波
seismic wave

斷層
fault

震源
focus

震源深度
depth of focus

洞穴
CAVE

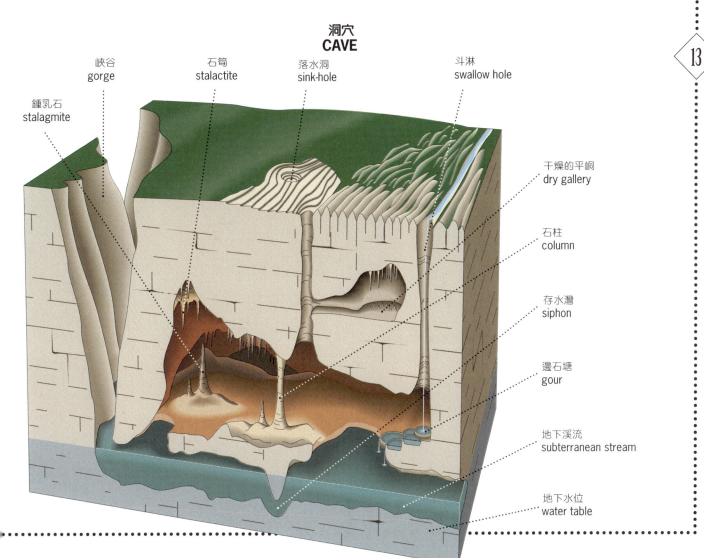

峽谷
gorge

石筍
stalactite

落水洞
sink-hole

斗淋
swallow hole

鍾乳石
stalagmite

干燥的平峒
dry gallery

石柱
column

存水灣
siphon

邊石塘
gour

地下溪流
subterranean stream

地下水位
water table

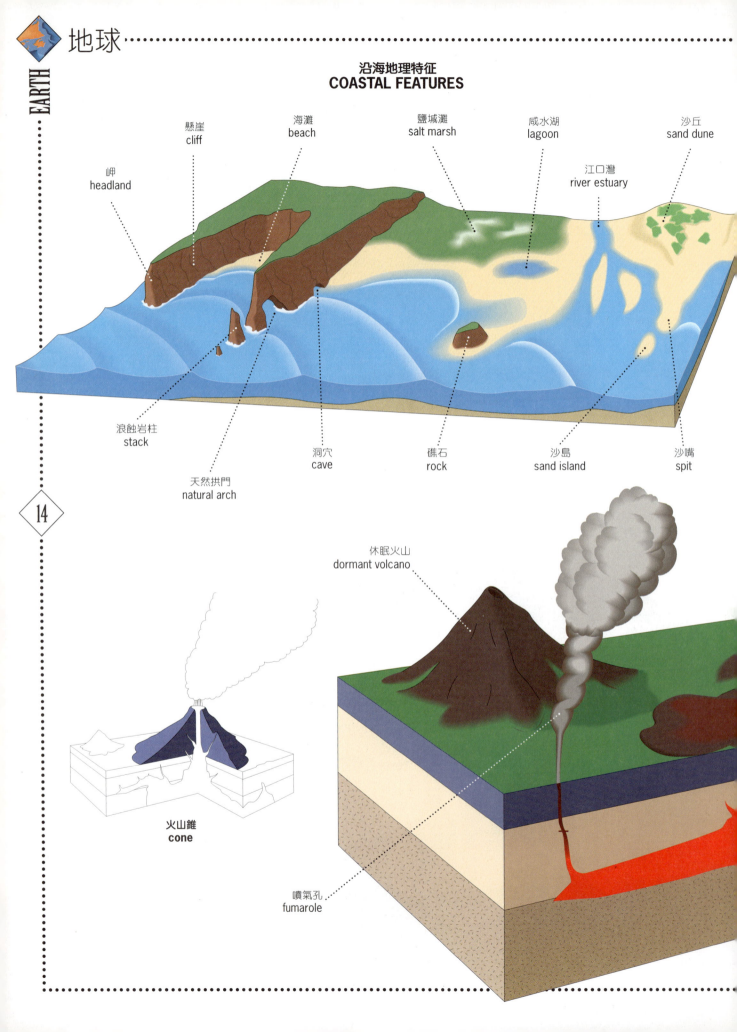

沿海地理特征
COASTAL FEATURES

岬
headland

懸崖
cliff

海灘
beach

鹽域灘
salt marsh

咸水湖
lagoon

江口灣
river estuary

沙丘
sand dune

浪蝕岩柱
stack

天然拱門
natural arch

洞穴
cave

礁石
rock

沙島
sand island

沙嘴
spit

火山錐
cone

休眠火山
dormant volcano

噴氣孔
fumarole

14

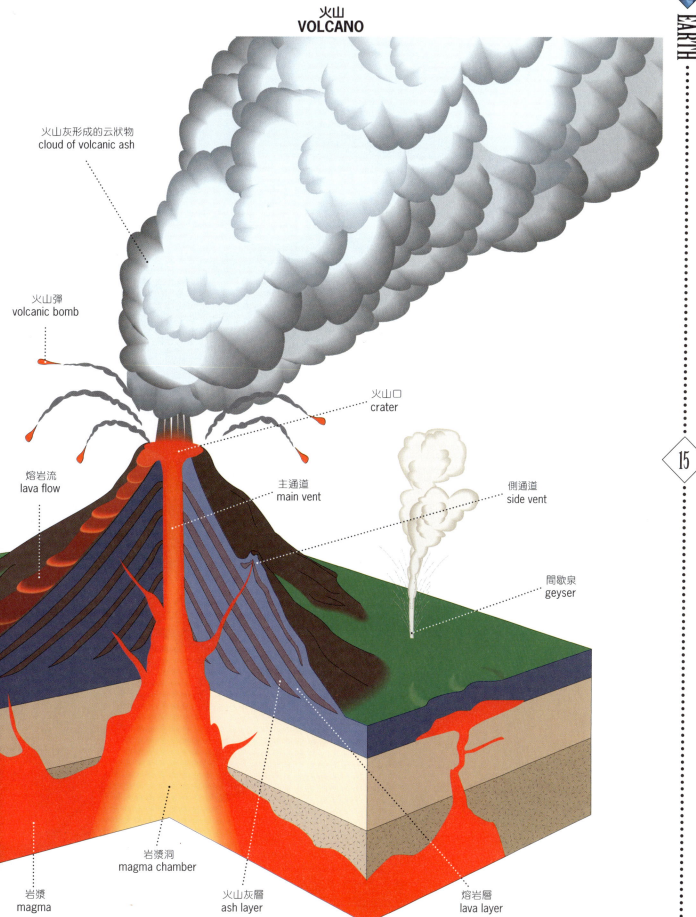

火山
VOLCANO

火山灰形成的云狀物
cloud of volcanic ash

火山彈
volcanic bomb

火山口
crater

熔岩流
lava flow

主通道
main vent

側通道
side vent

間歇泉
geyser

岩漿洞
magma chamber

岩漿
magma

火山灰層
ash layer

熔岩層
lava layer

冰川
GLACIER

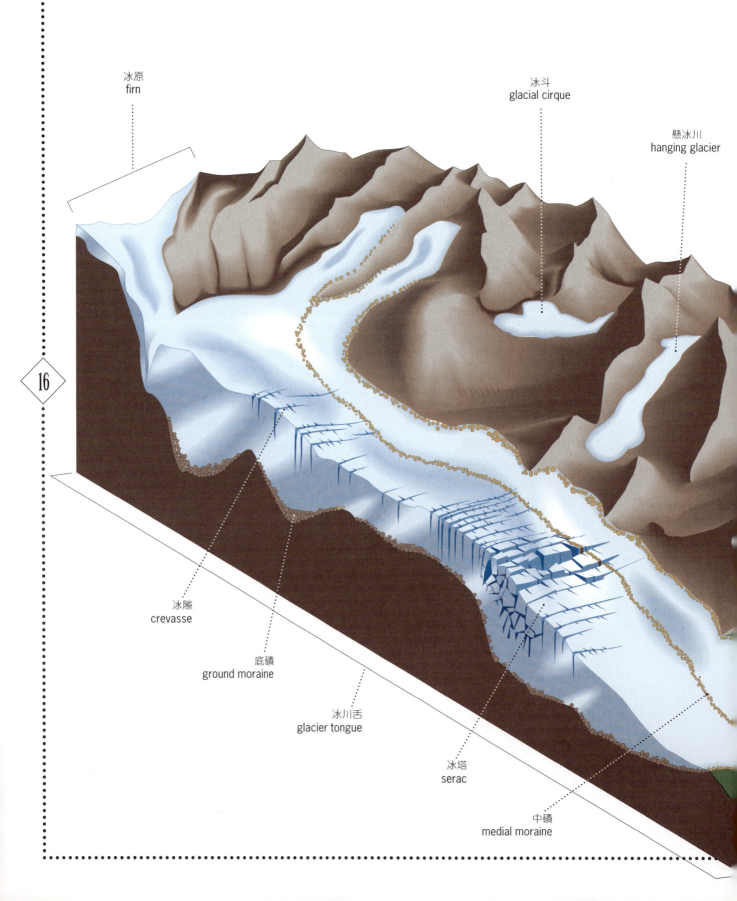

冰原
firn

冰斗
glacial cirque

懸冰川
hanging glacier

16

冰隙
crevasse

底磧
ground moraine

冰川舌
glacier tongue

冰塔
serac

中磧
medial moraine

山脈
MOUNTAIN

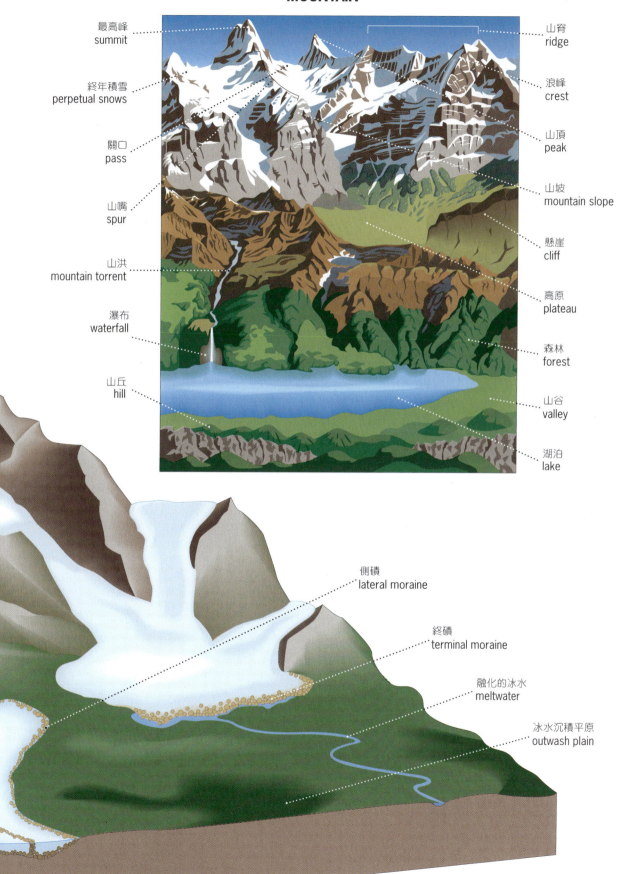

最高峰
summit

終年積雪
perpetual snows

關口
pass

山嘴
spur

山洪
mountain torrent

瀑布
waterfall

山丘
hill

山脊
ridge

浪峰
crest

山頂
peak

山坡
mountain slope

懸崖
cliff

高原
plateau

森林
forest

山谷
valley

湖泊
lake

側磧
lateral moraine

終磧
terminal moraine

融化的冰水
meltwater

冰水沉積平原
outwash plain

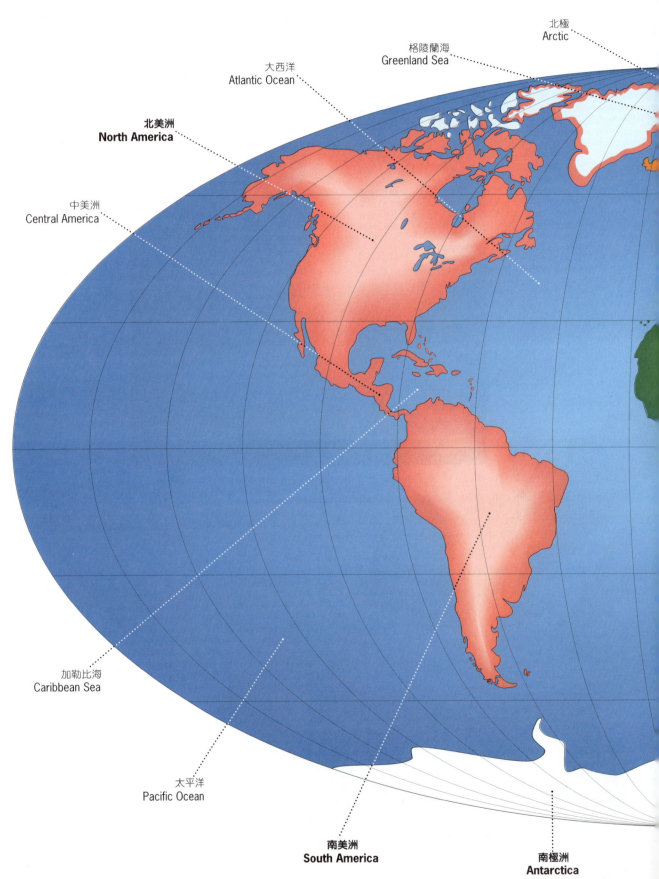

大陸
THE CONTINENTS

北極
Arctic

格陵蘭海
Greenland Sea

大西洋
Atlantic Ocean

北美洲
North America

中美洲
Central America

加勒比海
Caribbean Sea

太平洋
Pacific Ocean

南美洲
South America

南極洲
Antarctica

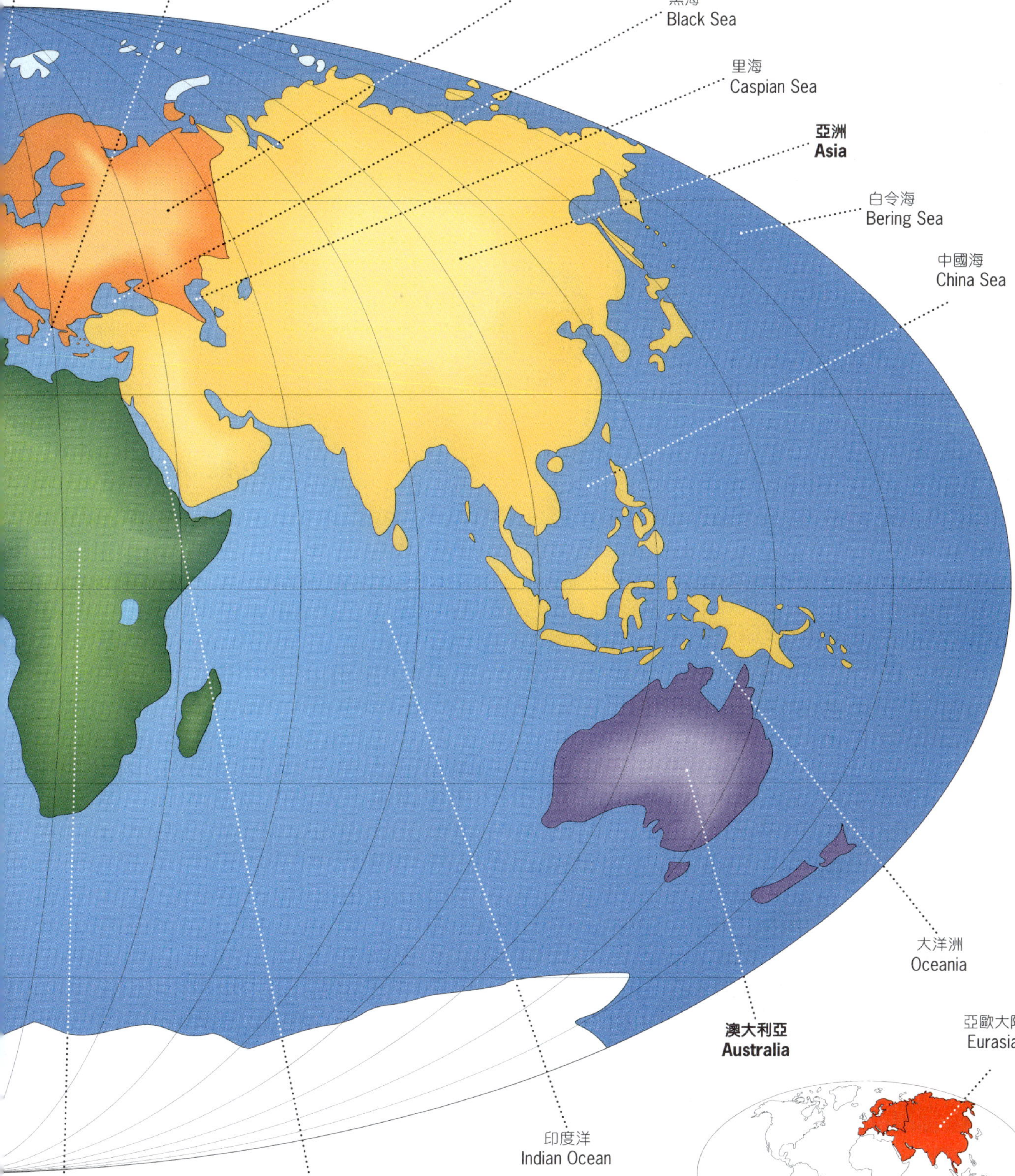

北海
North Sea

地中海
Mediterranean Sea

北冰洋
Arctic Ocean

歐洲
Europe

黑海
Black Sea

里海
Caspian Sea

亞洲
Asia

白令海
Bering Sea

中國海
China Sea

大洋洲
Oceania

亞歐大陸
Eurasia

印度洋
Indian Ocean

澳大利亞
Australia

非洲
Africa

紅海
Red Sea

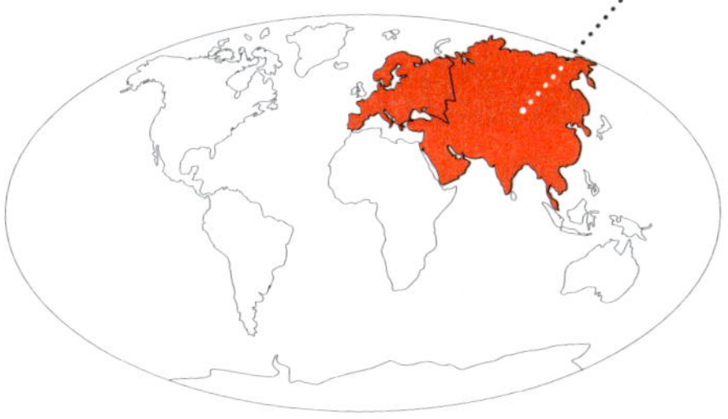

地球 ·

EARTH

一年四季
SEASONS OF THE YEAR

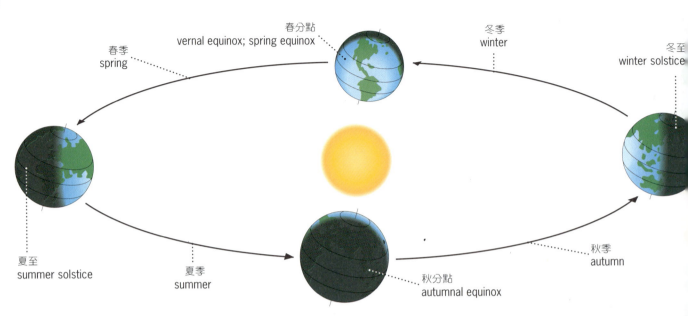

春季
spring

春分點
vernal equinox; spring equinox

冬季
winter

冬至
winter solstice

夏至
summer solstice

夏季
summer

秋分點
autumnal equinox

秋季
autumn

生物圈的構成
STRUCTURE OF THE BIOSPHERE

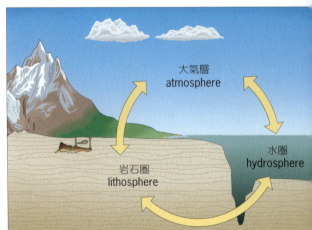

大氣層
atmosphere

岩石圈
lithosphere

水圈
hydrosphere

海拔地帶與植被
ELEVATION ZONES AND VEGETATION

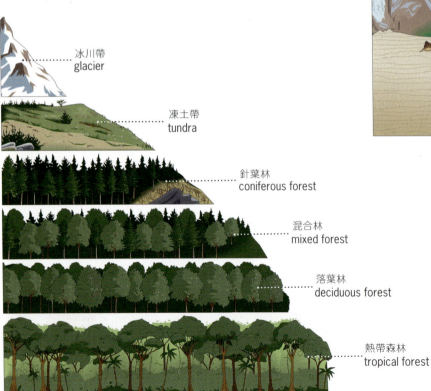

冰川帶
glacier

凍土帶
tundra

針葉林
coniferous forest

混合林
mixed forest

落葉林
deciduous forest

熱帶森林
tropical forest

世界氣候
CLIMATES OF THE WORLD

熱帶氣候
tropical climates

熱帶雨林氣候
tropical rain forest

熱帶大草原氣候
tropical savanna

大平原氣候
steppe

沙漠氣候
desert

溫帶氣候
temperate climates

長濕夏季氣候
humid - long summer

短濕夏季氣候
humid - short summer

海洋氣候
marine

極地氣候
polar climates

極地凍土帶氣候
polar tundra

極地冰冠氣候
polar ice cap

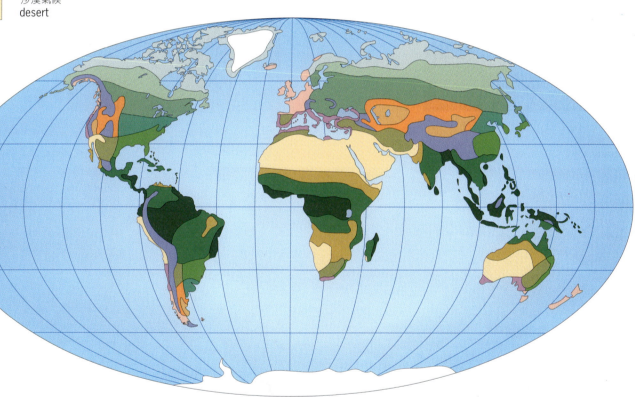

亞熱帶氣候
subtropical climates

地中海亞熱帶氣候
Mediterranean subtropical

亞熱帶潮濕氣候
humid subtropical

亞熱帶干燥氣候
dry subtropical

大陸性氣候
continental climates

大陸性干燥氣候
dry continental - arid

大陸性半干燥氣候
dry continental - semiarid

高原氣候
highland climates

高原氣候
highland climates

亞北極氣候
subarctic climates

亞北極氣候
subarctic climates

天氣
WEATHER

薄霧
mist

濃霧
fog

露水
dew

霜凍
glazed frost

暴風雨天氣
stormy sky

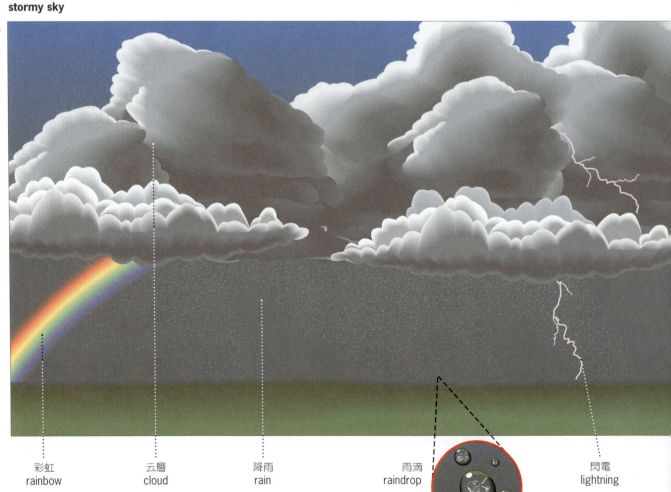

彩虹
rainbow

云層
cloud

降雨
rain

雨滴
raindrop

閃電
lightning

氣象觀測儀器
METEOROLOGICAL MEASURING INSTRUMENTS

風力測量
MEASURE OF WIND STRENGTH

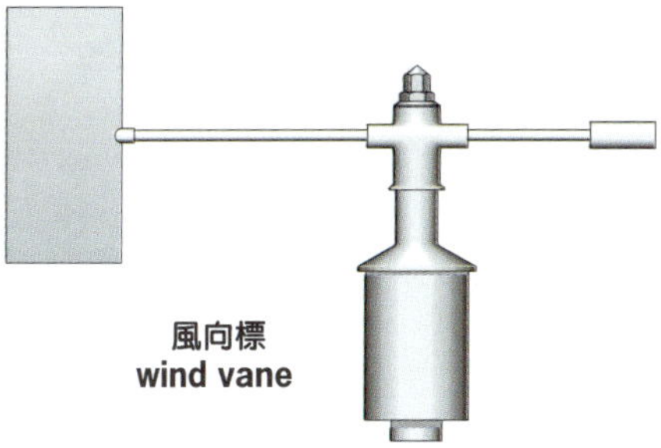

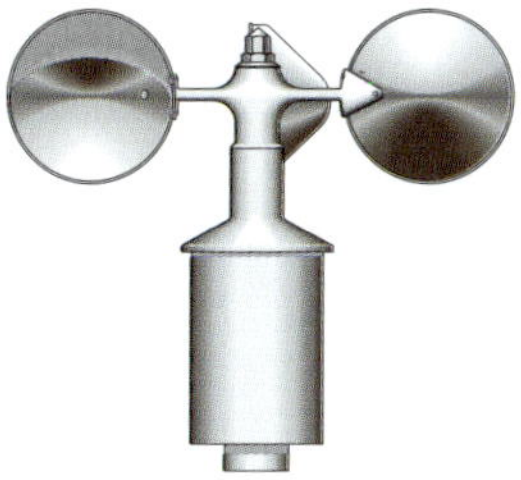

濕度測量
MEASURE OF HUMIDITY

風向標
wind vane

風速表
anemometer

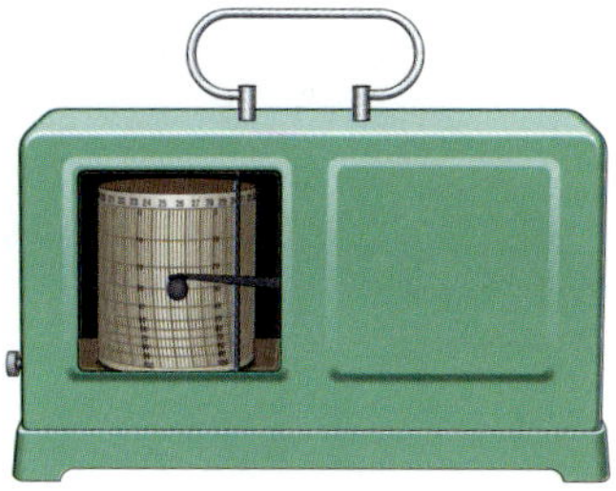

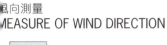

濕度計
hygrograph

降雨量測量
MEASURE OF RAINFALL

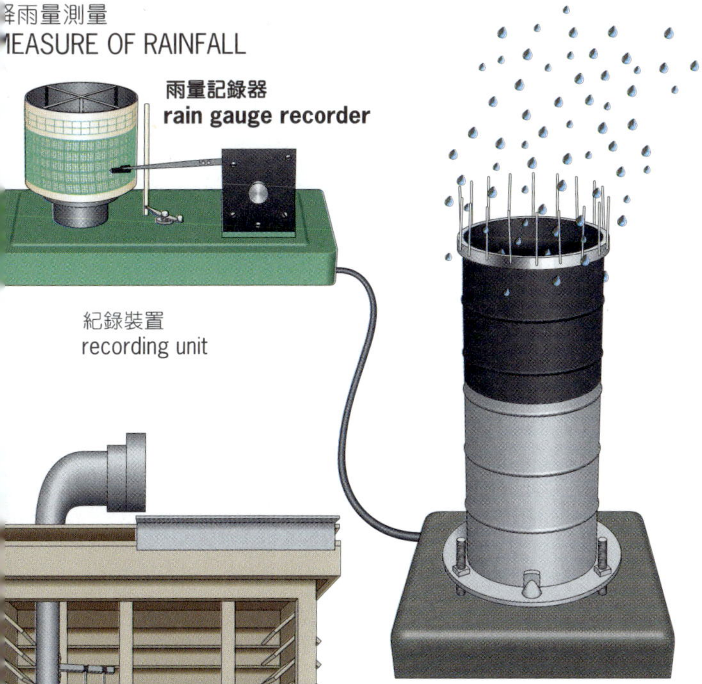

雨量記錄器
rain gauge recorder

紀錄裝置
recording unit

雨量直讀器
direct-reading rain gauge

雨水收集漏斗
collecting funnel

測量管
measuring tube

密封帶
tightening band

容器
container

支撐物
support

雨水收集器
collecting vessel

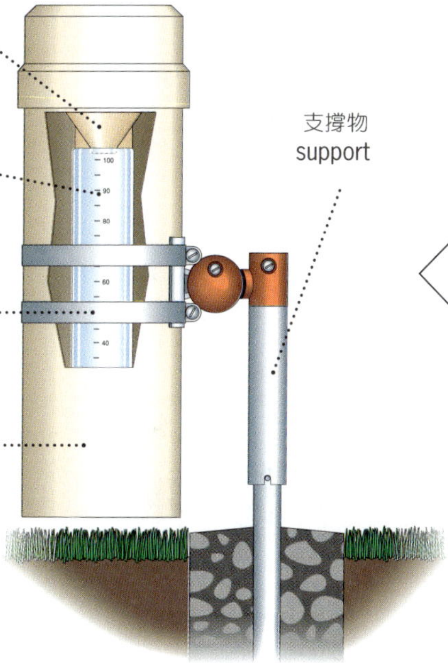

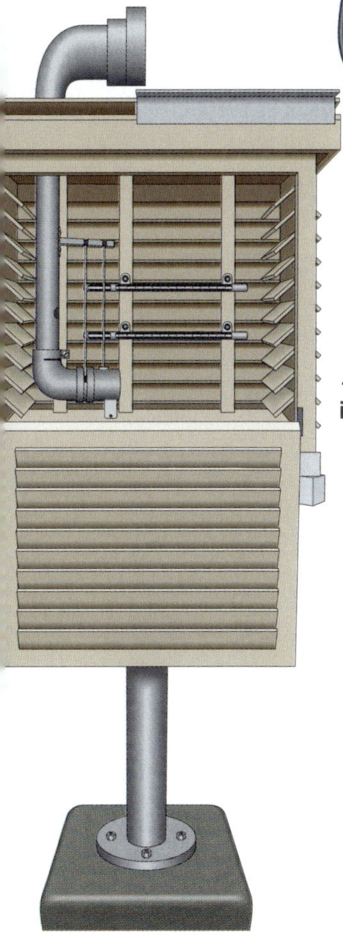

儀器箱
instrument shelter

氣壓測量
MEASURE OF AIR PRESSURE

氣溫測量
MEASURE OF TEMPERATURE

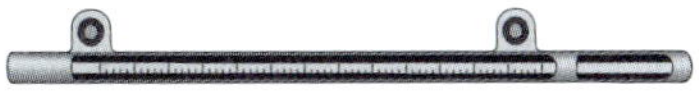

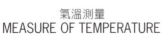

最低溫度計
minimum thermometer

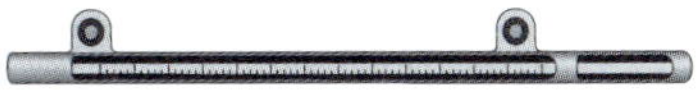

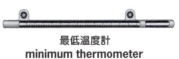

最高溫度計
maximum thermometer

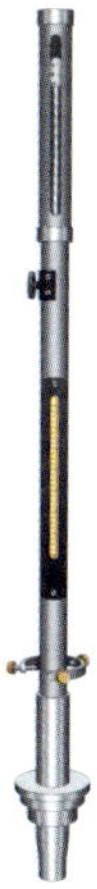

水銀氣壓表
mercury barometer

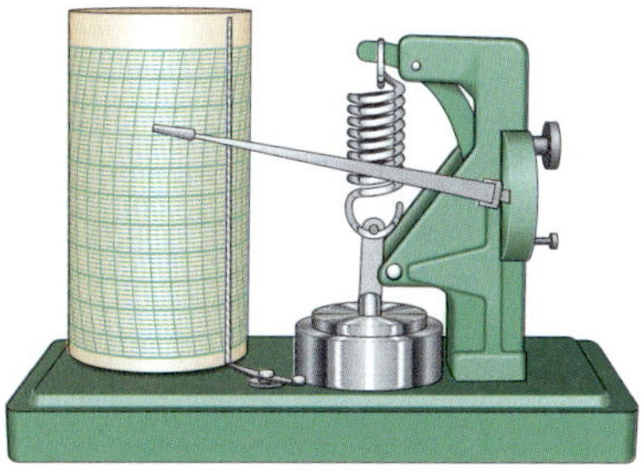

氣壓表
barograph

制圖學
CARTOGRAPHY

半球
hemispheres

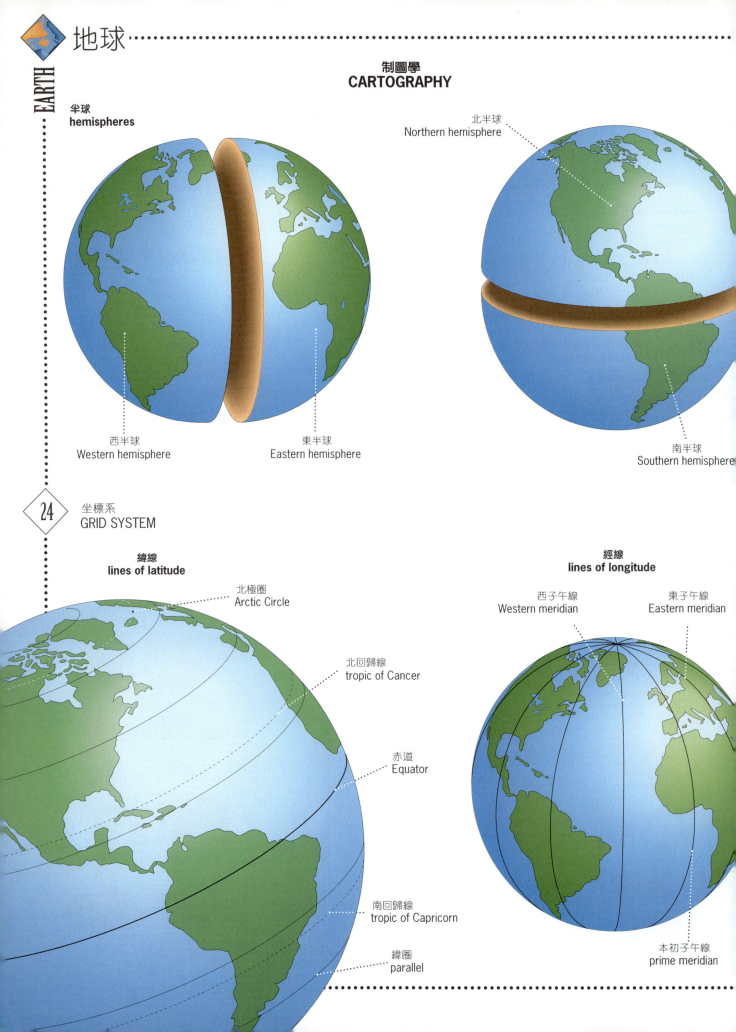

北半球
Northern hemisphere

西半球
Western hemisphere

東半球
Eastern hemisphere

南半球
Southern hemisphere

24

坐標系
GRID SYSTEM

緯線
lines of latitude

北極圈
Arctic Circle

北回歸線
tropic of Cancer

赤道
Equator

南回歸線
tropic of Capricorn

緯圈
parallel

經線
lines of longitude

西子午線
Western meridian

東子午線
Eastern meridian

本初子午線
prime meridian

地圖投影
MAP PROJECTIONS

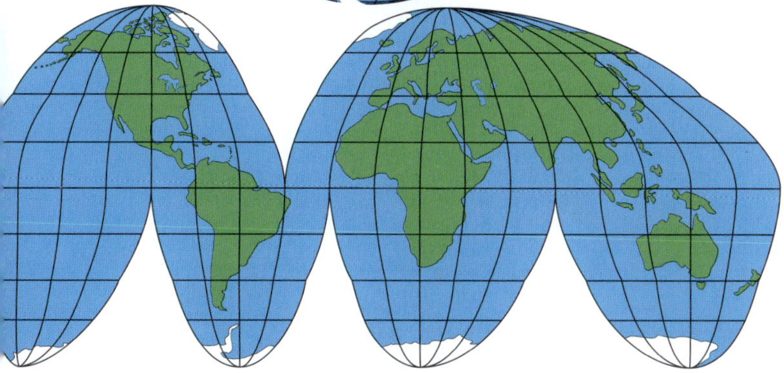

中斷投影
interrupted projection

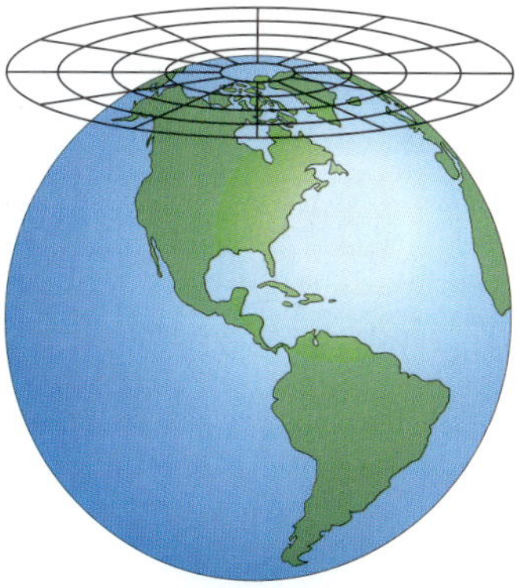

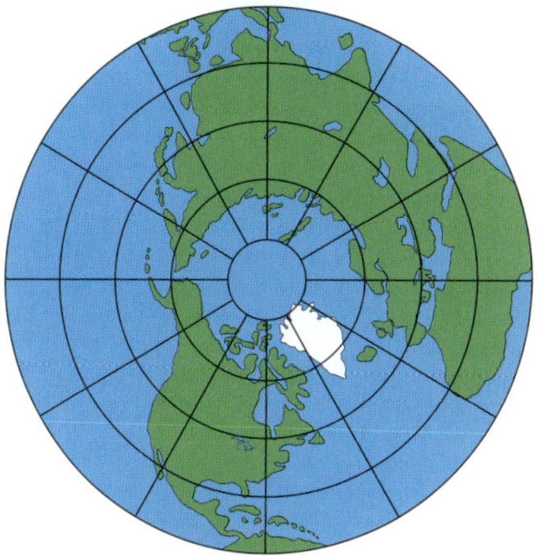

平面投影
plane projection

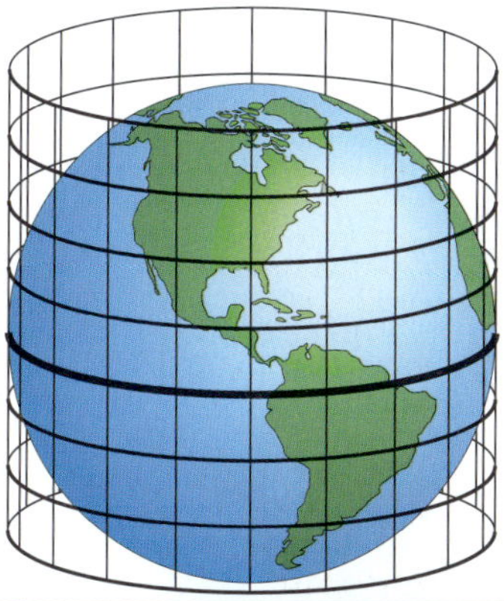

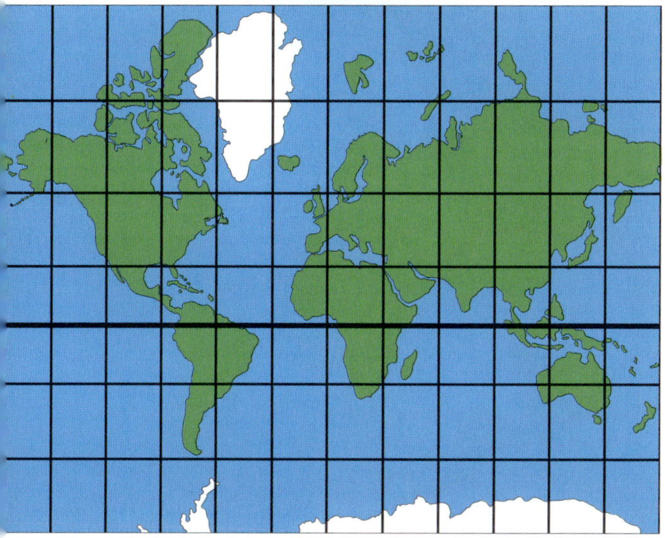

圓柱形投影
cylindrical projection

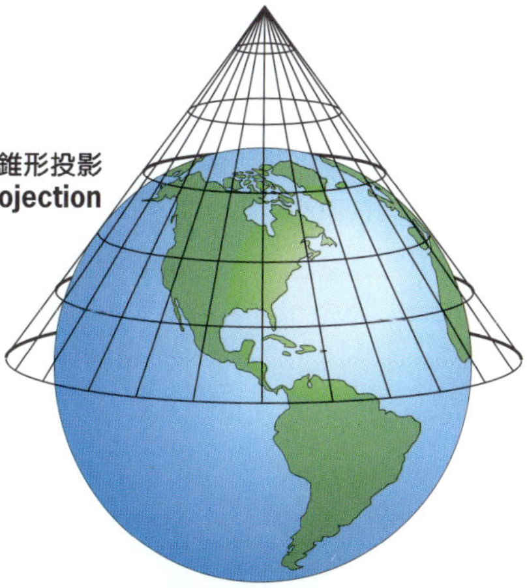

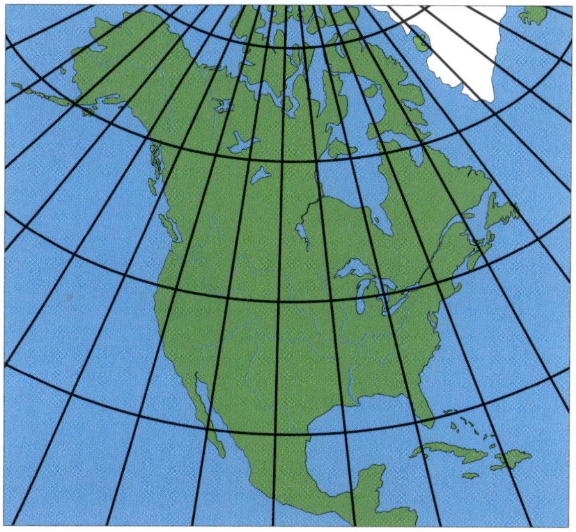

圓錐形投影
conical projection

EARTH

制圖學
CARTOGRAPHY

行政地圖
political map

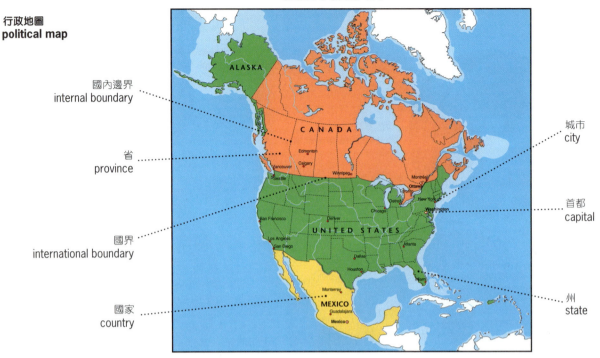

國內邊界
internal boundary

省
province

國界
international boundary

國家
country

城市
city

首都
capital

州
state

自然地圖
physical map

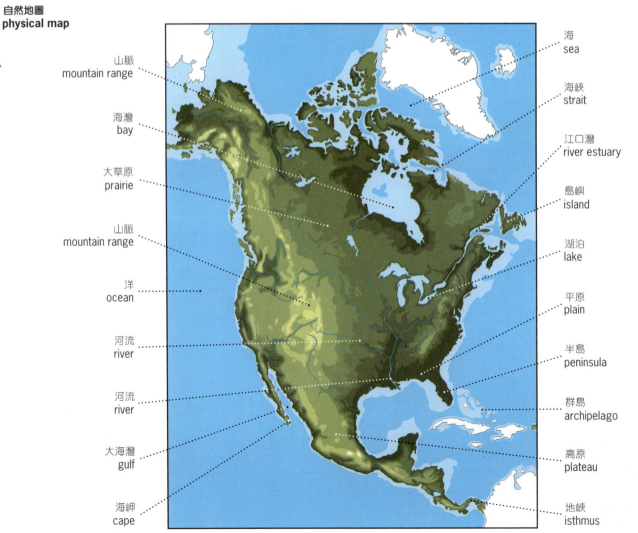

山脈
mountain range

海灣
bay

大草原
prairie

山脈
mountain range

洋
ocean

河流
river

河流
river

大海灣
gulf

海岬
cape

海
sea

海峽
strait

江口灣
river estuary

島嶼
island

湖泊
lake

平原
plain

半島
peninsula

群島
archipelago

高原
plateau

地峽
isthmus

公路地圖
road map

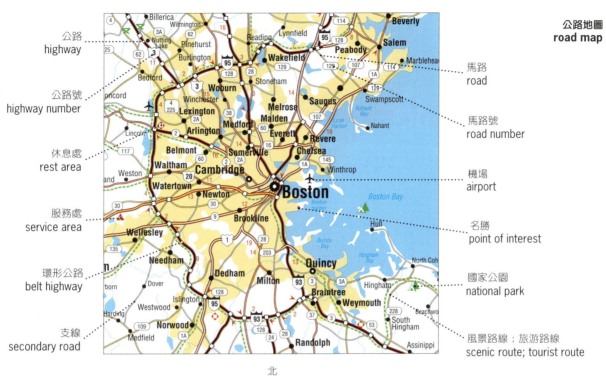

公路
highway

公路號
highway number

休息處
rest area

服務處
service area

環形公路
belt highway

支線
secondary road

馬路
road

馬路號
road number

機場
airport

名勝
point of interest

國家公園
national park

風景路線；旅游路線
scenic route; tourist route

羅盤盤面
COMPASS CARD

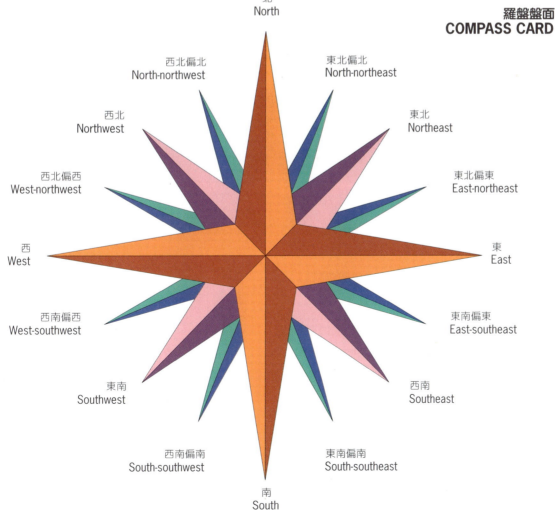

北
North

西北偏北
North-northwest

東北偏北
North-northeast

西北
Northwest

東北
Northeast

西北偏西
West-northwest

東北偏東
East-northeast

西
West

東
East

西南偏西
West-southwest

東南偏東
East-southeast

東南
Southwest

西南
Southeast

西南偏南
South-southwest

東南偏南
South-southeast

南
South

EARTH

生態學
ECOLOGY

温室效應
greenhouse effect

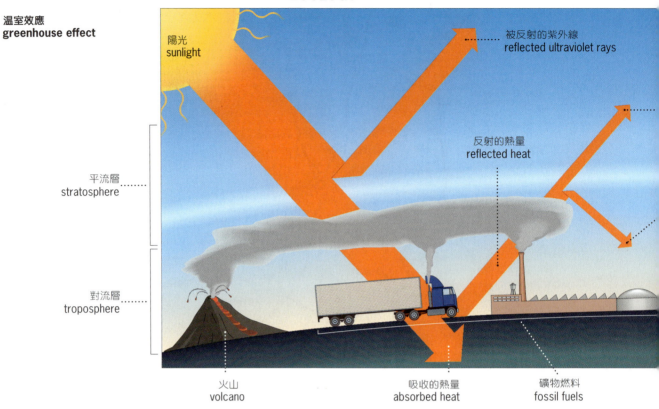

陽光
sunlight

被反射的紫外線
reflected ultraviolet rays

反射的熱量
reflected heat

平流層
stratosphere

對流層
troposphere

火山
volcano

吸收的熱量
absorbed heat

礦物燃料
fossil fuels

食物鏈
food chain

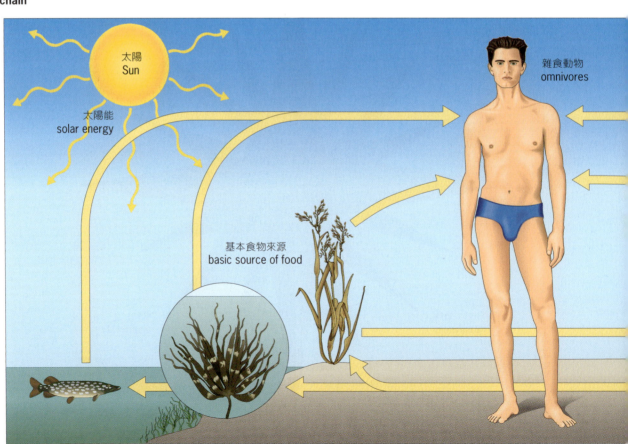

太陽
Sun

雜食動物
omnivores

太陽能
solar energy

基本食物來源
basic source of food

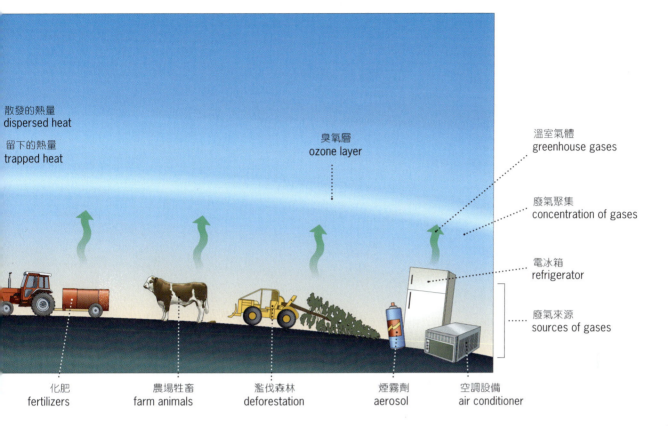

散發的熱量 dispersed heat
留下的熱量 trapped heat
臭氧層 ozone layer
溫室氣體 greenhouse gases
廢氣聚集 concentration of gases
電冰箱 refrigerator
廢氣來源 sources of gases
化肥 fertilizers
農場牲畜 farm animals
濫伐森林 deforestation
煙霧劑 aerosol
空調設備 air conditioner

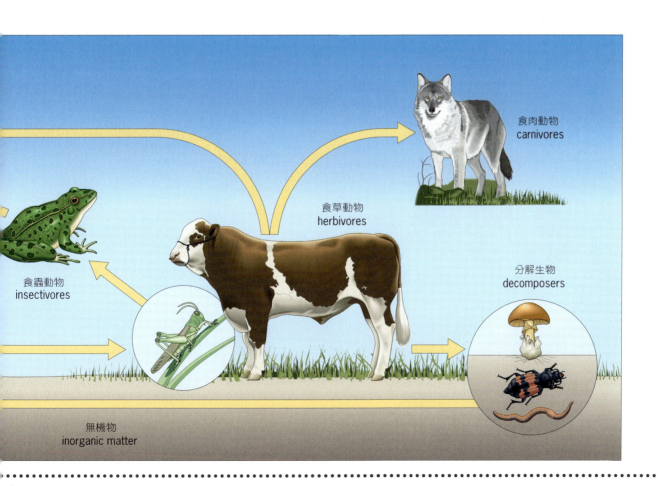

食肉動物 carnivores
食草動物 herbivores
分解生物 decomposers
食蟲動物 insectivores
無機物 inorganic matter

生態學
ECOLOGY

大氣污染
atmospheric pollution

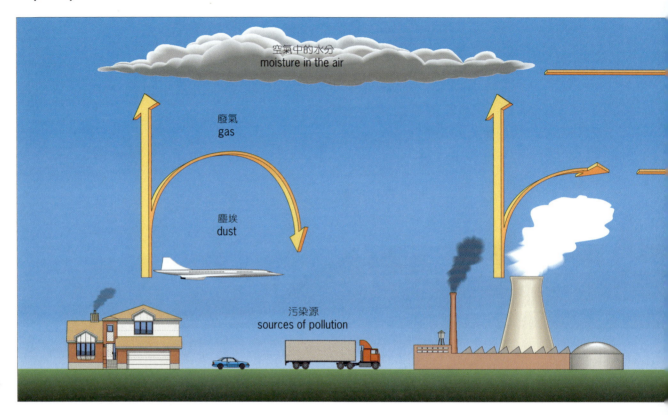

空氣中的水分
moisture in the air

廢氣
gas

塵埃
dust

污染源
sources of pollution

水的循環
water cycle

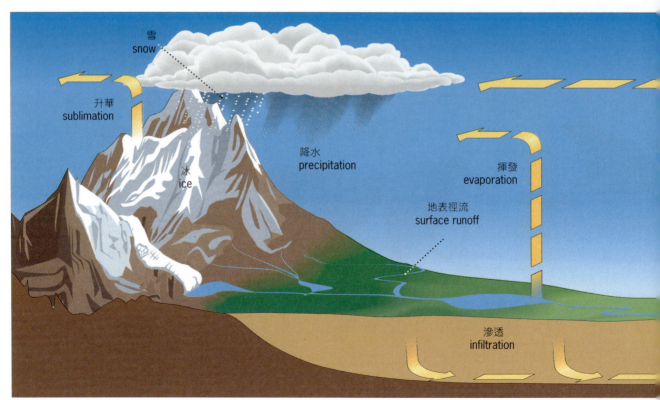

雪
snow

升華
sublimation

冰
ice

降水
precipitation

揮發
evaporation

地表徑流
surface runoff

滲透
infiltration

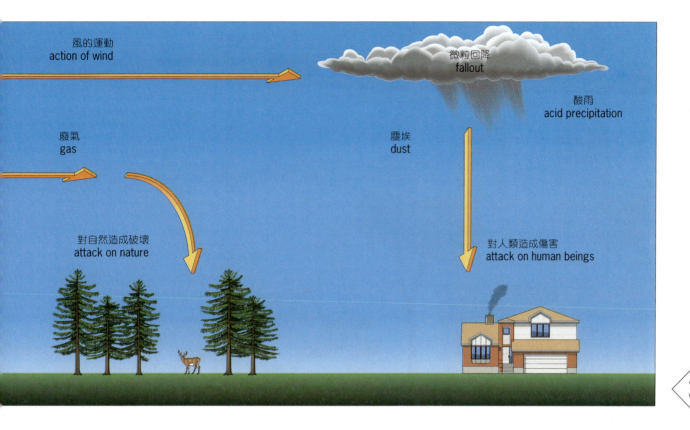

風的運動
action of wind

微粒回降
fallout

酸雨
acid precipitation

廢氣
gas

塵埃
dust

對自然造成破壞
attack on nature

對人類造成傷害
attack on human beings

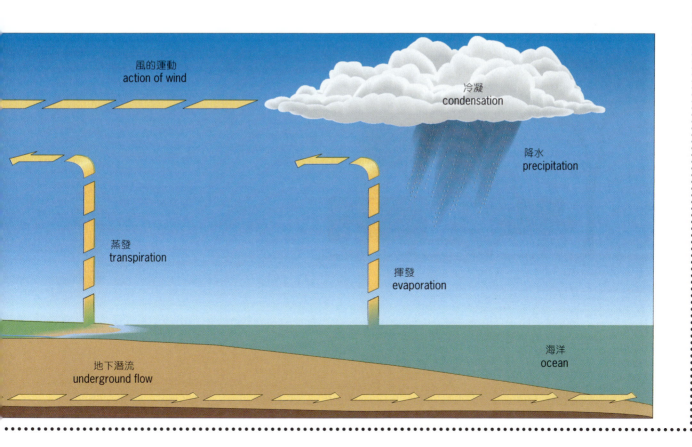

風的運動
action of wind

冷凝
condensation

降水
precipitation

蒸發
transpiration

揮發
evaporation

海洋
ocean

地下潛流
underground flow

生態學
ECOLOGY

地面食物污染
food pollution on ground

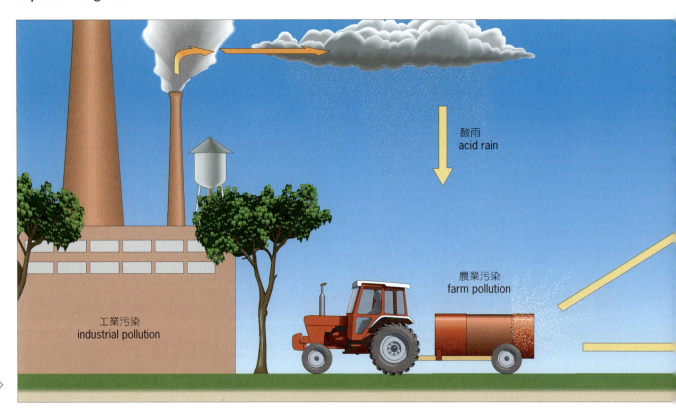

酸雨
acid rain

農業污染
farm pollution

工業污染
industrial pollution

水中食物污染
food pollution in water

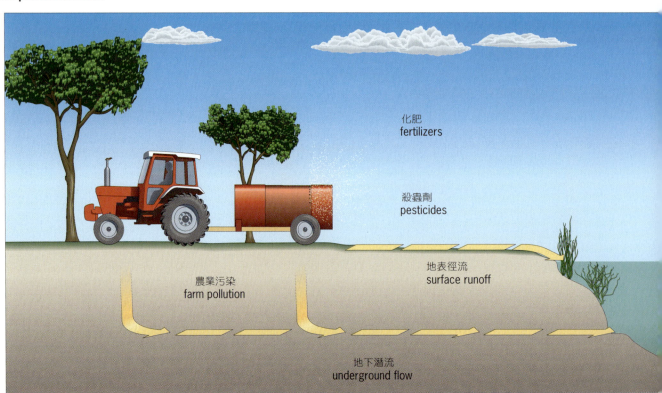

化肥
fertilizers

殺蟲劑
pesticides

地表徑流
surface runoff

農業污染
farm pollution

地下潛流
underground flow

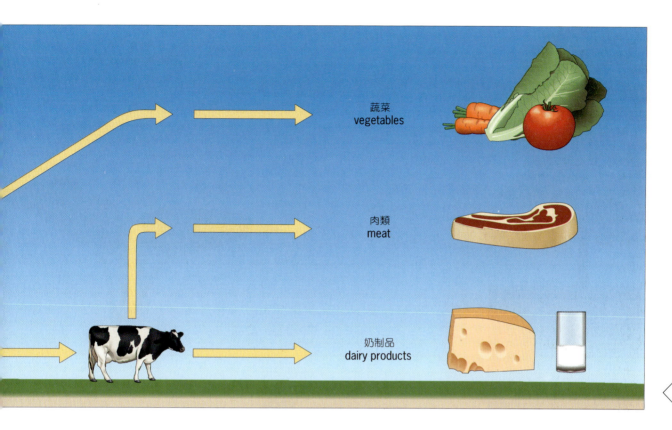

蔬菜
vegetables

肉類
meat

奶制品
dairy products

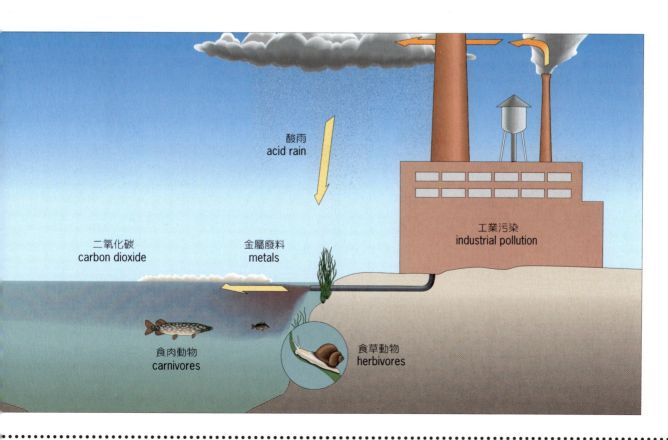

酸雨
acid rain

二氧化碳
carbon dioxide

金屬廢料
metals

工業污染
industrial pollution

食肉動物
carnivores

食草動物
herbivores

植物王國

植物與土壤
PLANT AND SOIL

土壤剖面圖
SOIL PROFILE

發芽
GERMINATION

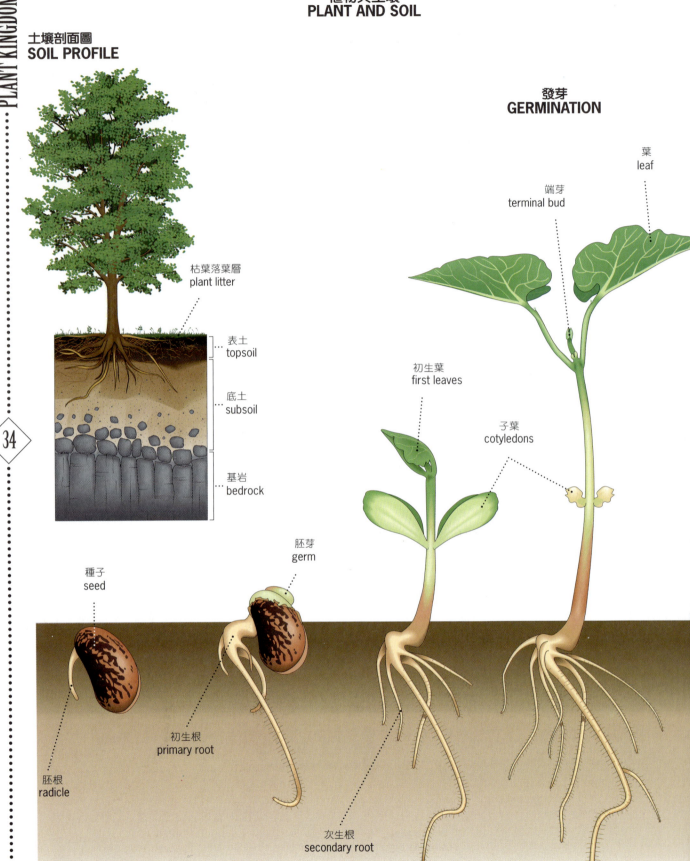

枯葉落葉層
plant litter

表土
topsoil

底土
subsoil

基岩
bedrock

葉
leaf

端芽
terminal bud

初生葉
first leaves

子葉
cotyledons

胚芽
germ

種子
seed

初生根
primary root

胚根
radicle

次生根
secondary root

根毛
root hairs

蘑菇
MUSHROOM

蘑菇的構造
structure of a mushroom

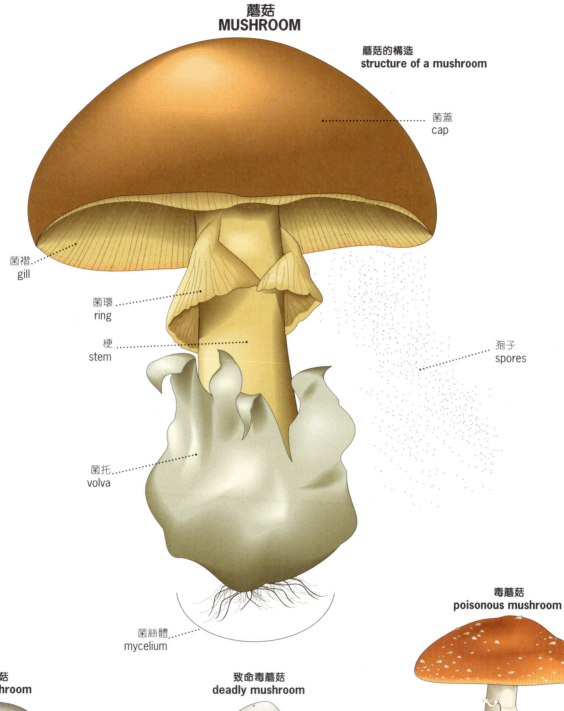

菌蓋
cap

菌褶
gill

菌環
ring

梗
stem

孢子
spores

菌托
volva

菌絲體
mycelium

毒蘑菇
poisonous mushroom

食用蘑菇
edible mushroom

致命毒蘑菇
deadly mushroom

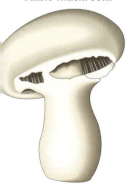

人工栽培蘑菇
cultivated mushroom

鬼筆鵝膏
destroying angel

蛤蟆菌
fly agaric

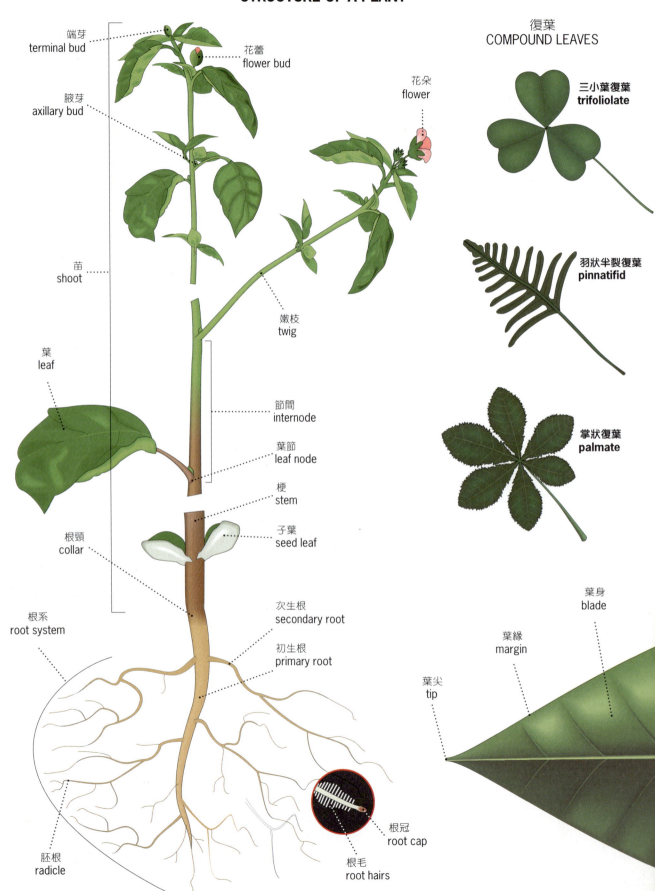

36

植物的構造
STRUCTURE OF A PLANT

端芽
terminal bud

花蕾
flower bud

腋芽
axillary bud

花朵
flower

苗
shoot

嫩枝
twig

葉
leaf

節間
internode

葉節
leaf node

梗
stem

子葉
seed leaf

根頸
collar

次生根
secondary root

初生根
primary root

根系
root system

胚根
radicle

根冠
root cap

根毛
root hairs

復葉
COMPOUND LEAVES

三小葉復葉
trifoliolate

羽狀半裂復葉
pinnatifid

掌狀復葉
palmate

葉身
blade

葉緣
margin

葉尖
tip

單葉
SIMPLE LEAVES

葉緣
LEAF MARGINS

線形單葉
linear

矛尖狀單葉
lanceolate

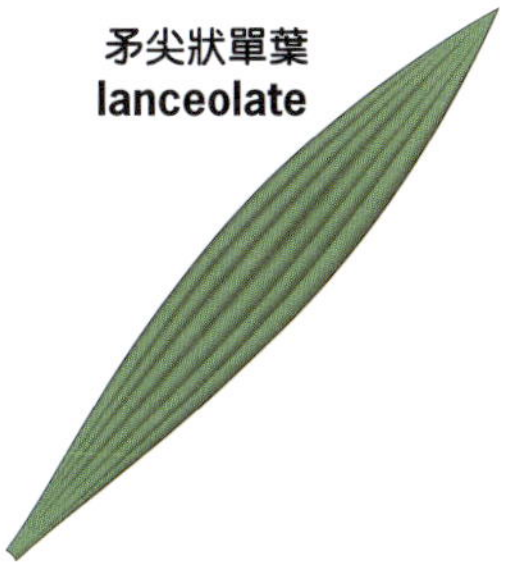

圓形單葉
orbiculate

繐毛葉
ciliate

圓齒葉
crenate

全緣葉
entire

裂片狀葉
lobate

齒狀葉
dentate

37

葉脈
vein

中脈
midrib

葉
leaf

葉柄
petiole

鞘
sheath

托葉
stipule

葉腋
leaf axil

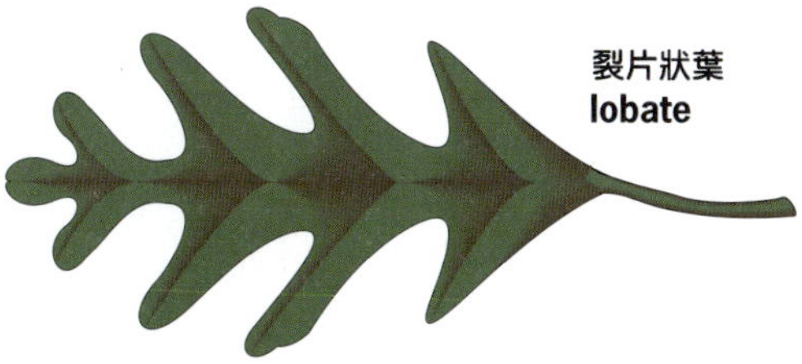

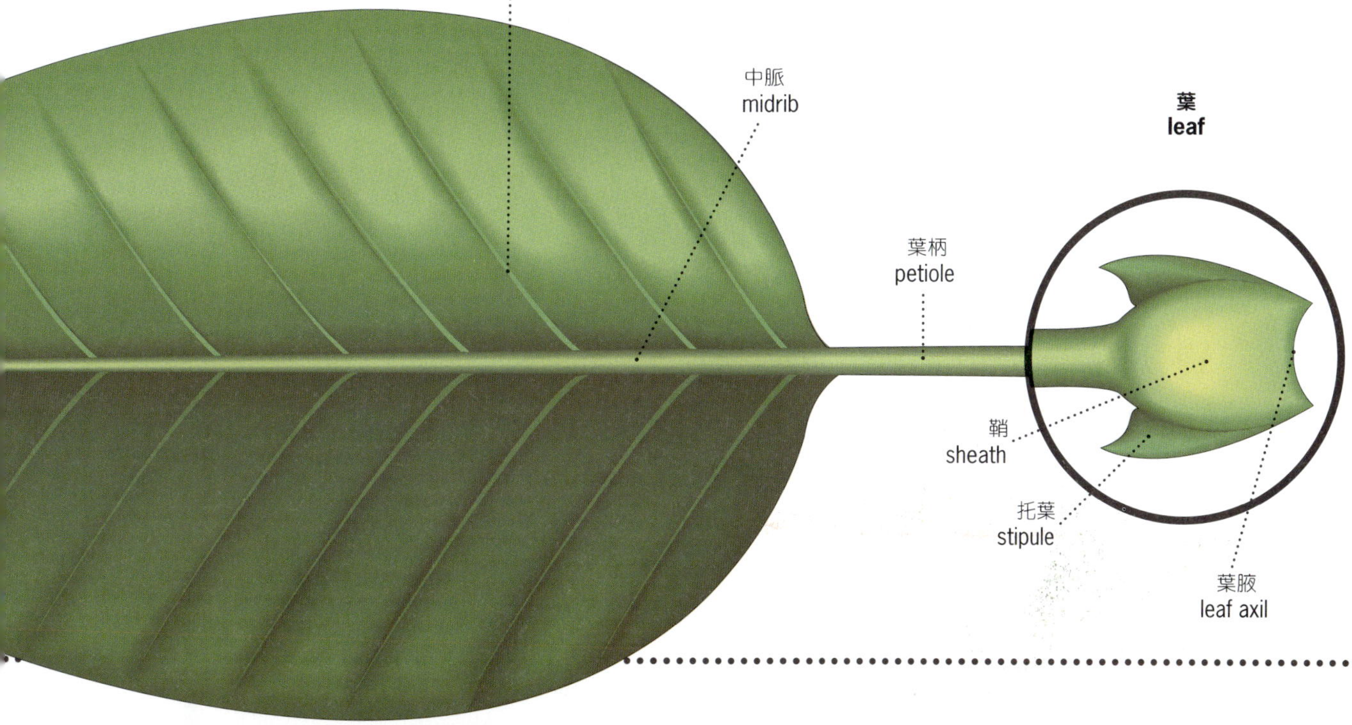

植物王國 ·

PLANT KINGDOM

花
FLOWERS

花的構造
structure of a flower

柱頭
stigma

花絲
filament

花瓣
petal

花冠
corolla

雄蕊
stamen

雌蕊
pistil

花萼
calyx

萼片
sepal

花托
receptacle

花藥
anther

子房
ovary

花柱
style

胚珠
ovule

花梗
pedicel

38

部分花朵
EXAMPLES OF FLOWERS

蘭花
orchid

鬱金香
tulip

紫羅蘭
violet

罌粟花
poppy

玫瑰
rose

秋海棠
begonia

百合
lily

鈴蘭
lily of the valley

向日葵
sunflower

39

藏紅花
crocus

乃馨
rnation

黃水仙
daffodil

植物王國
PLANT KINGDOM

植物王國

40

樹木
TREE

樹的構造
structure of a tree

枝
branches

葉
foliage

樹梢
top

樹冠
crown

樹枝
branch

細枝
twig

主枝
limb

直根
taproot

淺根
shallow root

胚根
radicle

樹干
trunk

根毛區
root-hair zone

樹椿
stump

新枝
shoot

樹干的橫切面
cross section of a trunk

年輪
annual ring

木髓
pith

表樹皮
outer bark

內樹皮
inner bark

形成層
cambium

液材
sapwood

心材
heartwood

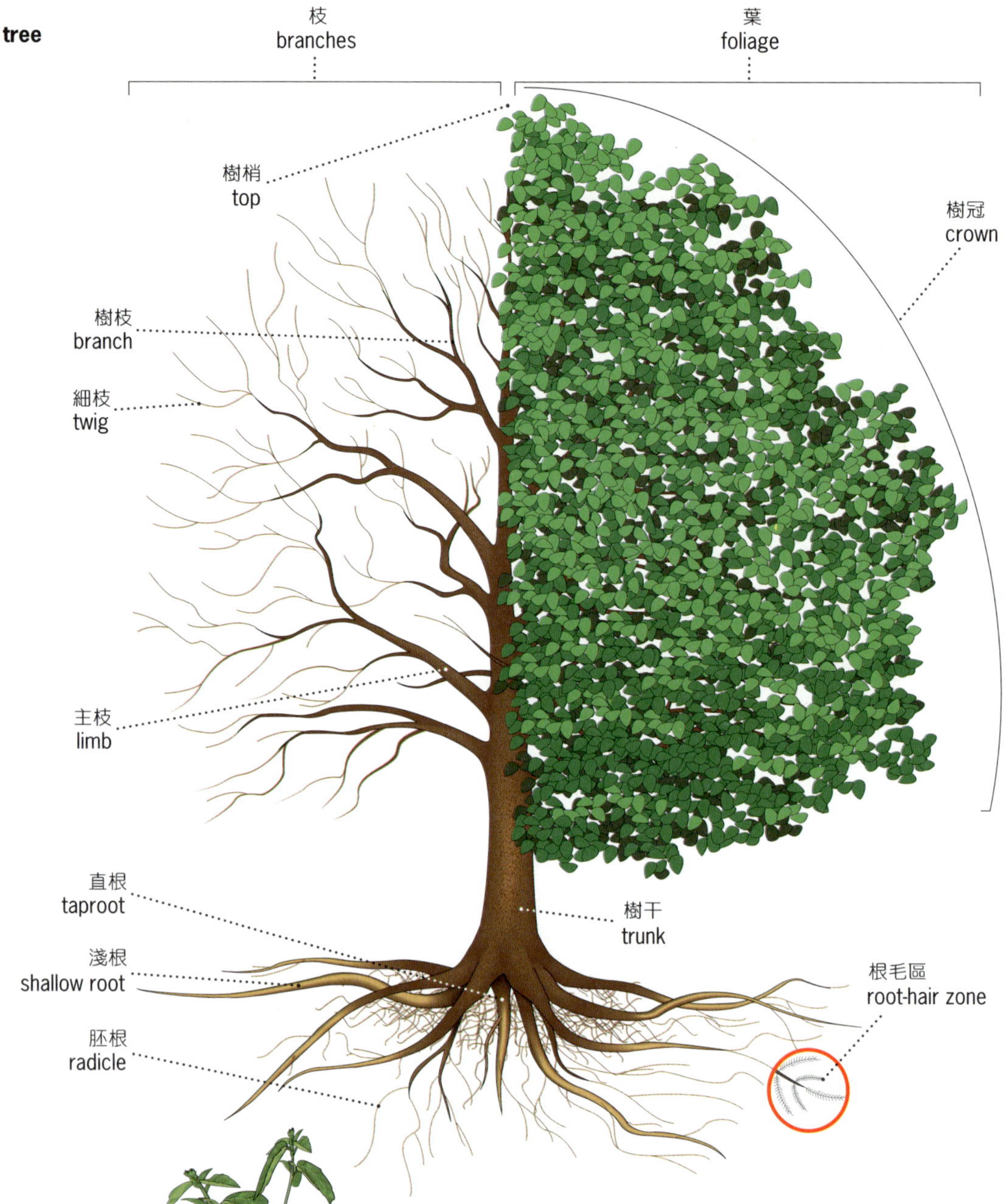

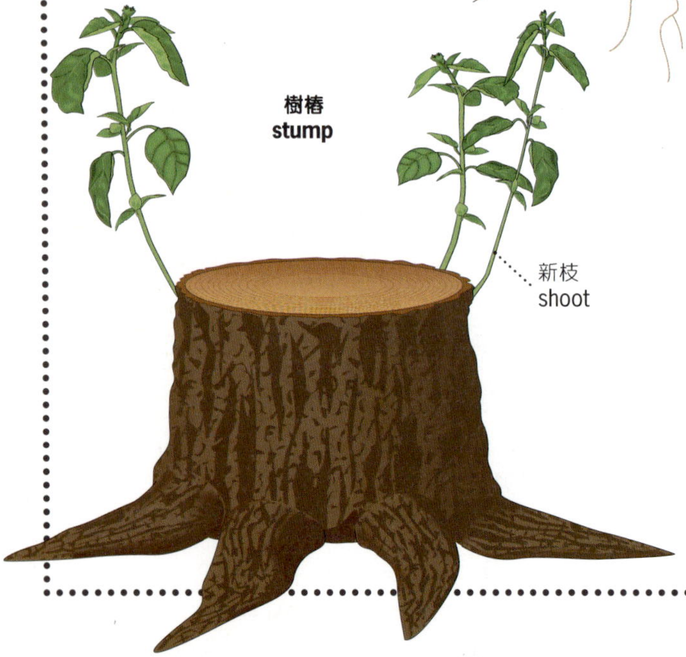

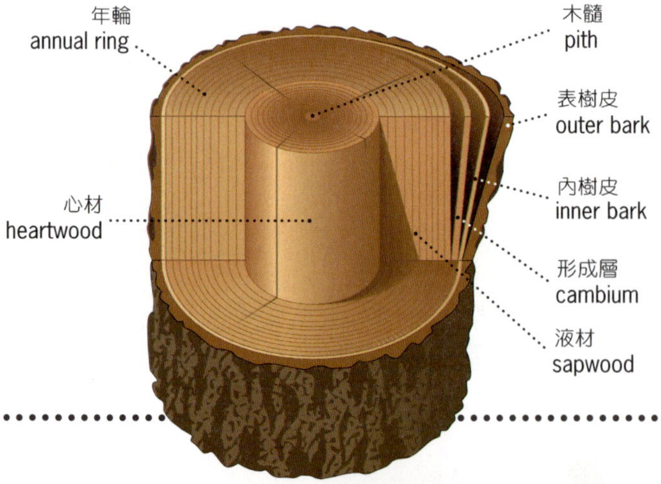

部分樹木
EXAMPLES OF TREES

白楊
poplar

橡樹
oak

楓樹
maple

棕櫚
palm tree

垂柳
weeping willow

白樺
birch

42

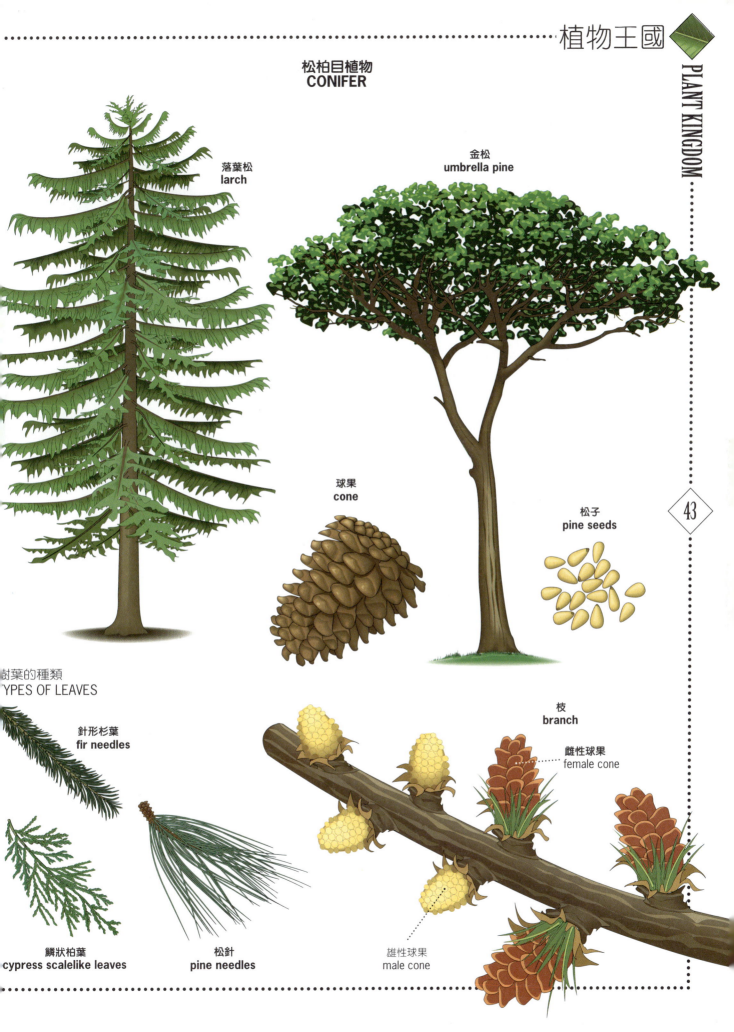

松柏目植物
CONIFER

落葉松
larch

金松
umbrella pine

球果
cone

松子
pine seeds

樹葉的種類
YPES OF LEAVES

針形杉葉
fir needles

枝
branch

雌性球果
female cone

鱗狀柏葉
cypress scalelike leaves

松針
pine needles

雄性球果
male cone

肉質果：漿果
FLESHY FRUITS: BERRY FRUITS

漿果橫切面
section of a berry

漿果的主要種類
MAJOR TYPES OF BERRIES

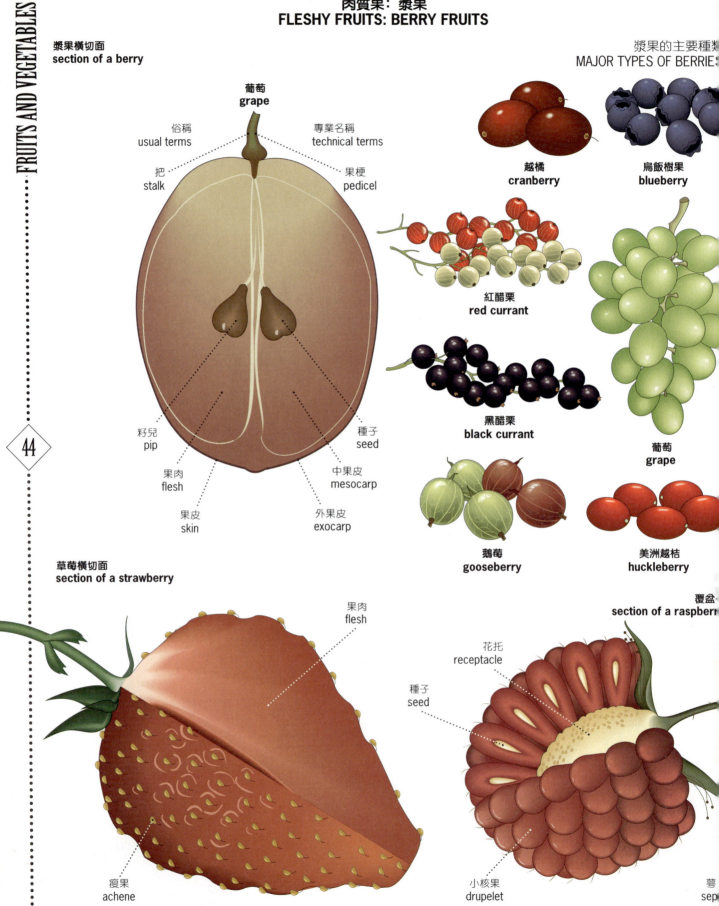

葡萄
grape

俗稱
usual terms

專業名稱
technical terms

把
stalk

果梗
pedicel

籽兒
pip

種子
seed

果肉
flesh

中果皮
mesocarp

果皮
skin

外果皮
exocarp

越橘
cranberry

烏飯樹果
blueberry

紅醋栗
red currant

黑醋栗
black currant

鵝莓
gooseberry

美洲越桔
huckleberry

葡萄
grape

草莓橫切面
section of a strawberry

果肉
flesh

種子
seed

瘦果
achene

覆盆
section of a raspberr

花托
receptacle

小核果
drupelet

萼
sep

肉質核果
FLESHY STONE FRUITS

核果橫切面
section of a stone fruit

桃子
peach

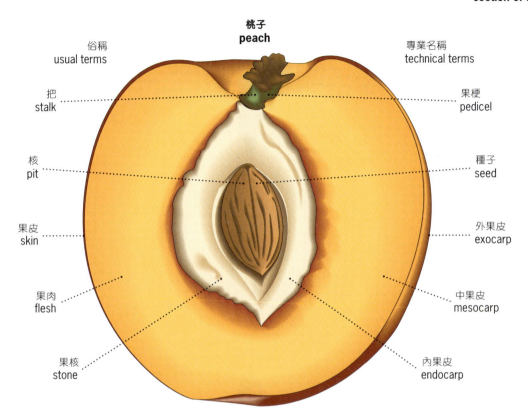

俗稱
usual terms

專業名稱
technical terms

把
stalk

果梗
pedicel

核
pit

種子
seed

果皮
skin

外果皮
exocarp

果肉
flesh

中果皮
mesocarp

果核
stone

內果皮
endocarp

核果的主要種類
MAJOR TYPES OF STONE FRUITS

蜜桃
nectarine

桃子
peach

芒果
mango

杏子
apricot

橄欖
olive

洋李
plum

棗
date

櫻桃
cherry

肉質梨果
FLESHY POME FRUITS

梨果橫切面
section of a pome fruit

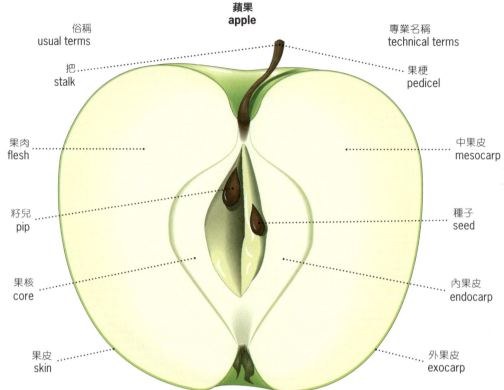

蘋果
apple

俗稱
usual terms

專業名稱
technical terms

把
stalk

果梗
pedicel

果肉
flesh

中果皮
mesocarp

籽兒
pip

種子
seed

果核
core

內果皮
endocarp

果皮
skin

外果皮
exocarp

梨果的主要種類
MAJOR TYPES OF POME FRUITS

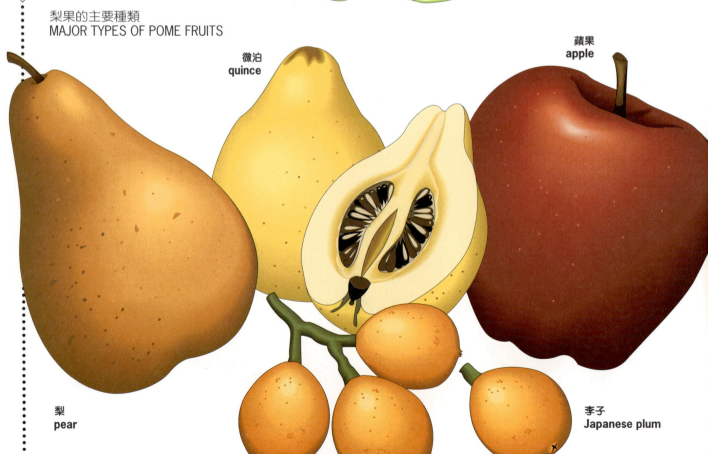

微泊
quince

蘋果
apple

梨
pear

李子
Japanese plum

肉質果：柑橘果
FLESHY FRUITS: CITRUS FRUITS

柑橘果橫切面
section of a citrus fruit

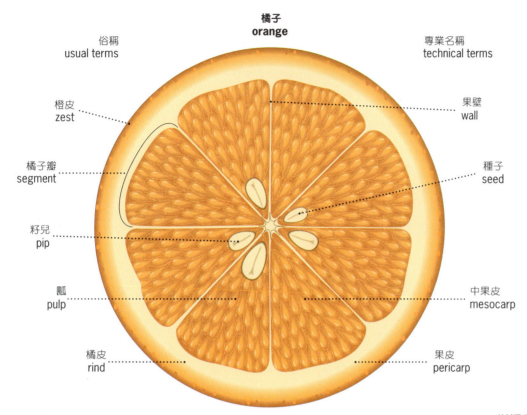

橘子
orange

俗稱
usual terms

專業名稱
technical terms

橙皮
zest

果壁
wall

橘子瓣
segment

種子
seed

籽兒
pip

瓤
pulp

中果皮
mesocarp

橘皮
rind

果皮
pericarp

柑橘果的主要種類
MAJOR TYPES OF CITRUS FRUITS

檸檬
lemon

酸橙
lime

橙子
orange

葡萄柚
grapefruit

柑橘
mandarin

熱帶水果
TROPICAL FRUITS

熱帶水果的主要種類
MAJOR TYPES OF TROPICAL FRUITS

荔枝
litchi

獼猴桃
kiwi

番石榴
guava

柿子
Japanese persimmon

印度無花果
Indian fig

番荔枝
cherimoya

無花果
fig

番木瓜
papaya

石榴
pomegranate

香蕉
banana

鱷梨
avocado

菠蘿
pineapple

蔬菜
VEGETABLES

開花蔬菜
INFLORESCENT VEGETABLES

花椰菜
cauliflower

甘藍
broccoli

洋薊
artichoke

瓜果
FRUIT VEGETABLES

西瓜
watermelon

倭瓜
autumn squash

南瓜
pumpkin

羅馬甜瓜
cantaloupe

香瓜
muskmelon

茄子
eggplant

密生西葫蘆
summer squash

黃瓜
cucumber

綠皮密生西葫蘆
**zucchini /
courgette**

羊角豆
okra

青菜豆
green bean

甜椒；青椒
sweet pepper; green pepper

西紅柿
tomato

辣椒
hot pepper; chilli

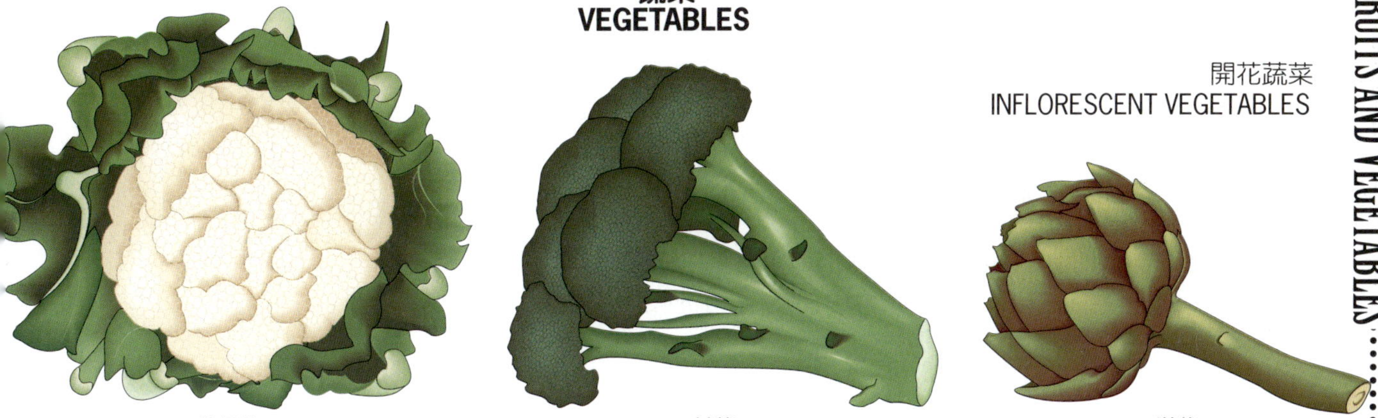

蔬菜
VEGETABLES

球莖橫切面
section of a bulb

芽
bud

珠芽
bulbil

鱗葉
scale leaf

葉肉
fleshy leaves

地下莖
underground stem

根
root

球莖蔬菜
BULB VEGETABLES

大蒜
garlic

韭蔥
leek

青蔥
shallot

黃洋蔥
yellow onion

小洋蔥
pickling onion

細香蔥
chives

蔥
scallion

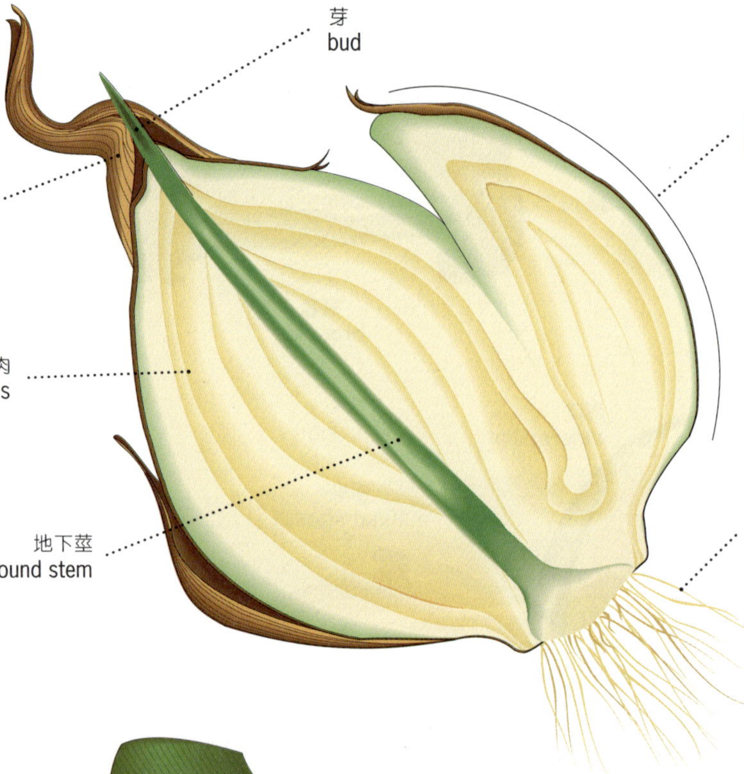

塊莖蔬菜
TUBER VEGETABLES

洋姜
Jerusalem artichoke

馬鈴薯
potato

甘薯
sweet potato

根莖蔬菜
ROOT VEGETABLES

撇藍
kohlrabi

塊莖芹
celeriac

瑞典蕪菁
swede

甜菜
beet

蕪菁
turnip

51

辣根
horseradish

歐洲蘿蔔
parsnip

胡蘿蔔
carrot

小蘿蔔
radish

波羅門參
salsify

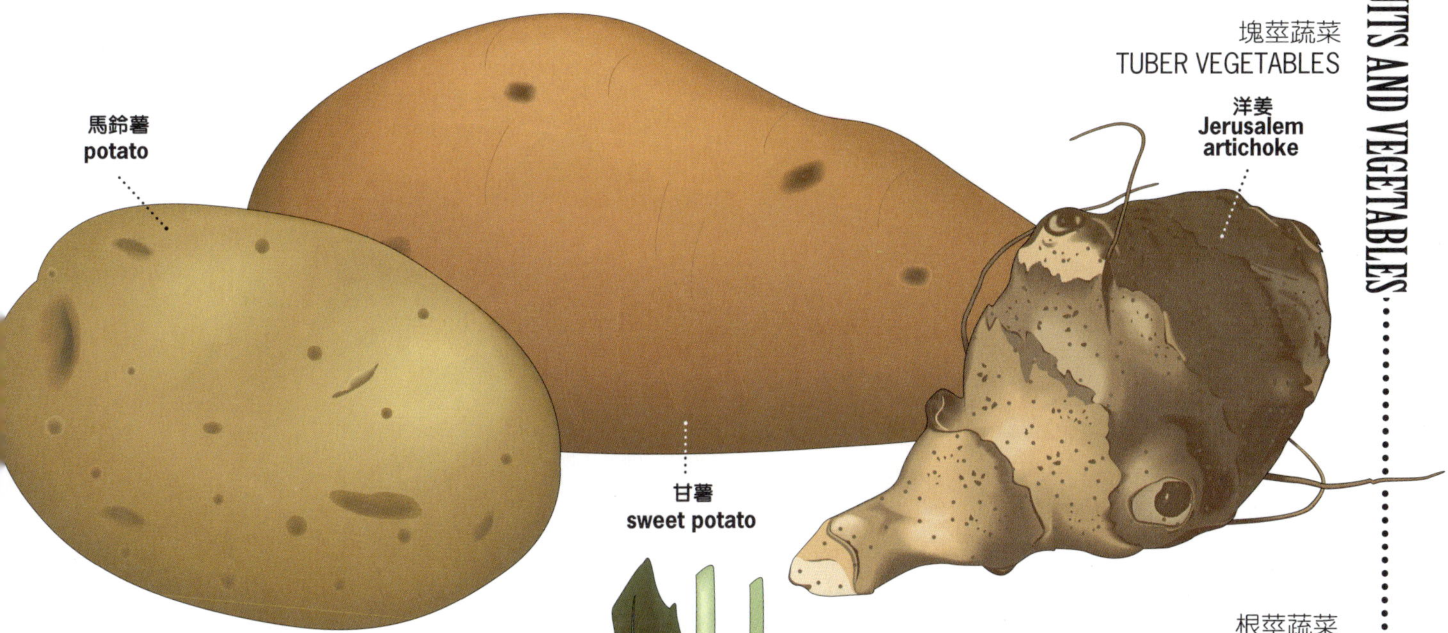

FRUITS AND VEGETABLES

蔬菜
VEGETABLES

莖葉蔬菜
STALK VEGETABLES

刺菜薊
cardoon

大黃
rhubarb

瑞士甜菜（厚皮菜）
Swiss chard

茴香
fennel

芹菜
celery

蘆筍
asparagus

豆類蔬菜
SEED VEGETABLES

甜玉米
sweet corn

鬻豆
broad beans

香豌豆
sweet peas

嫩豌豆
green peas

穗須
silk

玉米棒
cob

苞葉
husk

玉米粒
kernel

濱豆
lentils

鷹嘴豆
chick peas

大豆
soy beans

豆芽
bean sprouts

葉菜
LEAF VEGETABLES

青卷心菜
green cabbage

卷葉苣買菜
curly endive

白卷心菜
white cabbage

長葉萵苣
romaine lettuce

寬葉苣買菜
broad-leaved endive

卷心萵苣
cabbage lettuce

菠菜
spinach

菊苣
chicory

大白菜
Chinese cabbage

皺葉羽衣甘藍
curly kale

菜用酸模
garden sorrel

水田芥
watercress

藥蒲公英
dandelion

湯菜
Brussels sprouts

家獨活
corn salad

藤葉
vine leaf

53

園藝學
GARDENING

小鏟
trowel

手提叉
hand fork

園用手耘鋤
hand cultivator

整枝剪刀
pruning shears

54

園圃割草機
lawnmower

速度控制
speed control

點火開關鑰匙
ignition key

手柄
handle

安全手柄
safety handle

盛草箱
grassbox

導向器
deflector

罩
casing

啟動裝置
starter

發動機
motor

噴水壺
watering can

長柄耙
rake

園藝叉
garden fork

園藝鏟
spade

鐵鍬
shovel

草坪耙
lawn rake

獨輪車
wheelbarrow

堆肥箱
compost bin

昆蟲與蜘蛛
INSECTS AND SPIDER

螞蟻
ant

瓢蟲
ladybug

蒼蠅
fly

蜘蛛
spider

蝗蟲
grasshopper

56

蜻蜓
dragonfly

蝴蝶
BUTTERFLY

毛蟲
caterpillar

頭部
head

單眼
simple eye

大顎
mandible

步行足
walking leg

腹足
proleg

前翅
forewing

蝶蛹
chrysalis

翼脈
wing vein

翅室
cell

胸部
thorax

頭部
head

觸角
antenna

唇須
labial palp

復眼
compound eye

喙
proboscis

前腿
foreleg

中腿
middle leg

爪
claw

后翅
hind wing

腹部
abdomen

后腿
hind leg

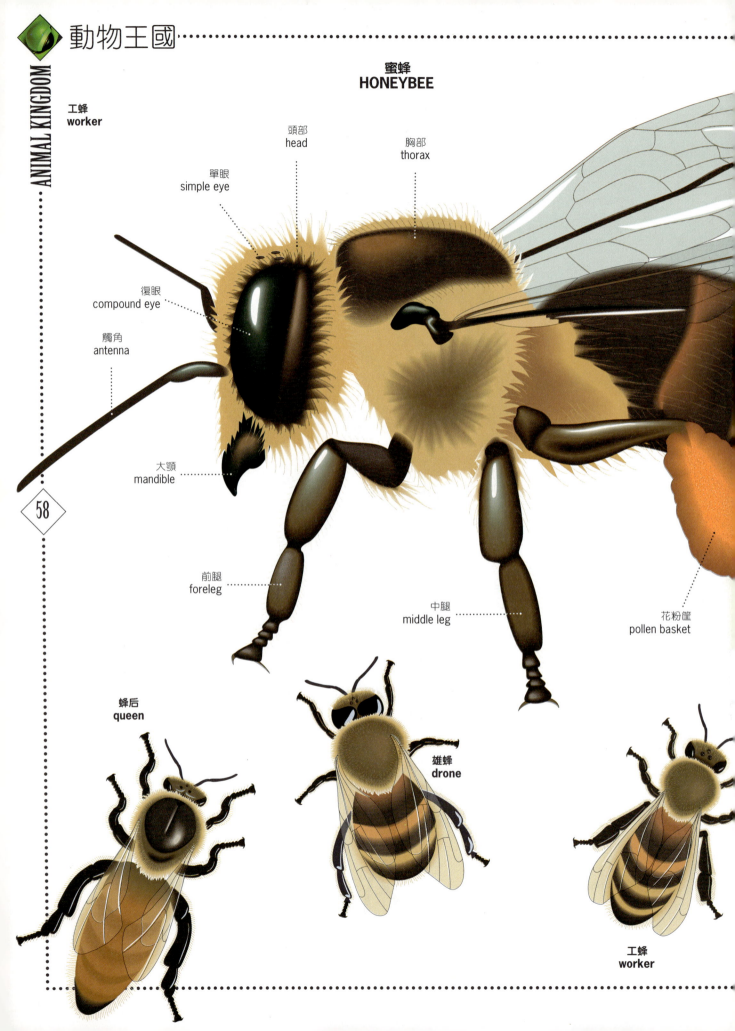

ANIMAL KINGDOM

蜜蜂
HONEYBEE

工蜂
worker

單眼
simple eye

頭部
head

胸部
thorax

復眼
compound eye

觸角
antenna

大顎
mandible

58

前腿
foreleg

中腿
middle leg

花粉筐
pollen basket

蜂后
queen

雄蜂
drone

工蜂
worker

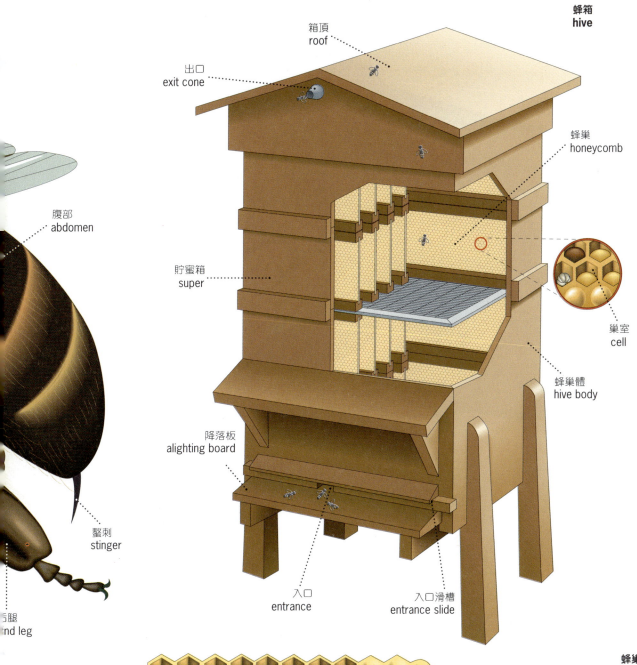

腹部
abdomen

螫刺
stinger

后腿
nd leg

箱頂
roof

出口
exit cone

蜂箱
hive

蜂巢
honeycomb

貯蜜箱
super

蜂巢體
hive body

巢室
cell

降落板
alighting board

入口
entrance

入口滑槽
entrance slide

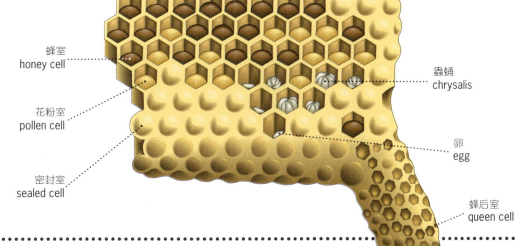

蜂巢橫切面
honeycomb section

蜂室
honey cell

花粉室
pollen cell

密封室
sealed cell

蟲蛹
chrysalis

卵
egg

蜂后室
queen cell

兩棲動物
AMPHIBIANS

青蛙
frog

上眼瞼
upper eyelid

吻
snout

鼻孔
nostril

眼球
eyeball

嘴
mouth

下眼瞼
lower eyelid

皮膚
skin

耳膜
eardrum

前肢
forelimb

趾
digit

蹼足
webbed foot

蹼
web

后肢
hind limb

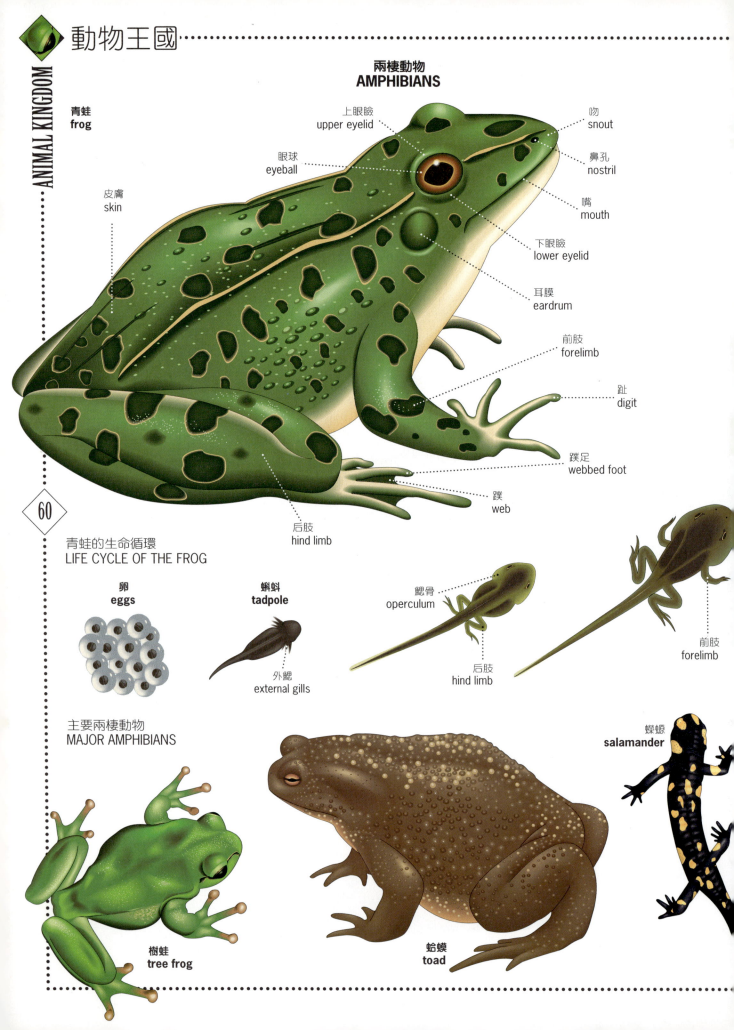

60

青蛙的生命循環
LIFE CYCLE OF THE FROG

卵
eggs

蝌蚪
tadpole

鰓骨
operculum

外鰓
external gills

后肢
hind limb

前肢
forelimb

主要兩棲動物
MAJOR AMPHIBIANS

蠑螈
salamander

樹蛙
tree frog

蛤蟆
toad

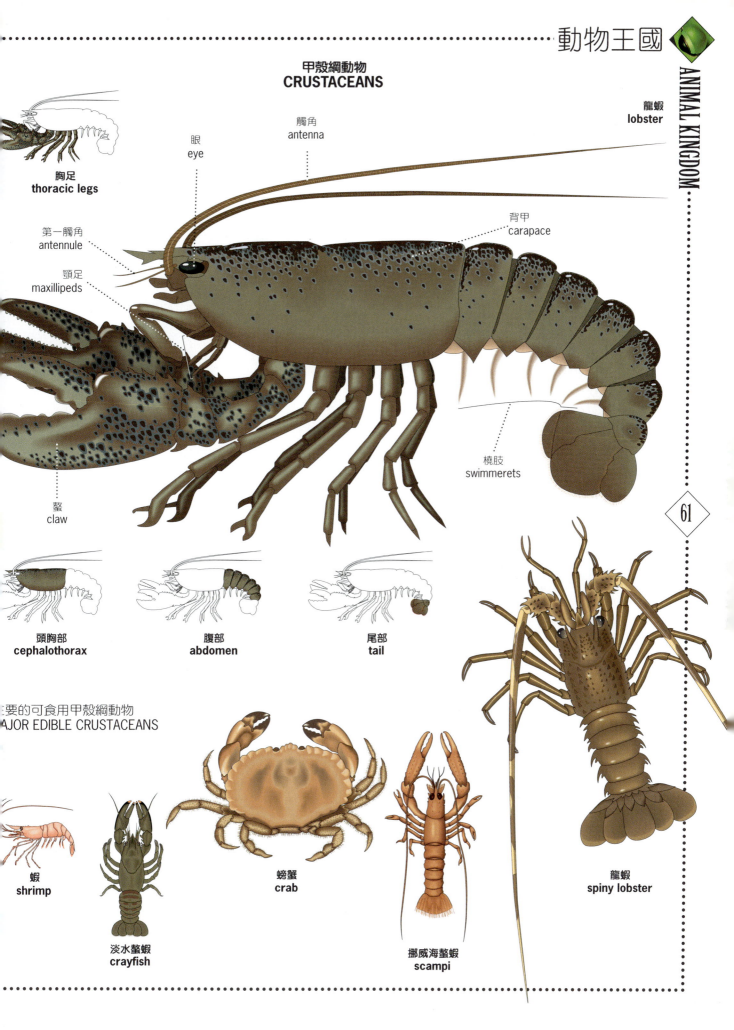

甲殼綱動物
CRUSTACEANS

胸足
thoracic legs

眼
eye

觸角
antenna

龍蝦
lobster

第一觸角
antennule

顎足
maxillipeds

背甲
carapace

螯
claw

橈肢
swimmerets

頭胸部
cephalothorax

腹部
abdomen

尾部
tail

要的可食用甲殼綱動物
AJOR EDIBLE CRUSTACEANS

蝦
shrimp

淡水螯蝦
crayfish

螃蟹
crab

挪威海螯蝦
scampi

龍蝦
spiny lobster

動物王國

形態
MORPHOLOGY

魚類
FISHES

第一背鰭
first dorsal fin

鼻孔
nostril

鰓
gills

下頜
mandible

上頜
maxilla

胸鰭
pectoral fin

腹鰭
pelvic fin

海馬
sea horse

62

鮭魚
trout

箭魚
swordfish

金槍魚
tuna

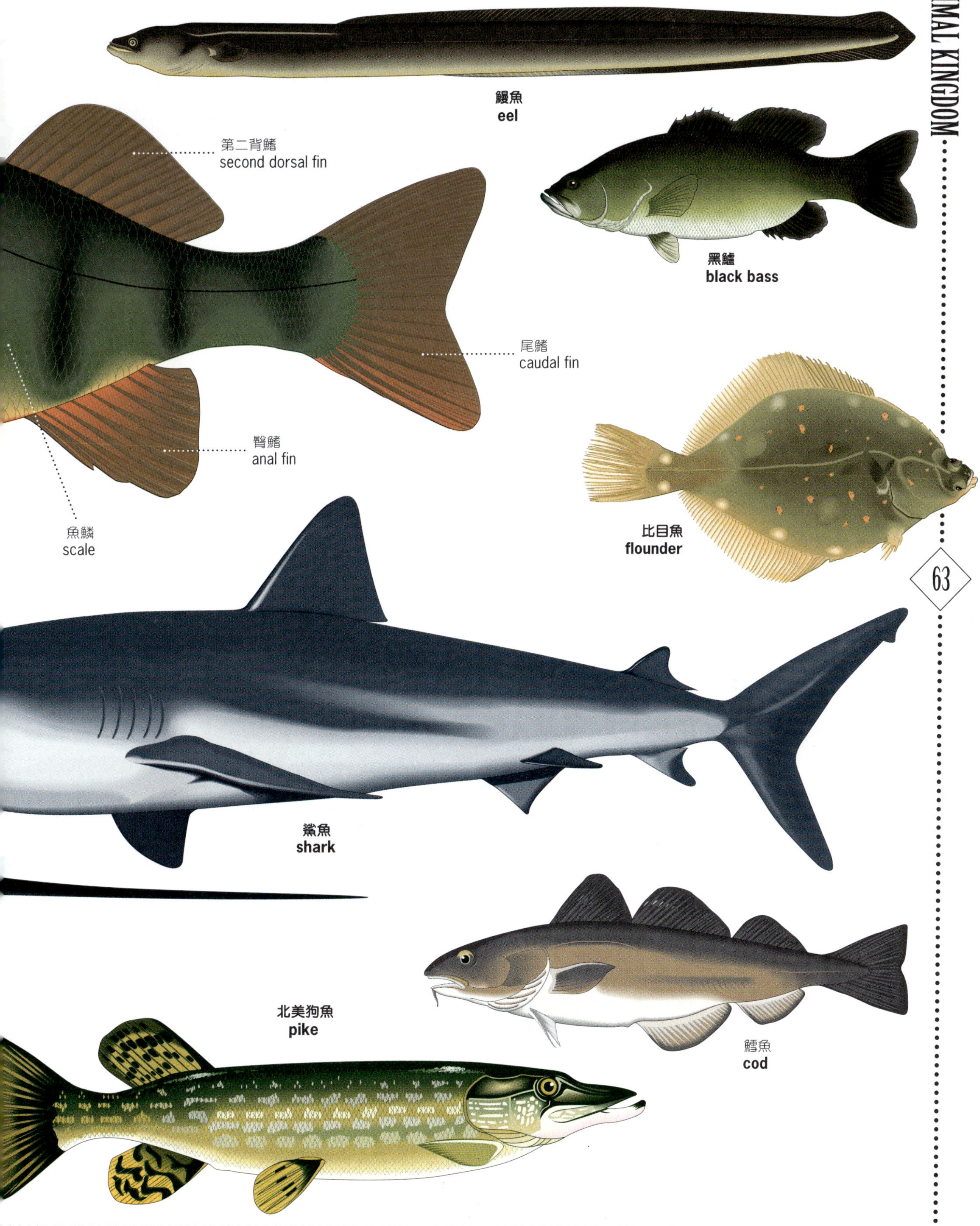

鰻魚
eel

第二背鰭
second dorsal fin

黑鱸
black bass

尾鰭
caudal fin

臀鰭
anal fin

比目魚
flounder

魚鱗
scale

63

鯊魚
shark

北美狗魚
pike

鱈魚
cod

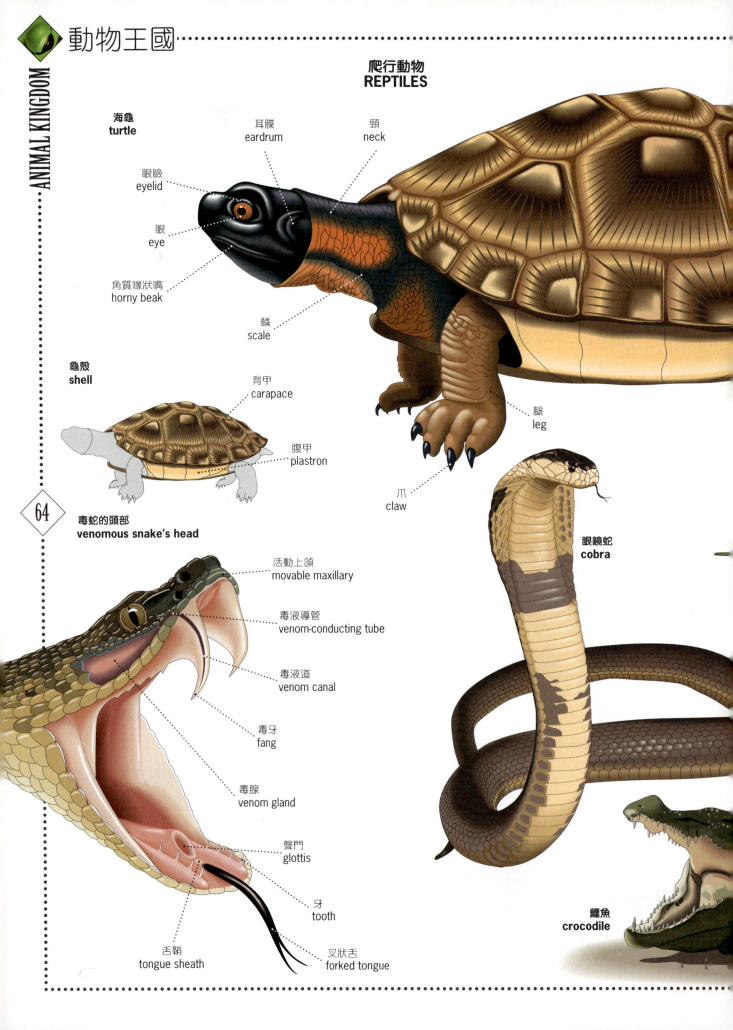

爬行動物
REPTILES

海龜
turtle

耳膜
eardrum

頸
neck

眼瞼
eyelid

眼
eye

角質喙狀嘴
horny beak

鱗
scale

龜殼
shell

背甲
carapace

腹甲
plastron

腿
leg

爪
claw

毒蛇的頭部
venomous snake's head

活動上頜
movable maxillary

毒液導管
venom-conducting tube

毒液道
venom canal

毒牙
fang

毒腺
venom gland

聲門
glottis

牙
tooth

舌鞘
tongue sheath

叉狀舌
forked tongue

眼鏡蛇
cobra

鱷魚
crocodile

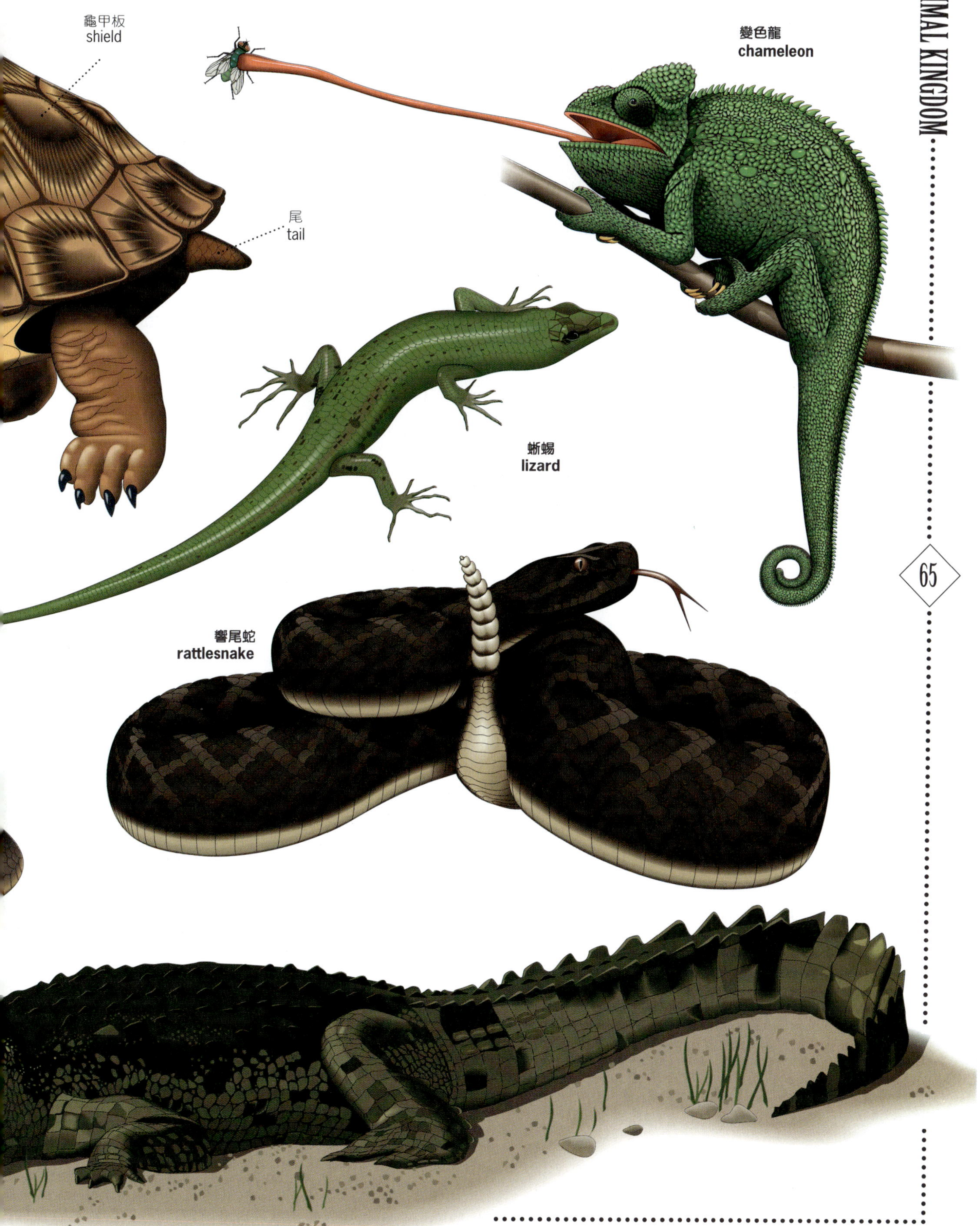

龜甲板
shield

尾
tail

變色龍
chameleon

蜥蜴
lizard

響尾蛇
rattlesnake

貓
CAT

須
whiskers

上眼瞼
upper eyelid

下眼瞼
lower eyelid

瞬膜
nictitating
membrane

胡須
whiskers

唇
lip

睫毛
eyelashes

瞳孔
pupil

鼻頭皮
nose leather

吻
muzzle

犬
DOG

額鼻間的凹痕
stop

吻
muzzle

上唇兩邊的下垂部分
flews

頰
cheek

廦甲
withers

背部
back

形態
MORPHOLOGY

大腿
thigh

肩部
shoulder

陰莖鞘
sheath

肘部
elbow

跗關節
hock

前腿
forearm

前爪
dog's forepaw

掌墊
palmar pad

趾墊
digital pad

爪
claw

殘留趾
dewclaw

趾
toe

腕
wrist

趾
toe

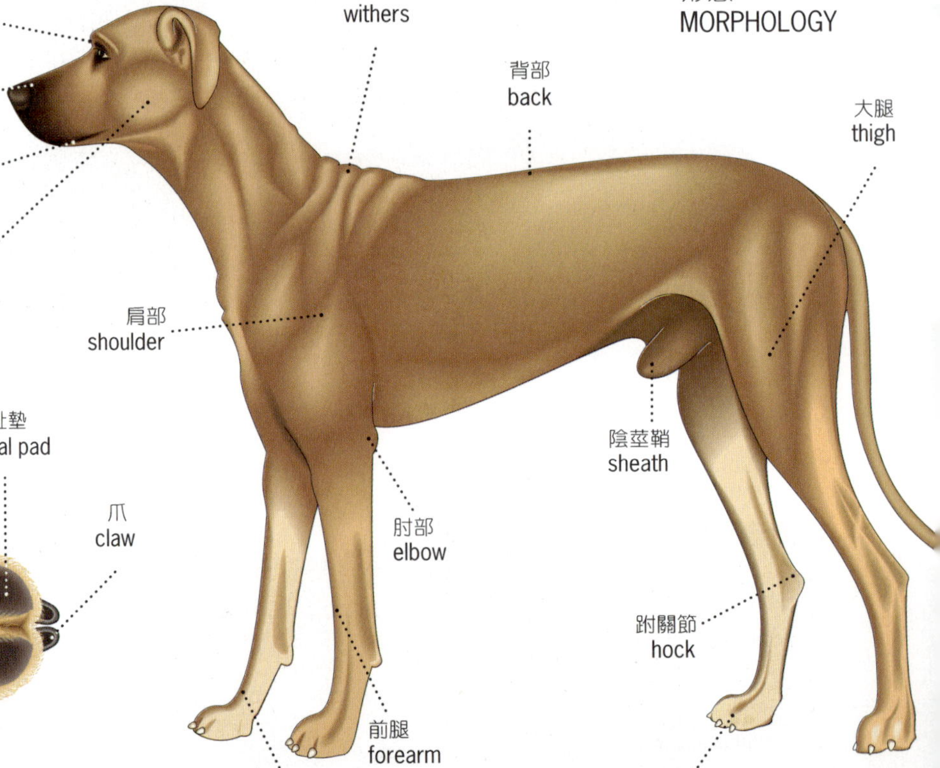

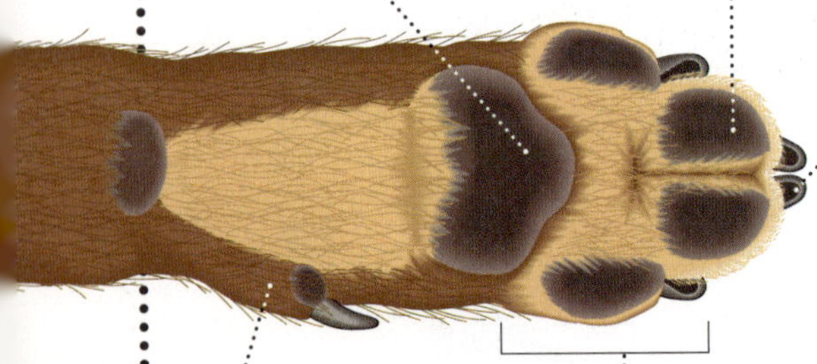

馬
HORSE

門鬃
forelock

鼻
nose

鼻孔
nostril

吻
muzzle

唇
lip

鬃
mane

鬐甲
withers

背部
back

肋腹
flank

腰
loin

臀
croup

尾
tail

頸
neck

肩
shoulder

胸
chest

前腿
arm

肘
elbow

膝
knee

角質胼胝
chestnut

球節
fetlock joint

蹄冠
coronet

距毛
fetlock

腹
belly

陰莖鞘
sheath

大腿
thigh

后腿上部
gaskin

骨交
pastern

蹄
hoof

跗關節
hock

炮骨
cannon

67

家禽與家畜
FARM ANIMALS

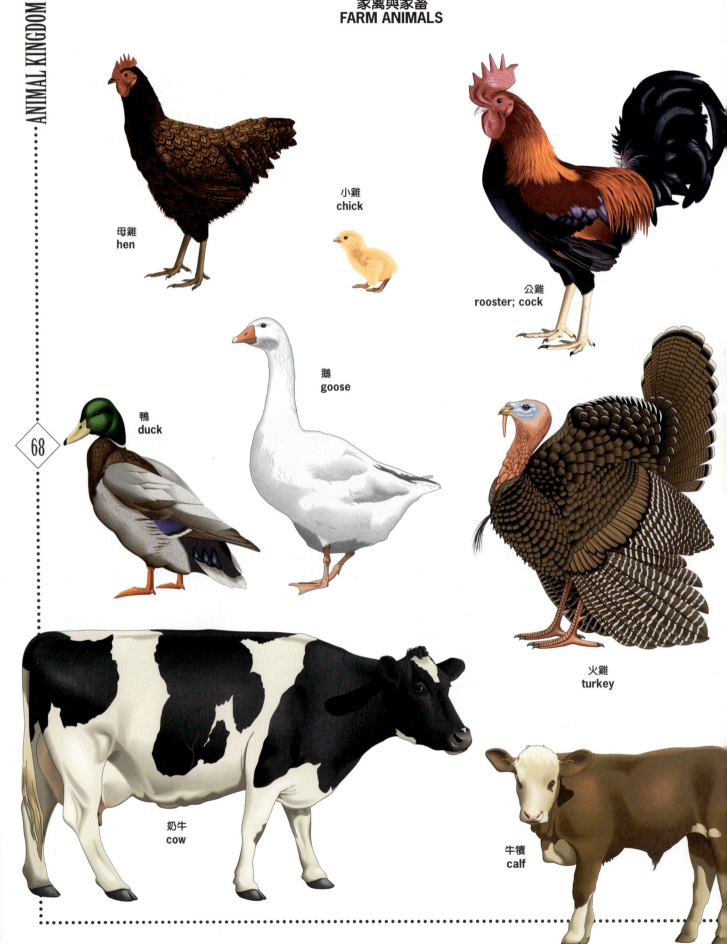

母雞
hen

小雞
chick

公雞
rooster; cock

鴨
duck

鵝
goose

火雞
turkey

68

奶牛
cow

牛犢
calf

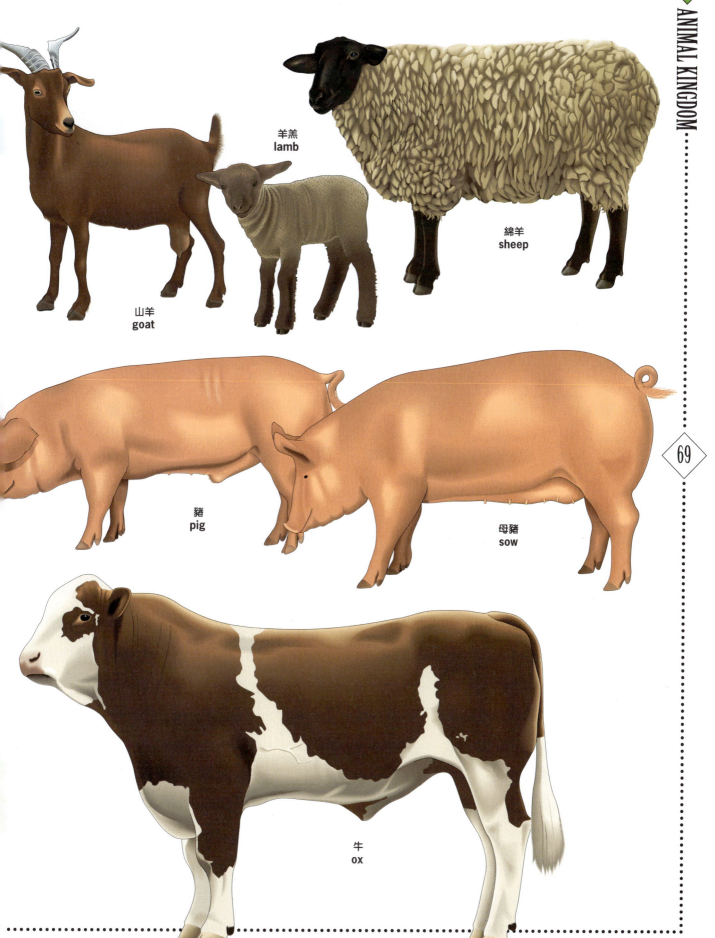

羊羔
lamb

綿羊
sheep

山羊
goat

豬
pig

母豬
sow

牛
ox

顎的種類
TYPES OF JAWS

齧齒目動物的顎
rodent's jaw

河狸
beaver

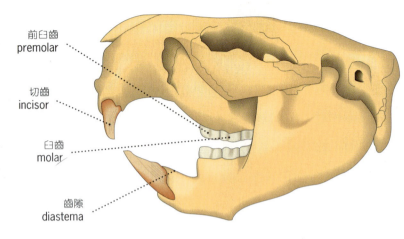

前臼齒
premolar

切齒
incisor

臼齒
molar

齒隙
diastema

食肉類動物的顎
carnivore's jaw

獅子
lion

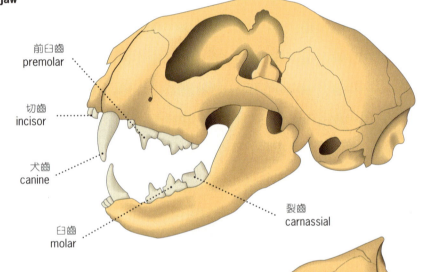

前臼齒
premolar

切齒
incisor

犬齒
canine

臼齒
molar

裂齒
carnassial

食草類動物的顎
herbivore's jaw

馬
horse

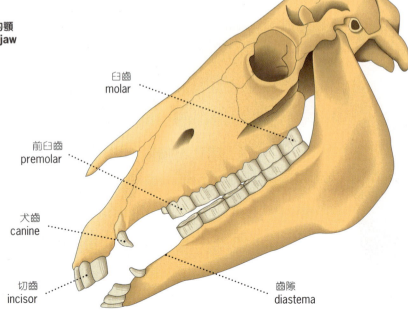

臼齒
molar

前臼齒
premolar

犬齒
canine

切齒
incisor

齒隙
diastema

70

角的主要種類
MAJOR TYPES OF HORNS

歐洲盤羊的角
horns of mouflon

長頸鹿的角
horns of giraffe

犀牛的角
horns of rhinoceros

獠牙的主要種類
MAJOR TYPES OF TUSKS

海象的長牙
tusks of walrus

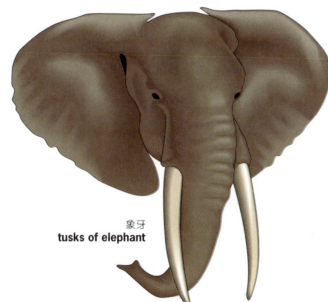

象牙
tusks of elephant

疣豬的獠牙
tusks of wart hog

蹄的主要種類
TYPES OF HOOFS

單趾蹄
one-toe hoof

雙趾蹄
two-toed hoof

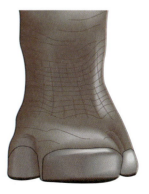

三趾蹄
three-toed hoof

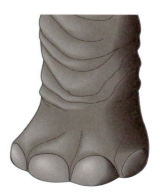

四趾蹄
four-toed hoof

動物王國

野生動物
WILD ANIMALS

長頸鹿
giraffe

北極熊
polar bear

猴子
monkey

獅子
lion

海豚
dolphin

鯨魚
whale

袋鼠
kangaroo

大象
elephant

斑馬
zebra

單峰駱駝；阿拉伯駱駝
dromedary;
Arabian camel

弗吉尼亞鹿（白尾鹿）
white-tailed deer

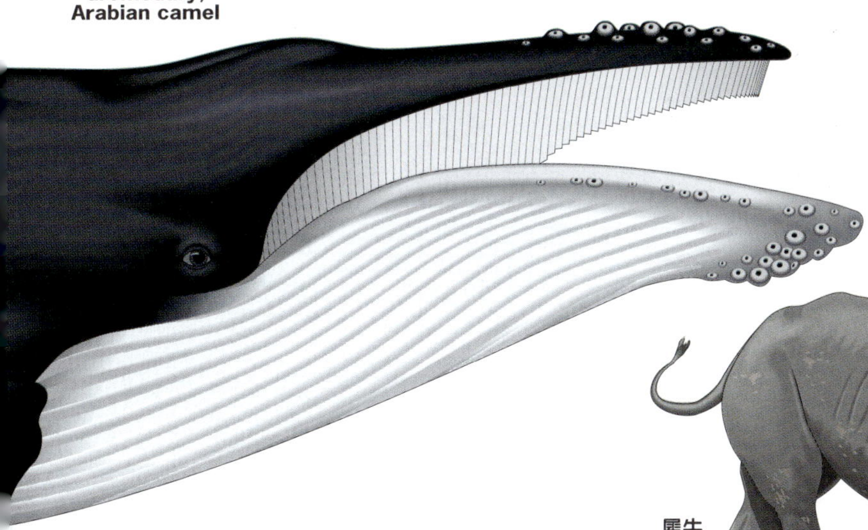

犀牛
rhinoceros

鳥類
BIRD

鳥啄的主要種類
PRINCIPAL TYPES OF BILLS

水生鳥類
aquatic bird

食蟲鳥類
insectivorous bird

涉禽
wading bird

食谷鳥類
granivorous bird

猛禽
bird of prey

形態
MORPHOLOG

肉冠
crown

前額
forehead

喙
bill

眼
eye

頦
chin

喉
throat

胸
breast

腹
abdomen

鳥爪的主要種類
PRINCIPAL TYPES OF FEET

猛禽
bird of prey

爪
talon

鱗
scale

水生鳥類
aquatic bird

蹼趾
webbed toe

蹼
web

水生鳥類
aquatic bird

瓣蹼
lobe

瓣蹼趾
lobate toe

棲禽
perching bird

趾
toe

中趾
middle toe

外趾
outer toe

鳥巢
bird's nest

鳥房
birdhouse

喂鳥器
bird feeder

圓筒
cylinder

鳥食
seeds

棲木
perch

后頸
nape

背部
back

翅膀
wing

腰部
rump

尾部
tail

肋腹
flank

尾下覆羽
under tail covert

尾上覆羽
upper tail covert

卵
egg

腿
foot

胚盤
blastodisc

蛋殼
shell

后趾
hind toe

空氣
air space

爪
claw

蛋黃
yolk

蛋白
albumen

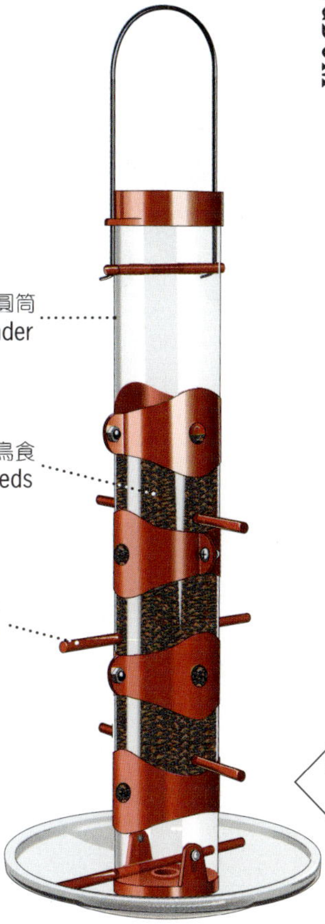

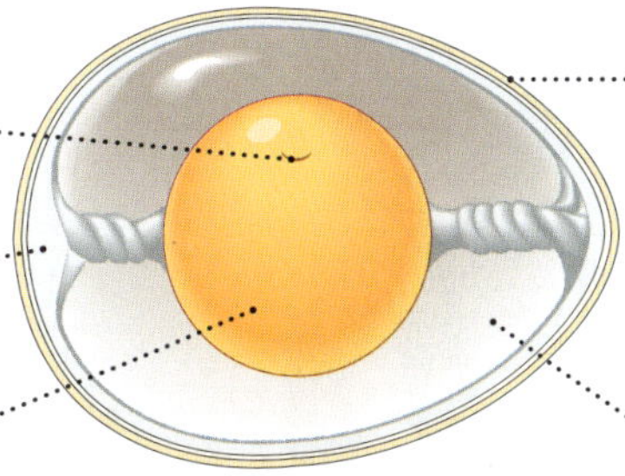

動物王國

部分鳥類
EXAMPLES OF BIRDS

烏鴉
crow

鸚鵡
parrot

鸛
stork

燕
swallow

火烈鳥
flamingo

鴕鳥
ostrich

76

知更鳥
robin

藍背堅倌
blue jay

貓頭鷹
owl

夜鶯
nightingale

蜂鳥
hummingbird

孔雀
peacock

人體：正面圖
HUMAN BODY, ANTERIOR VIEW

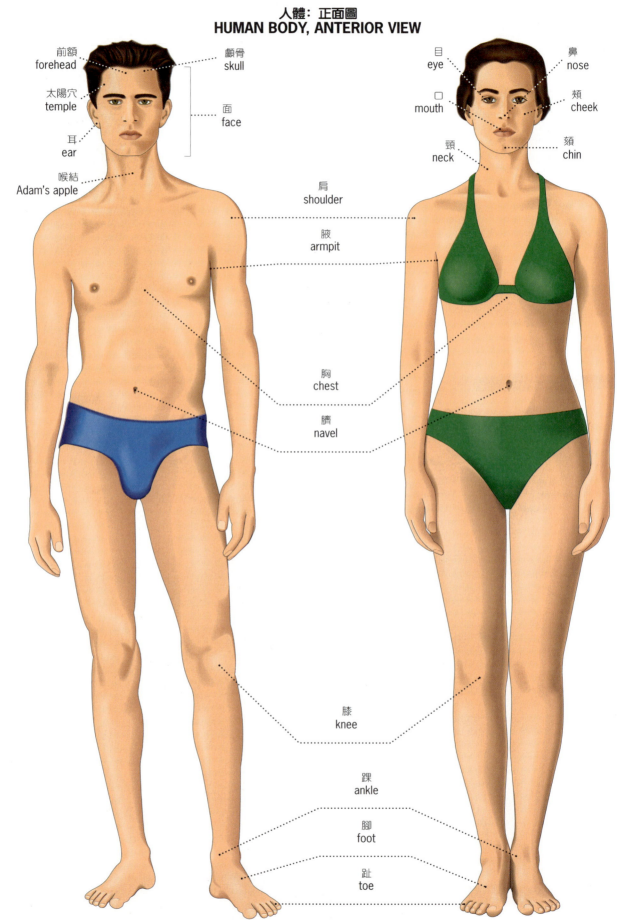

前額
forehead

顱骨
skull

太陽穴
temple

面
face

耳
ear

喉結
Adam's apple

目
eye

鼻
nose

口
mouth

頰
cheek

頸
neck

頦
chin

肩
shoulder

腋
armpit

胸
chest

臍
navel

膝
knee

踝
ankle

腳
foot

趾
toe

78

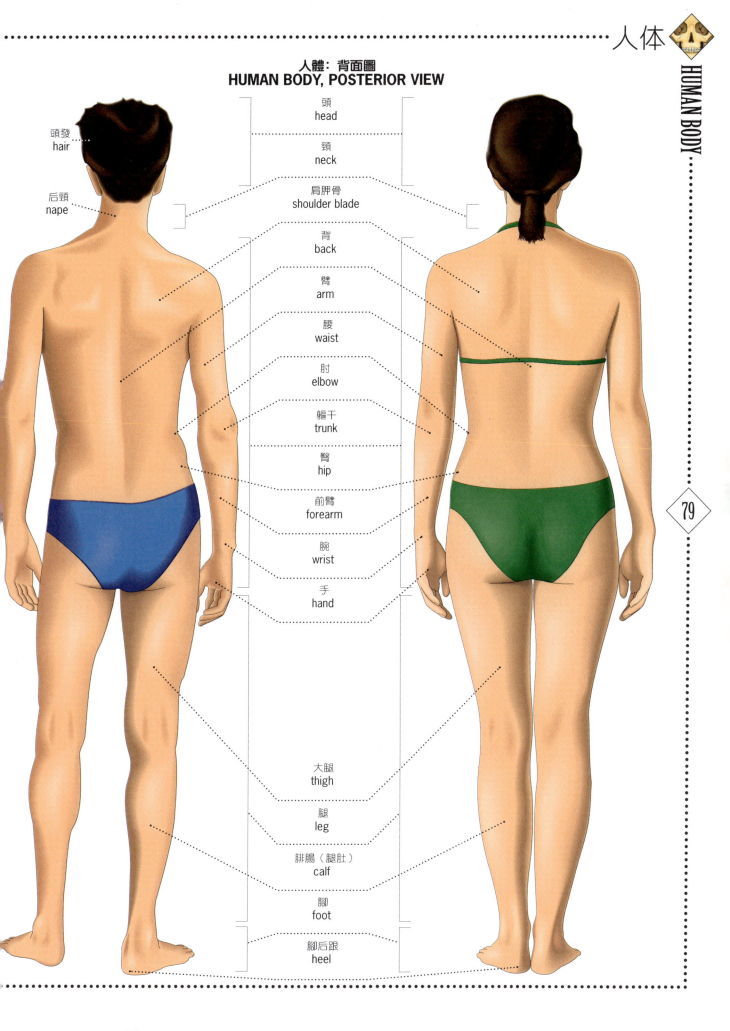

人體：背面圖
HUMAN BODY, POSTERIOR VIEW

頭發
hair

后頸
nape

頭
head

頸
neck

肩胛骨
shoulder blade

背
back

臂
arm

腰
waist

肘
elbow

軀干
trunk

臀
hip

前臂
forearm

腕
wrist

手
hand

大腿
thigh

腿
leg

腓腸（腿肚）
calf

腳
foot

腳后跟
heel

人体

骨骼
SKELETON

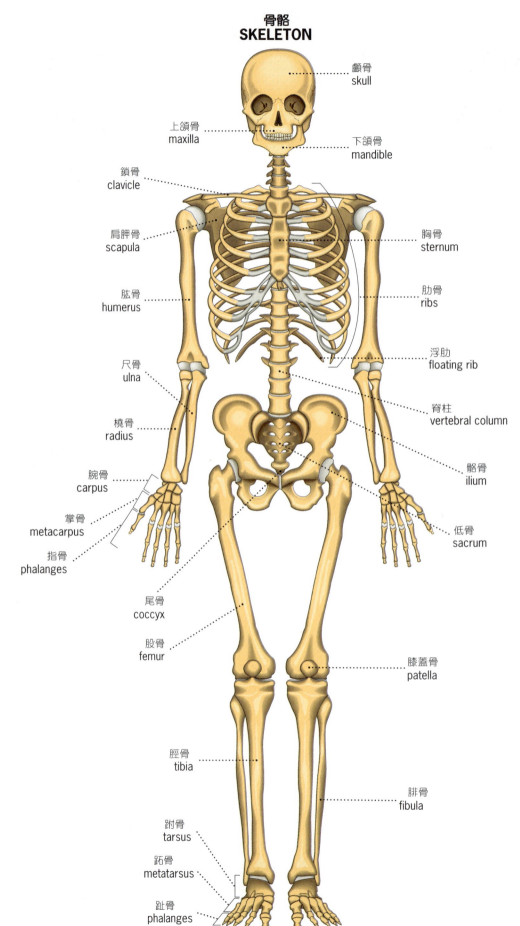

顱骨
skull

上頜骨
maxilla

下頜骨
mandible

鎖骨
clavicle

肩胛骨
scapula

胸骨
sternum

肱骨
humerus

肋骨
ribs

尺骨
ulna

浮肋
floating rib

橈骨
radius

脊柱
vertebral column

腕骨
carpus

髂骨
ilium

掌骨
metacarpus

指骨
phalanges

骶骨
sacrum

尾骨
coccyx

股骨
femur

膝蓋骨
patella

脛骨
tibia

腓骨
fibula

跗骨
tarsus

跖骨
metatarsus

趾骨
phalanges

人體解剖圖
HUMAN ANATOMY

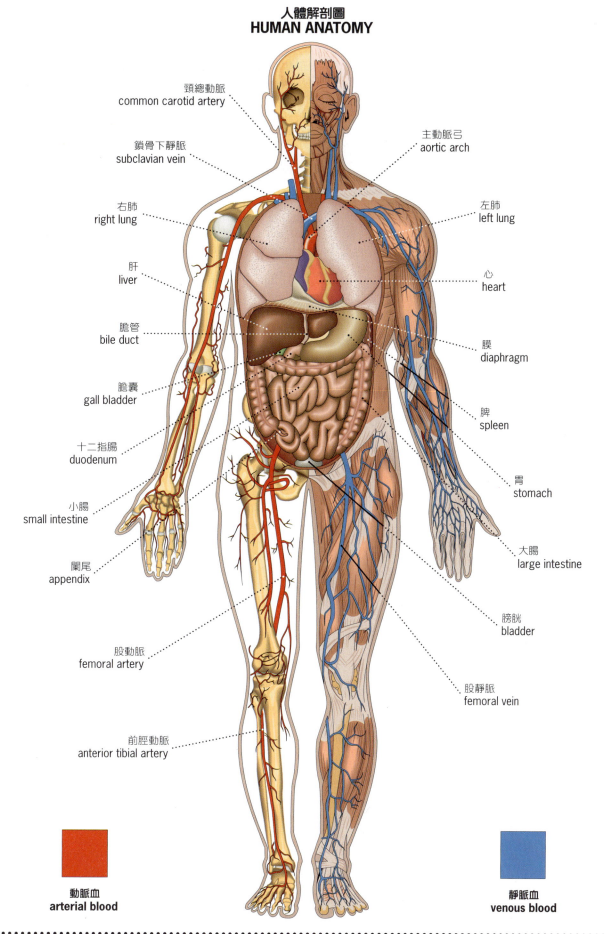

頸總動脈
common carotid artery

鎖骨下靜脈
subclavian vein

右肺
right lung

肝
liver

膽管
bile duct

膽囊
gall bladder

十二指腸
duodenum

小腸
small intestine

闌尾
appendix

股動脈
femoral artery

前脛動脈
anterior tibial artery

主動脈弓
aortic arch

左肺
left lung

心
heart

膜
diaphragm

脾
spleen

胃
stomach

大腸
large intestine

膀胱
bladder

股靜脈
femoral vein

動脈血
arterial blood

靜脈血
venous blood

眼睛：視覺器官
EYE: THE ORGAN OF SIGHT

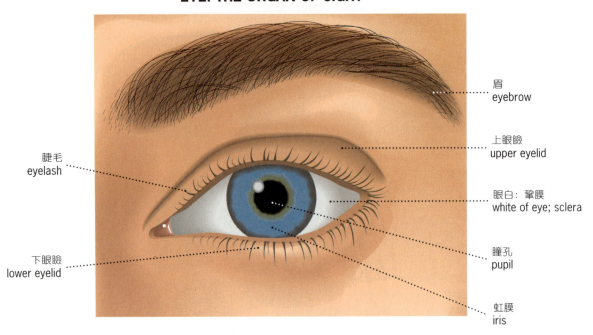

眉
eyebrow

上眼瞼
upper eyelid

眼白：鞏膜
white of eye; sclera

瞳孔
pupil

虹膜
iris

睫毛
eyelash

下眼瞼
lower eyelid

手：觸覺器官
HAND: THE ORGAN OF TOUCH

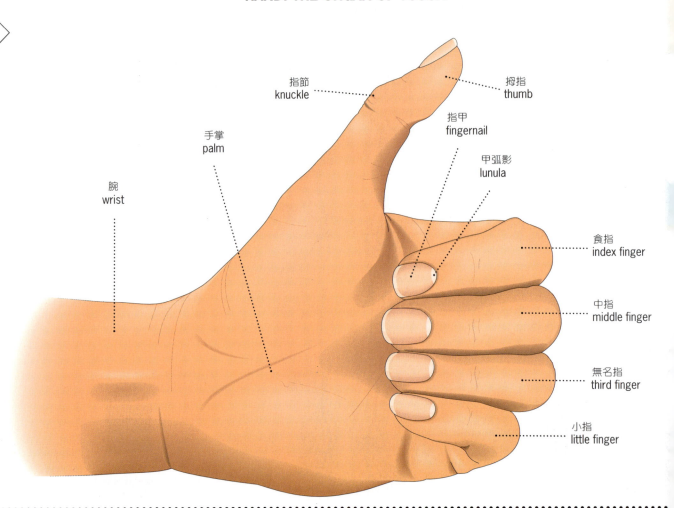

指節
knuckle

拇指
thumb

指甲
fingernail

甲弧影
lunula

手掌
palm

腕
wrist

食指
index finger

中指
middle finger

無名指
third finger

小指
little finger

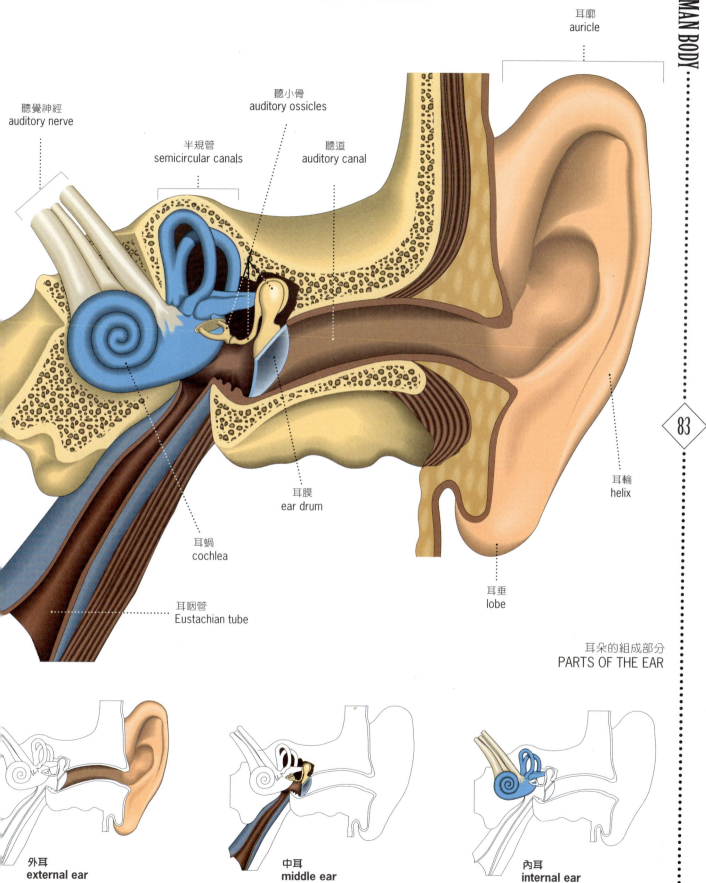

耳：聽覺器官
EAR: THE ORGAN OF HEARING

耳廓
auricle

聽覺神經
auditory nerve

聽小骨
auditory ossicles

半規管
semicircular canals

聽道
auditory canal

耳輪
helix

耳膜
ear drum

耳蝸
cochlea

耳垂
lobe

耳咽管
Eustachian tube

耳朵的組成部分
PARTS OF THE EAR

外耳
external ear

中耳
middle ear

內耳
internal ear

鼻：嗅覺器官
NOSE: THE ORGAN OF SMELL

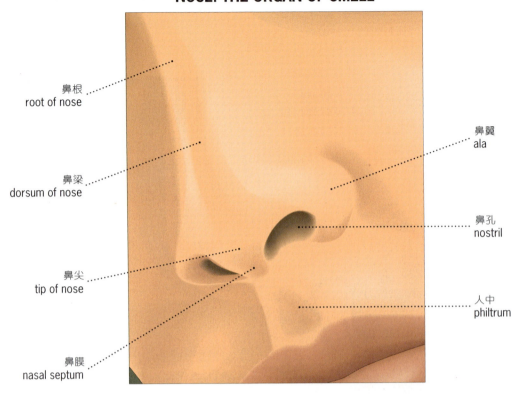

鼻根
root of nose

鼻梁
dorsum of nose

鼻尖
tip of nose

鼻膜
nasal septum

鼻翼
ala

鼻孔
nostril

人中
philtrum

口：味覺器官
MOUTH: THE ORGAN OF TASTE

味覺
taste sensations

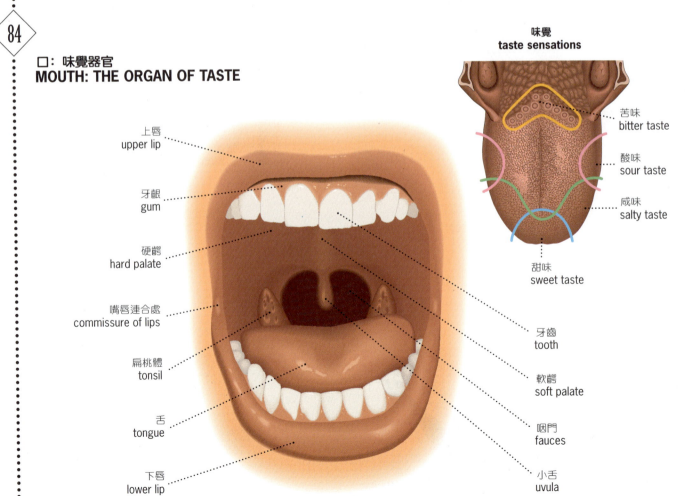

上唇
upper lip

牙齦
gum

硬齶
hard palate

嘴唇連合處
commissure of lips

扁桃體
tonsil

舌
tongue

下唇
lower lip

苦味
bitter taste

酸味
sour taste

咸味
salty taste

甜味
sweet taste

牙齒
tooth

軟齶
soft palate

咽門
fauces

小舌
uvula

人的牙齒
HUMAN DENTURE

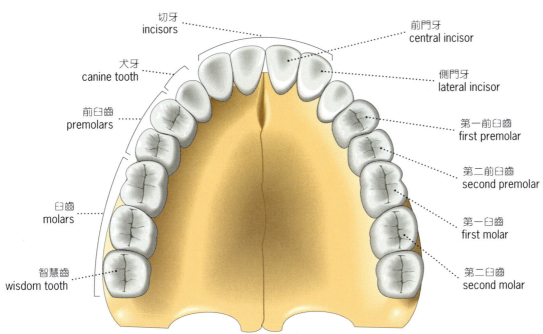

切牙
incisors

犬牙
canine tooth

前臼齒
premolars

臼齒
molars

智慧齒
wisdom tooth

前門牙
central incisor

側門牙
lateral incisor

第一前臼齒
first premolar

第二前臼齒
second premolar

第一臼齒
first molar

第二臼齒
second molar

臼齒橫切面
cross section of a molar

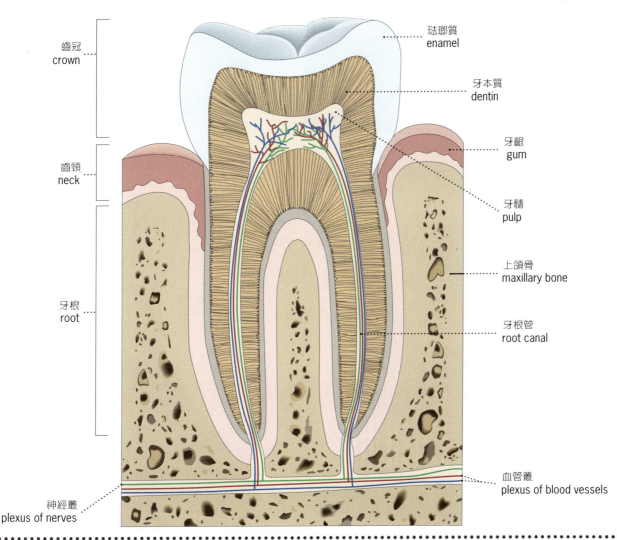

齒冠
crown

齒頸
neck

牙根
root

珐瑯質
enamel

牙本質
dentin

牙齦
gum

牙髓
pulp

上頜骨
maxillary bone

牙根管
root canal

血管叢
plexus of blood vessels

神經叢
plexus of nerves

傳統房屋
TRADITIONAL HOUSES

愛斯基摩冰屋
igloo

印第安棚屋
wigwam

小木屋
log cabin

小土屋
mud hut

吊腳樓
house on stilts

印第安圓錐帳篷
tepee

茅舍
hut

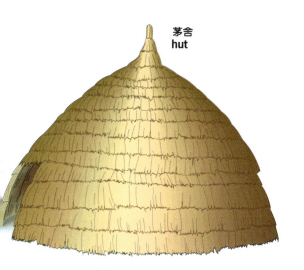

蒙古包
yurt

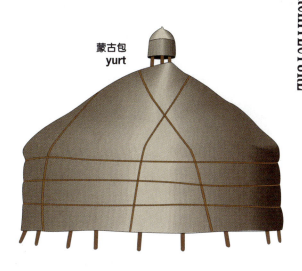

清眞寺
MOSQUE

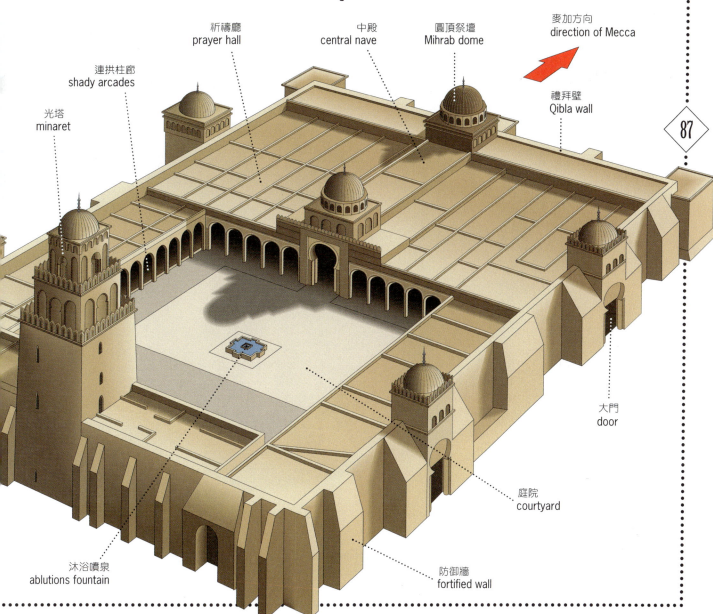

祈禱廳
prayer hall

中殿
central nave

圓頂祭壇
Mihrab dome

麥加方向
direction of Mecca

連拱柱廊
shady arcades

禮拜壁
Qibla wall

光塔
minaret

大門
door

庭院
courtyard

沐浴噴泉
ablutions fountain

防御牆
fortified wall

87

城堡
CASTLE

88

槍眼
machicolation

垛口
crenel

城齒
merlon

觀察孔
loophole

角
corner tow

懸牆
curtain wall

城堡
castle

塔樓
turret

城郭
bailey

掩蔽胸牆走廊
covered parapet walk

雉堞
battlement

城堡主樓
keep

小教堂
chapel

風障
brattice

護城河
moat

監獄
guardhouse

步行橋
footbridge

吊橋
drawbridge

防御土牆
rampart

側
flanking tow

柵欄
stockade

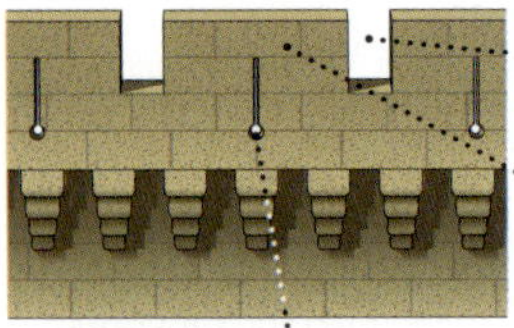

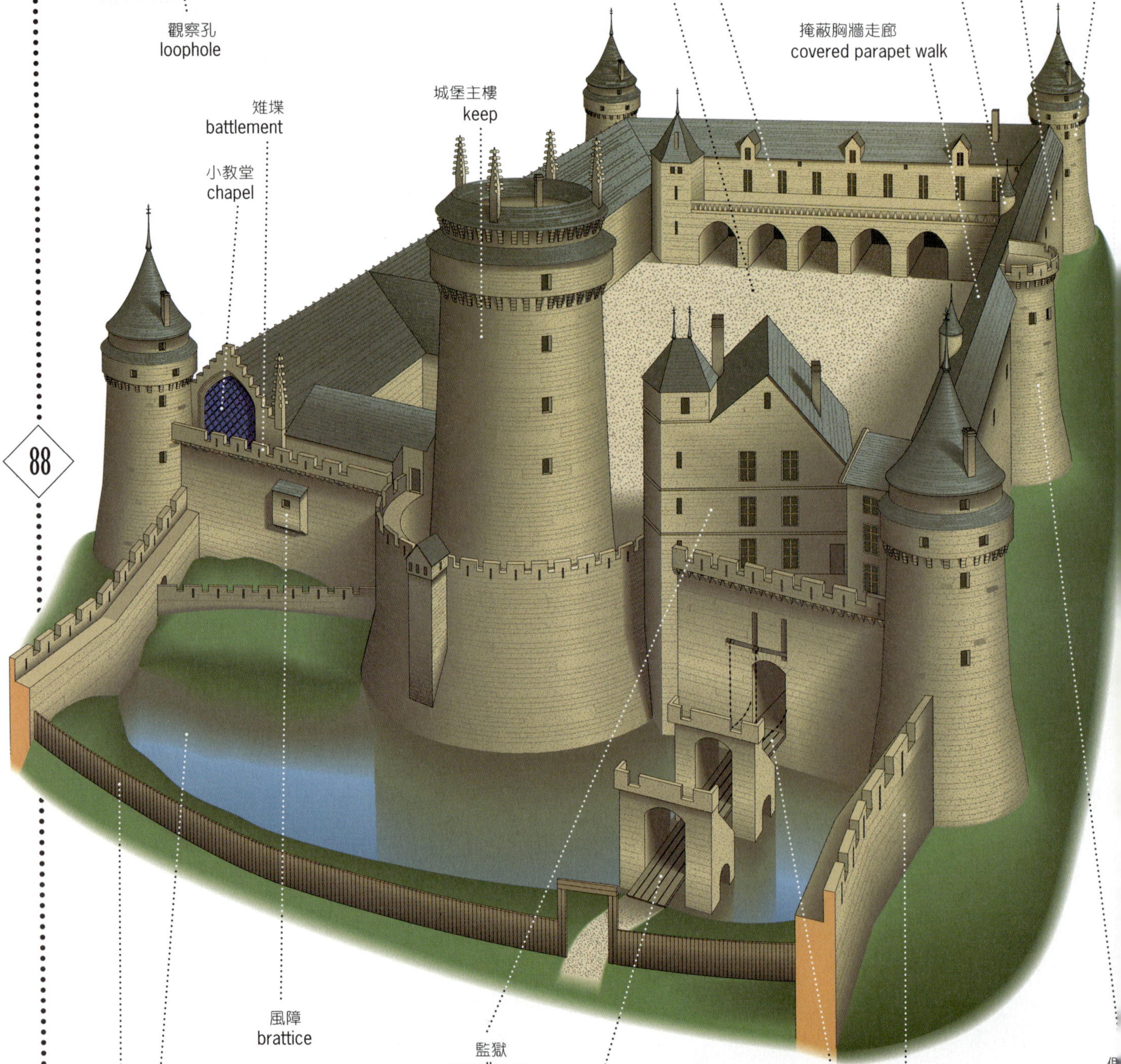

哥特式大教堂
GOTHIC CATHEDRAL

臨街正面
facade

鍾塔
bell tower

百葉窗板
louver-board

樓座
gallery

尖塔
spire

圓花窗
rose window

山牆飾內的三角面部分
tympanum

大門
portal

鍾樓
elfry

塔
tower

中殿
nave

耳堂尖塔
transept spire

耳堂
transept

圓室
chevet

拱扶垛
flying buttress

側翼教堂
side chapel

中殿與翼部相交處
crossing

支柱
pillar

高壇
choir

回廊
ambulatory

聖母堂
Lady chapel

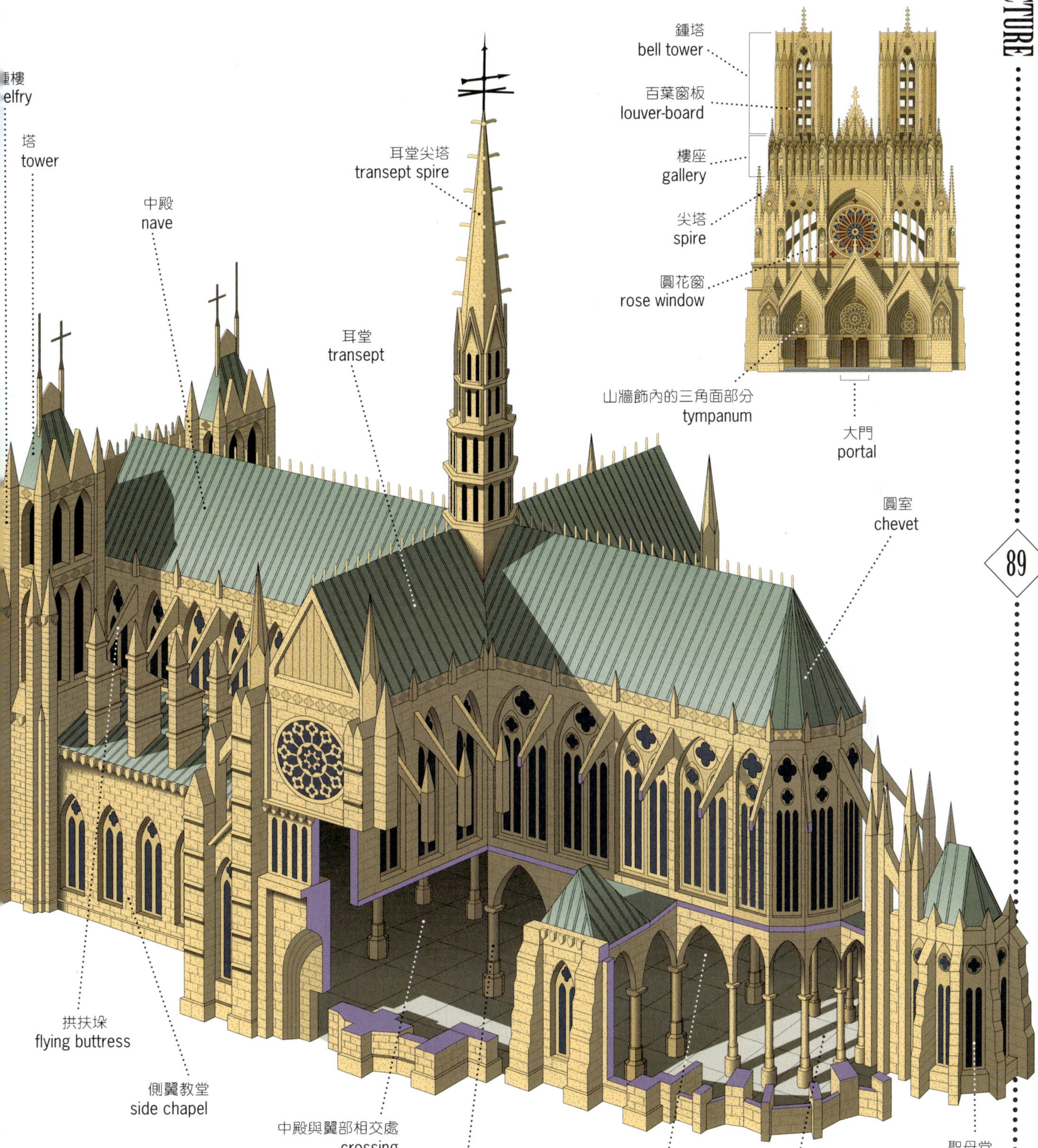

市中心
DOWNTOWN

廣場
square

公園
park

教堂
cathedral

會議廳
convention center

火車站
railroad station

高層辦公大樓
office tower

中央分隔帶
median strip

天文館
planetarium

鐵軌
railroad

交通島
traffic island

林蔭大道
boulevard / high street

街道
street

送貨斜坡
delivery ramp

高速公路
freeway / dual carriageway

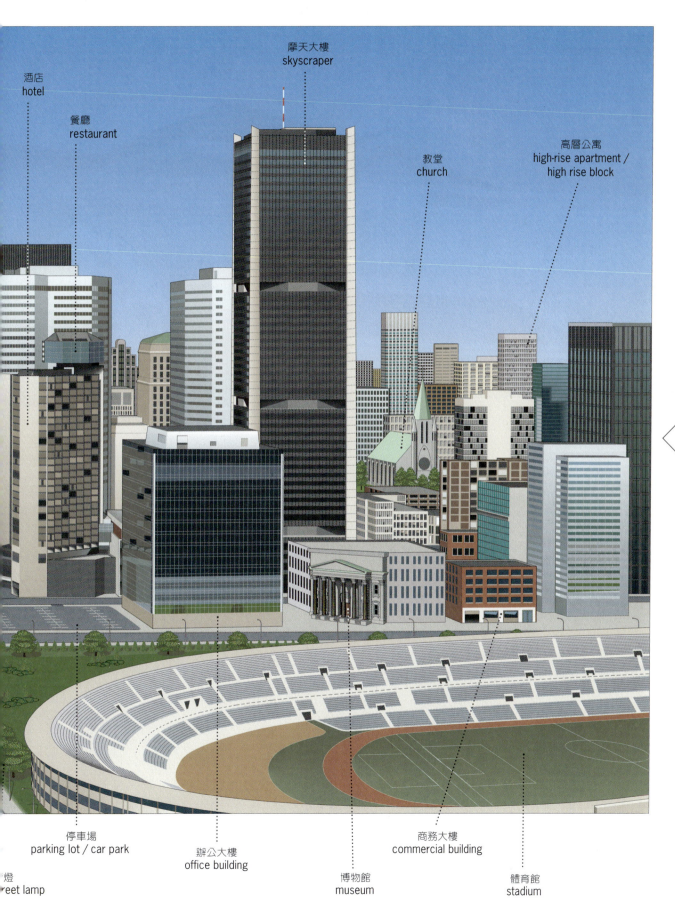

摩天大樓
skyscraper

酒店
hotel

餐廳
restaurant

教堂
church

高層公寓
high-rise apartment /
high rise block

停車場
parking lot / car park

辦公大樓
office building

商務大樓
commercial building

博物館
museum

體育館
stadium

燈
eet lamp

房屋
HOUSE

房屋的外觀
exterior of a house

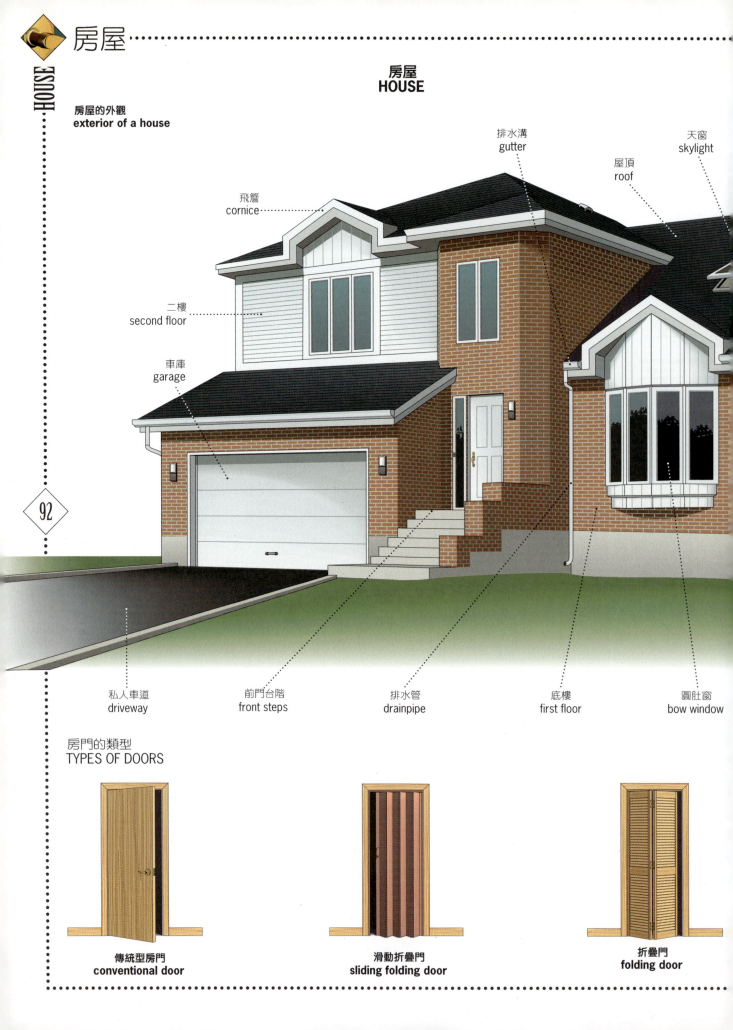

排水溝
gutter

天窗
skylight

屋頂
roof

飛簷
cornice

二樓
second floor

車庫
garage

92

私人車道
driveway

前門台階
front steps

排水管
drainpipe

底樓
first floor

圓肚窗
bow window

房門的類型
TYPES OF DOORS

傳統型房門
conventional door

滑動折疊門
sliding folding door

折疊門
folding door

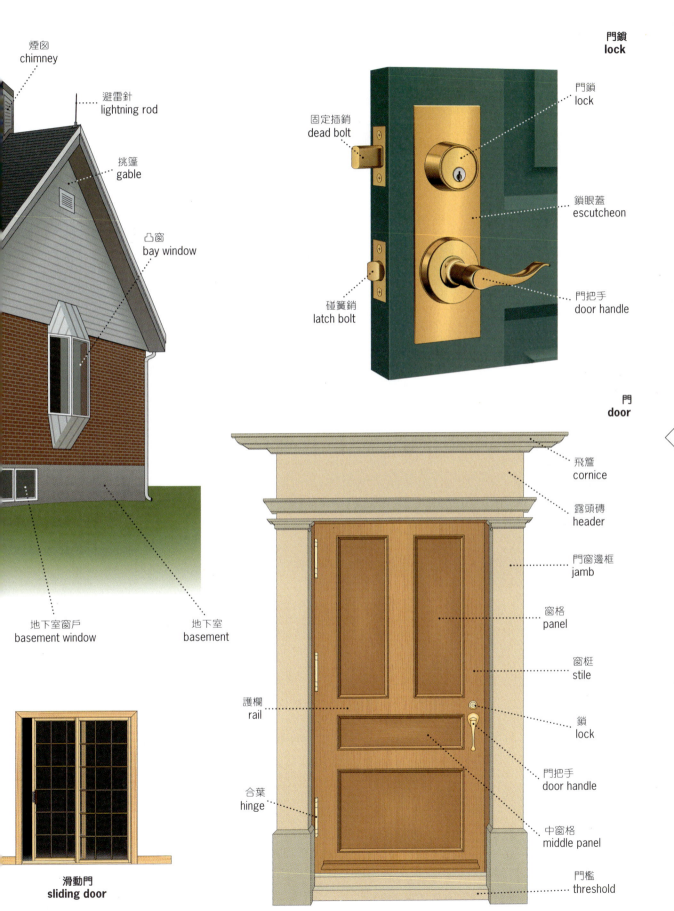

煙囪
chimney

避雷針
lightning rod

挑篷
gable

凸窗
bay window

門鎖
lock

固定插銷
dead bolt

門鎖
lock

鎖眼蓋
escutcheon

碰簧銷
latch bolt

門把手
door handle

門
door

地下室窗戶
basement window

地下室
basement

飛簷
cornice

露頭磚
header

門窗邊框
jamb

窗格
panel

窗梃
stile

護欄
rail

鎖
lock

合葉
hinge

門把手
door handle

中窗格
middle panel

滑動門
sliding door

門檻
threshold

窗戶
WINDOW

窗玻璃
pane

窗芯子
muntin

窗框
frame

頂欄
top rail

固定百葉窗；板條百葉窗
jalousie; slatted shutter

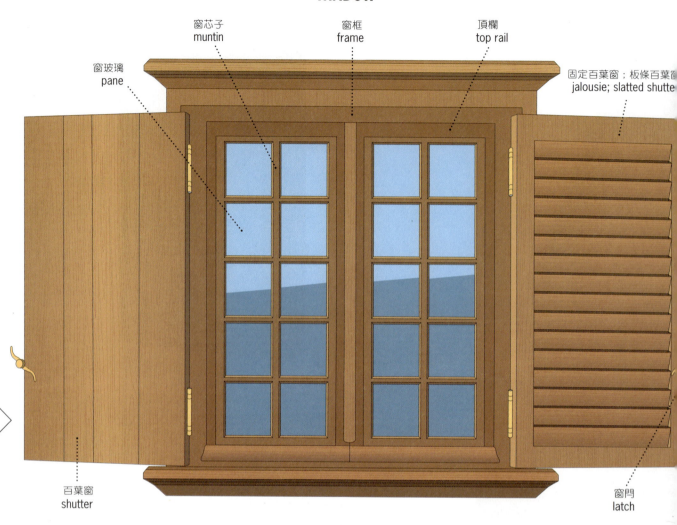

百葉窗
shutter

窗閂
latch

窗戶的類型
TYPES OF WINDOWS

豎鉸鏈窗（內開式）
**casement window
(inward opening)**

豎鉸鏈窗（外開式）
**casement window
(outward opening)**

水平軸窗
horizontal pivoting window

滑動窗
sliding window

滑動折疊窗
sliding folding window

豎軸窗
vertical pivoting window

推拉窗
sash window

煙窗
louvred window

床
BED

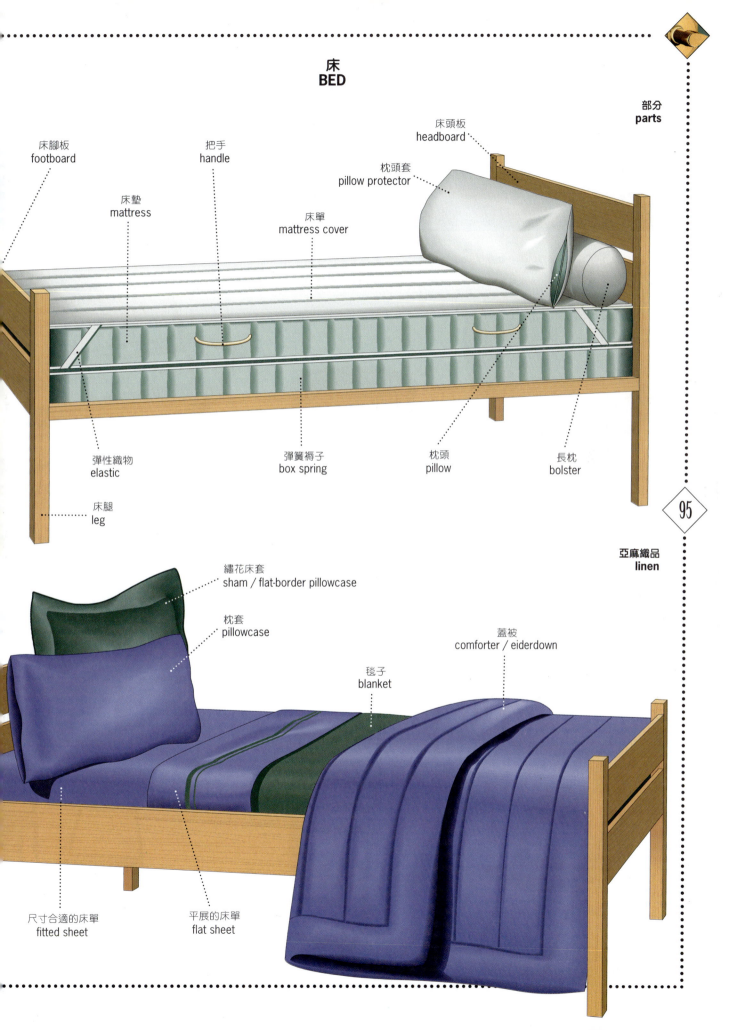

床腳板
footboard

把手
handle

床墊
mattress

床單
mattress cover

枕頭套
pillow protector

床頭板
headboard

彈性織物
elastic

彈簧褥子
box spring

枕頭
pillow

長枕
bolster

床腿
leg

95

繡花床套
sham / flat-border pillowcase

枕套
pillowcase

蓋被
comforter / eiderdown

毯子
blanket

尺寸合適的床單
fitted sheet

平展的床單
flat sheet

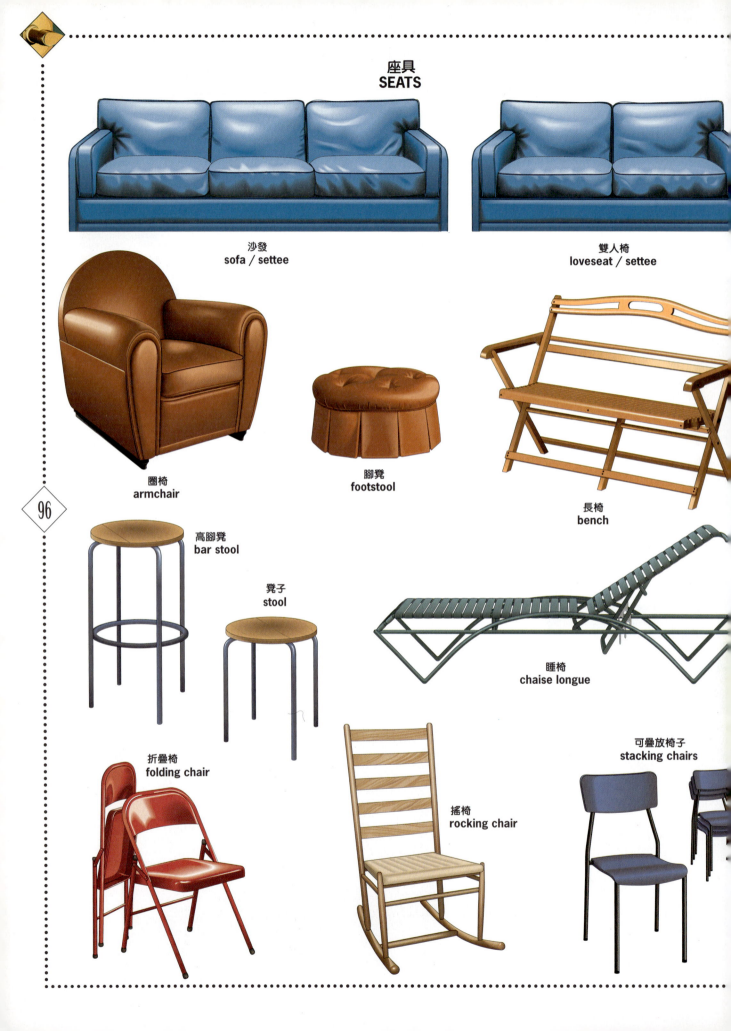

沙發
sofa / settee

雙人椅
loveseat / settee

圈椅
armchair

腳凳
footstool

長椅
bench

高腳凳
bar stool

凳子
stool

睡椅
chaise longue

可疊放椅子
stacking chairs

折疊椅
folding chair

搖椅
rocking chair

桌椅
TABLE AND CHAIRS

無扶手單人椅
side chair

捏把
ear

扶手
rail

椅背
back

梃
stile

座椅
seat

圍裙
apron

紡錘形立柱
spindle

椅腿
leg

支架
support

圈椅
armchair

靠手
arm

旋鈕
knob

抽屜
drawer

桌面
top

桌子
table

垂板
drop-leaf

桌腿
leg

橫檔
crosspiece

燈具
LIGHTS

活動式投射燈
track lighting

滑軌
track

變壓器
transformer

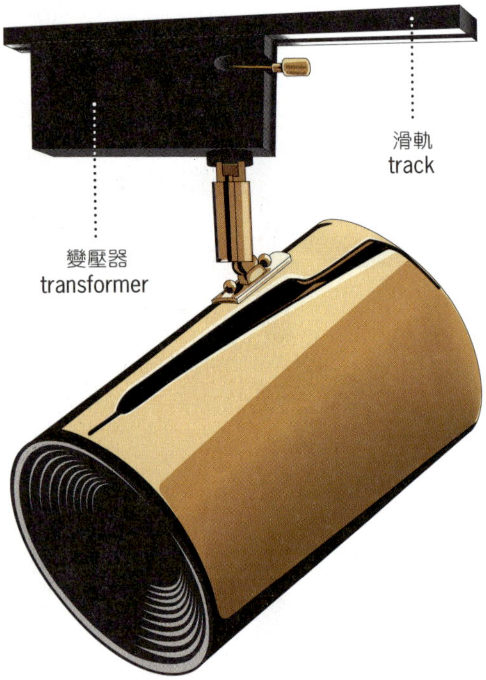

落地燈
floor lamp

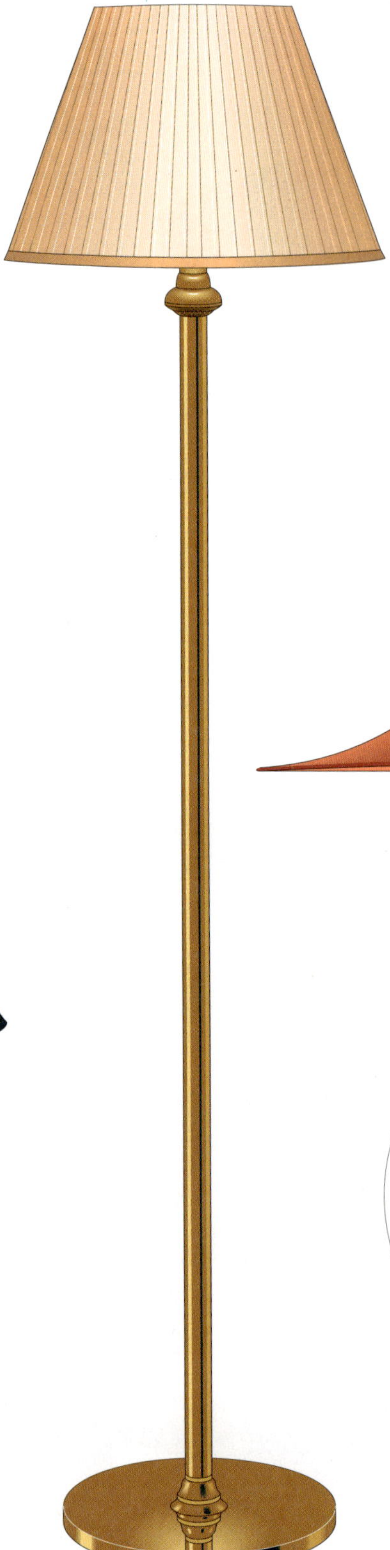

天花板固定燈
ceiling fixture

台燈
table lamp

燈罩
shade

燈座
stand

吊燈
hanging pendant

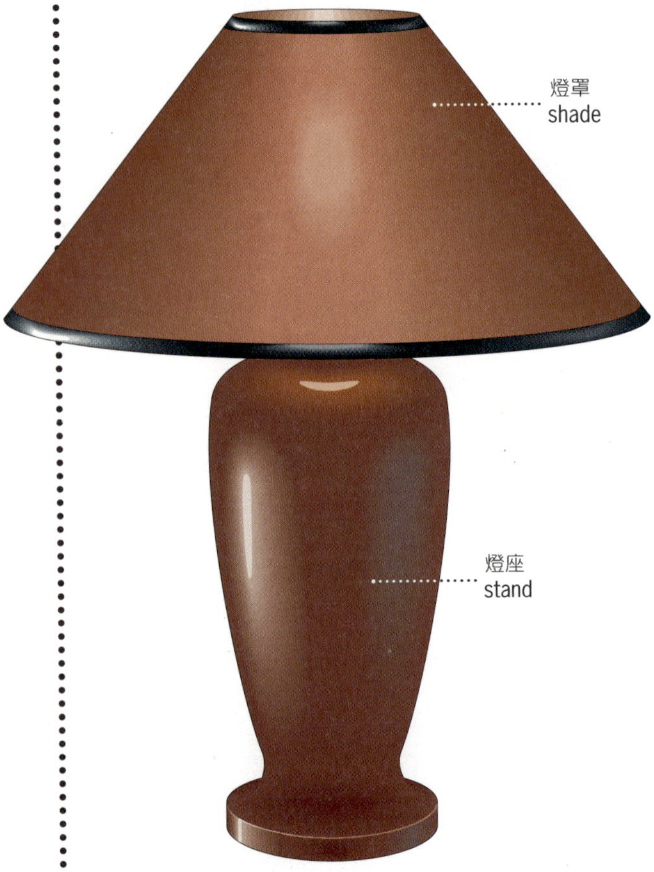

壁燈
wall fixture

照明設施
LIGHTING

白熾燈
candescent lamp

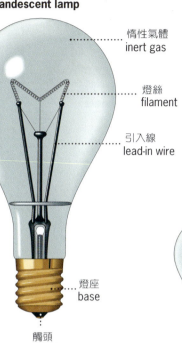

惰性氣體
inert gas

燈絲
filament

引入線
lead-in wire

燈座
base

觸頭
contact

燈泡
bulb

螺絲燈座
screw base

卡口燈座
bayonet base

絲鹵素燈泡
ngsten-halogen lamp

銷子
pin

燈座
base

熒光燈管
fluorescent tube

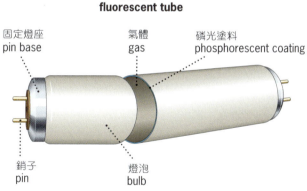

固定燈座
pin base

氣體
gas

磷光塗料
phosphorescent coating

銷子
pin

燈泡
bulb

節能燈泡
energy saving bulb

燈泡
bulb

熒光燈管
fluorescent tube

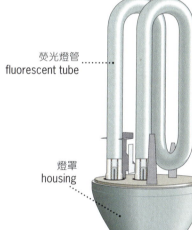

燈罩
housing

燈座
base

開關
switch

電源插座
outlet

歐式插座
European plug

罩子
cover

銷子
pin

美式插座
American plug

銷子
pin

接地端子
grounding terminal

玻璃器皿
GLASSWARE

香檳酒瓶
champagne glass

白葡萄酒瓶
white wine glass

紅葡萄酒瓶
red wine glass

笛形香檳酒杯
champagne flute

平底玻璃杯
tumbler; glass

啤酒杯
beer mug

卡拉夫瓶
carafe

細頸盛水瓶
decanter

餐具
DINNERWARE

咖啡杯
coffee cup

小杯
cup

大杯
mug

奶盅
creamer

糖碗
sugar bowl

胡椒瓶
pepper shaker

鹽瓶
salt shaker

黃油碟
butter dish

飯碗
cereal bowl

湯碗
soup bowl

餐盤
dinner plate

沙拉盤
salad plate

面包黃油盤；側盤
bread and butter plate;
side plate

沙拉碟
salad dish

沙拉碗
salad bowl

茶壺
teapot

咖啡壺
coffee plunger

湯蓋碗
soup tureen

水壺
water pitcher

銀質餐具
SILVERWARE

餐刀
knife

刀背
back

刀鋒
blade

手柄
handle

刀口
cutting edge

餐道的種類
YPES OF KNIVES

黃油刀
butter knife

奶酪刀
cheese knife

餐刀
dinner knife

牛排刀
steak knife

餐叉
rk

手柄
handle

齒尖
tine

餐叉的種類
TYPES OF FORKS

餐叉
dinner fork

頭
int

涮肉叉
fondue fork

湯匙
spoon

手柄
handle

匙的種類
PES OF SPOONS

內側
inside

咖啡匙
coffee spoon

茶匙
teaspoon

勺
bowl

湯匙
soup spoon

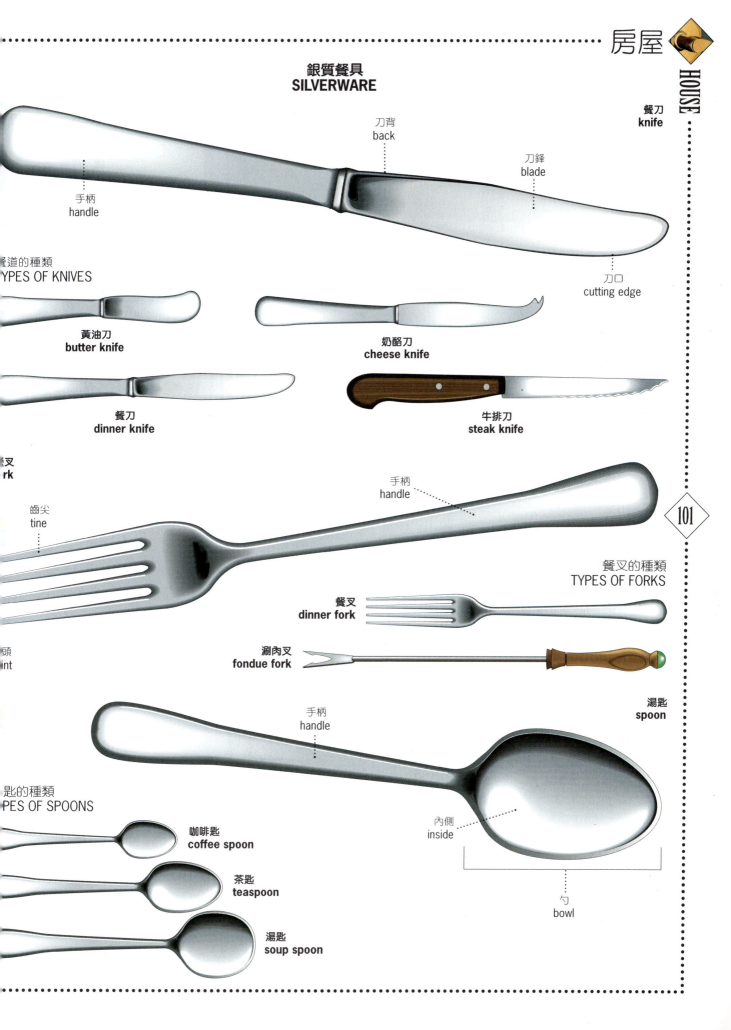

廚房用具
KITCHEN UTENSILS

長柄勺
ladle

馬鈴薯搗碎器
potato masher

抹刀
spatula

攪拌器
whisk

打蛋器
egg beater

量勺
measuring spoons

堅果鉗
nutcracker

啓瓶器
bottle opener

剝皮機
peeler

槓桿式瓶塞鑽
lever corkscrew

扞麵杖
rolling pin

罐頭起子
can opener

（意大利式細）面條夾
spaghetti tongs

漏斗
funnel

冰淇淋勺
ice-cream scoop

濾器
colander

檸檬榨汁機
lemon squeezer

沙拉攪拌器
salad spinner

篩網
strainer

磨碎機
grater

烹調用具
COOKING UTENSILS

煎鍋
frying pan

炒鍋
sauté pan

什錦鍋;砂鍋
stockpot; casserole

涮菜鍋具
fondue set

鑊子
wok

涮菜鍋
fondue pot

火爐
burner

雙層蒸鍋
double boiler

燉鍋
saucepan

蔬菜蒸籠
vegetable steame

烤鍋
roasting pans

高壓鍋
pressure cooker

高壓鍋調節閥
pressure regulator

安全閥
safety valve

廚房器具
KITCHEN APPLIANCES

自動滴漏咖啡煮具
utomatic drip coffee maker / automatic filter coffee maker

儲水器
reservoir

篢
basket

卡拉夫瓶
carafe

保溫盤
warming plate

開關
on-off switch

水壺
kettle

手動攪拌器
hand mixer

打蛋推出器
beater ejector

速度控制
speed control

打蛋器
beater

摻和器
lender

手動摻和器
hand blender

容器
container

切刀
cutting blade

按鈕
push button

烤面包爐
toaster

狹槽
slot

控制桿
lever

溫度控制
temperature control

冰箱
REFRIGERATOR

冷凍庫
freezer compartment

冰塊盤
ice cube tray

溫度自動調節器
thermostat control

蛋托
egg tray

黃油儲藏格
butter compartment

奶制品儲藏格
dairy compartment

保鮮儲藏格
crisper

冷藏庫
refrigerator compartment

護欄
guard rail

肉托
meat tray

玻璃罩
glass cover

擱板
shelf

儲藏室門
storage door

烹調器具
COOKING APPLIANCES

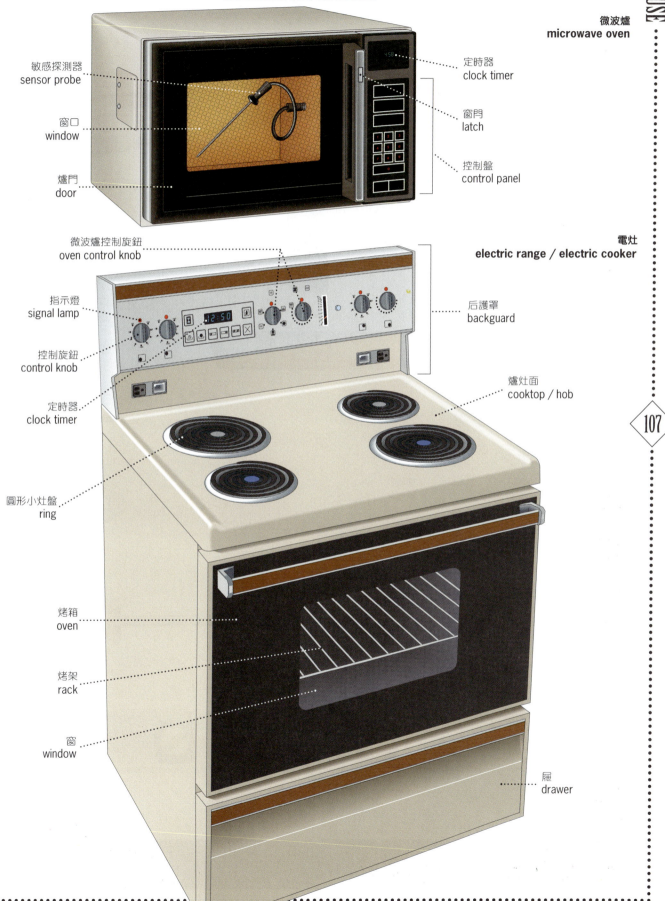

微波爐
microwave oven

敏感探測器
sensor probe

窗口
window

爐門
door

定時器
clock timer

窗閂
latch

控制盤
control panel

電灶
electric range / electric cooker

微波爐控制旋鈕
oven control knob

指示燈
signal lamp

控制旋鈕
control knob

定時器
clock timer

后護罩
backguard

爐灶面
cooktop / hob

圓形小灶盤
ring

烤箱
oven

烤架
rack

窗
window

屜
drawer

木工工具
CARPENTRY TOOLS

羊角槌頭
claw hammer

起釘器
claw

手柄
handle

木工錘
carpenter's hammer

鎚面
face

大頭錘
mallet

錘頭
head

卷
tape measu

尺盒
case

尺鎖
tape lock

刻度
scale

尺鉤
hook

卷尺
tape

釘子
nail

螺絲釘
screw

釘子頭
head

釘子頭
head

釘桿
shank

釘桿
shank

釘尖
tip

螺紋
thread

螺絲
screwdri

直角尺
framing square

水准儀
level

C形
C-clar

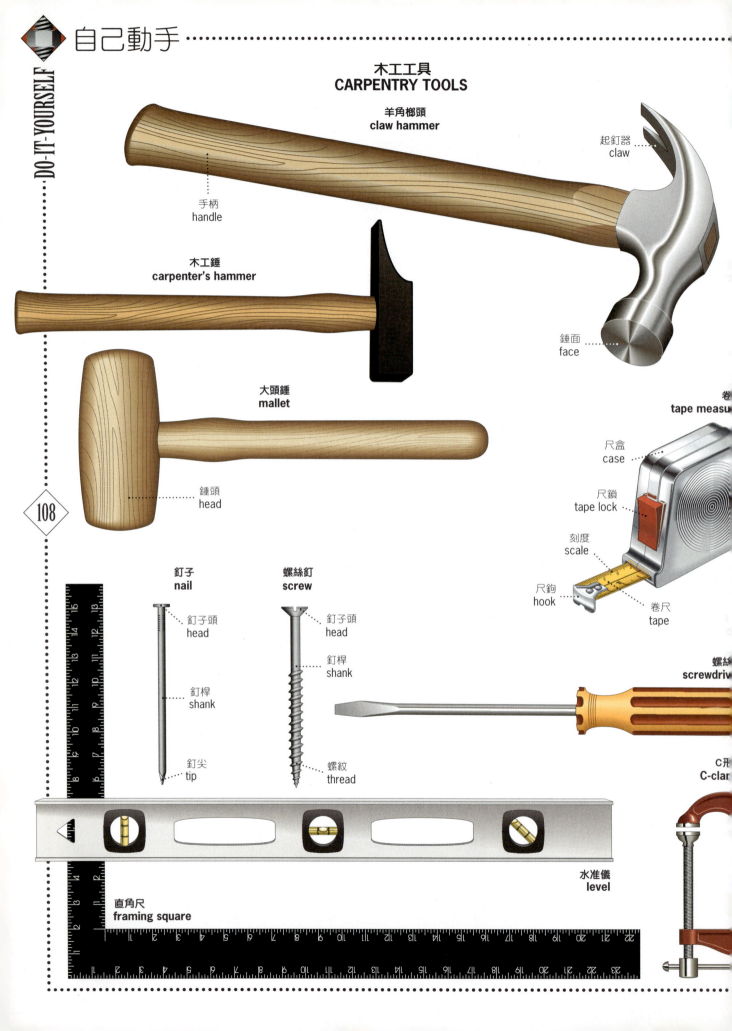

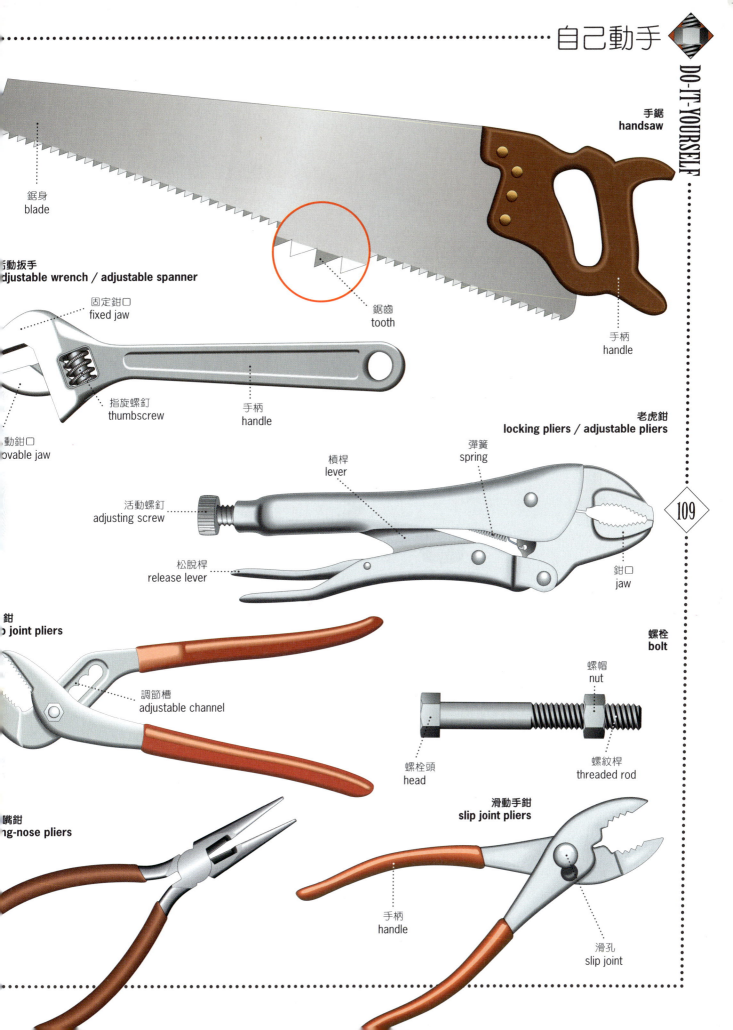

手鋸
handsaw

鋸身
blade

鋸齒
tooth

手柄
handle

活動扳手
adjustable wrench / adjustable spanner

固定鉗口
fixed jaw

指旋螺釘
thumbscrew

手柄
handle

活動鉗口
movable jaw

老虎鉗
locking pliers / adjustable pliers

彈簧
spring

槓桿
lever

活動螺釘
adjusting screw

松脫桿
release lever

鉗口
jaw

水泵鉗
slip joint pliers

調節槽
adjustable channel

螺栓
bolt

螺帽
nut

螺栓頭
head

螺紋桿
threaded rod

尖嘴鉗
long-nose pliers

滑動手鉗
slip joint pliers

手柄
handle

滑孔
slip joint

109

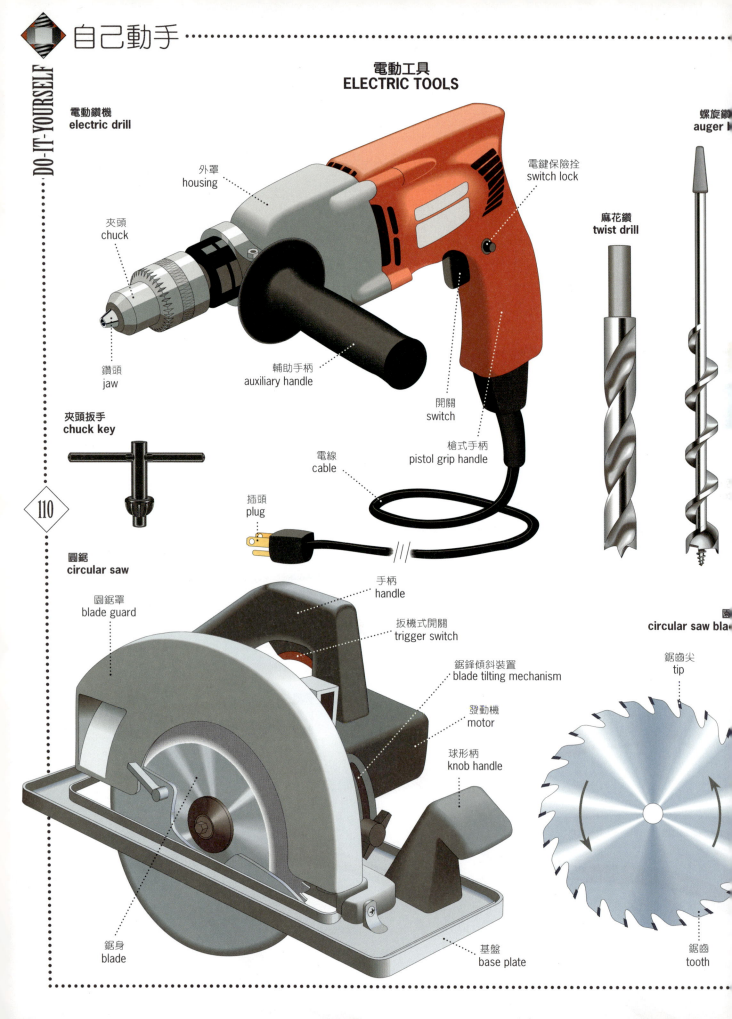

自己動手

電動工具
ELECTRIC TOOLS

電動鑽機
electric drill

外罩
housing

夾頭
chuck

鑽頭
jaw

電鍵保險拴
switch lock

螺旋鑽
auger

麻花鑽
twist drill

輔助手柄
auxiliary handle

開關
switch

槍式手柄
pistol grip handle

夾頭扳手
chuck key

電線
cable

插頭
plug

圓鋸
circular saw

手柄
handle

扳機式開關
trigger switch

圓鋸罩
blade guard

鋸鋒傾斜裝置
blade tilting mechanism

發動機
motor

球形柄
knob handle

鋸身
blade

基盤
base plate

circular saw blade

鋸齒尖
tip

鋸齒
tooth

粉刷維修
PAINTING UPKEEP

塗料輥
aint roller

塗料盤
tray

刮泥板
scraper

刮刀
blade

伸縮梯
extension ladder

輥輪
roller frame

手柄
handle

刷子
brush

輪套
roller cover

刷毛
bristles

扶手
side rail

梯
tepladder

滑輪
pulley

固定裝置
locking device

橫檔
rung

平台梯
platform ladder

升降繩
hoisting rope

防滑套
anti-slip shoe

男式服裝
MEN'S CLOTHING

襯衣
shirt

領扣
collar point

衣領
collar

叉口
placket

胸袋
breast pocket

假前胸
front

袖口
cuff

鈕扣
button

下擺
shirttail

吊褲
suspenders / brace

調節滑扣
adjustment slide

吊褲帶夾
suspender clip

環帶式鈕孔
button loop

皮質帶端
leather end

領帶
tie

后襟
rear apron

束頸
neck end

環扣
loop

前襟
front apron

褲子
pants / trousers

腰帶
waistband

口袋
pocket

遮紐蓋
fly

折痕
crease

皮帶
belt

皮帶扣
frame

皮帶孔
punch hole

皮帶套環
belt carrier

皮帶扣針舌
tongue

圓領背心
undershirt / vest

拳擊短褲
boxer shorts

貼身短褲
briefs

遮紐蓋
fly

褲襠墊布
crotch

腰帶
waistband

翻邊
cuff

雙排扣短上衣
double-breasted jacket

衣領
collar

襯里
lining

裝飾胸袋
breast welt pocket

袖
sleeve

暗包
concealed pocket

貼袋
patch pocket

口袋蓋
flap

帶帽大衣
duffle coat

兜帽
hood

盤花鈕扣
frog

木拴扣
toggle fastening

帽子
cap

帽冠
crown

帽簷
peak

絨線帽
stocking cap / bobble hat

獵帽
hunting cap

耳罩
ear flap

夾克
jacket

按扣
snap fastener

橡筋束腰
elastic waistband

風衣
windbreaker

束腰
waistband

拉繩
drawstring

女式服裝
WOMEN'S CLOTHING

無邊女帽
toque

針織帽
knitted hat

巴拉克拉發帽
balaclava

帽簷
peak

貝雷帽
beret

女套裝
suit

寬松女上衣
blouse

雙排扣短上衣
double-breasted jacket

短上衣
jacket

短裙
skirt

大衣
overcoat

南美披風
poncho

長裙
dress

牛仔褲
jeans

滑雪褲
ski pants

短褲
shorts

百慕大短褲
Bermuda shorts

腳帶
footstrap

直裙
straight skirt

裙褲
culottes

折疊裙
pleated skirt

女式服裝
WOMEN'S CLOTHING

睡衣
pajamas

胸罩
bra

肩帶
shoulder strap

罩杯
cup

短褲
pants / briefs

短襯裙
half-slip / waist slip

浴衣
bathrobe / dressing gown

毛衣
SWEATERS

水手領毛衣
crew neck sweater

套領毛衣
turtleneck / polo neck

開襟羊毛衫
cardigan

球衣
polo shirt

尖領開襟羊毛衫
V-neck cardigan

毛背心
sweater vest

掛衣環
hanger loop

尖領（V形領）
V-neck

袖
sleeve

鈕扣
button

口袋
pocket

稜紋
ribbing

手套與襪子
GLOVES AND STOCKINGS

手套
gloves

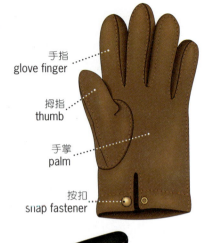

手指
glove finger

拇指
thumb

手掌
palm

按扣
snap fastener

縫合
stitching

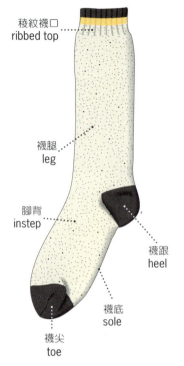

稜紋襪口
ribbed top

襪腿
leg

腳背
instep

襪跟
heel

襪底
sole

襪尖
toe

駕駛手套
driving glove

連指手套
mitten

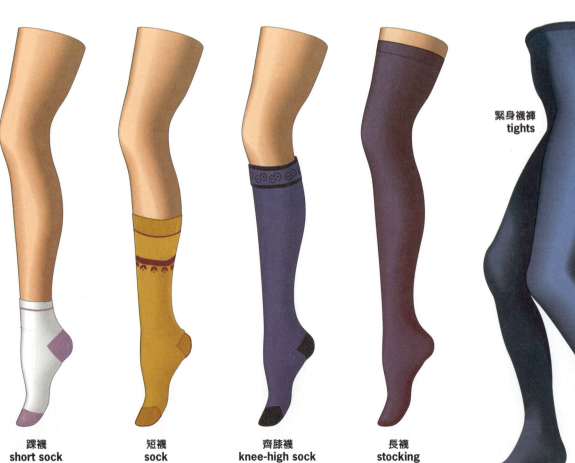

緊身襪褲
tights

踝襪
short sock

短襪
sock

齊膝襪
knee-high sock

長襪
stocking

鞋
SHOES

大頭鞋
**heavy duty boot /
walking boot**

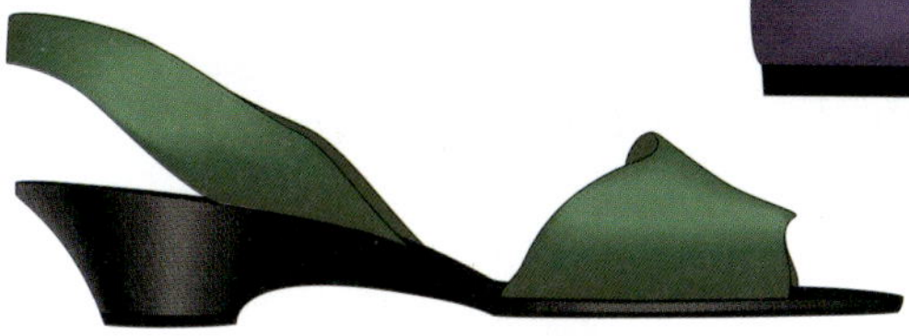

軟底低跟女便鞋
ballerina / pump

露跟女鞋
slingback

長筒靴
thigh-boot

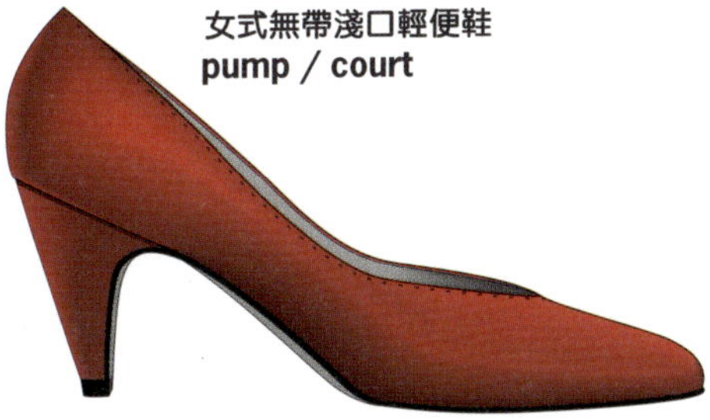

女式無帶淺口輕便鞋
pump / court

網球鞋
tennis shoe

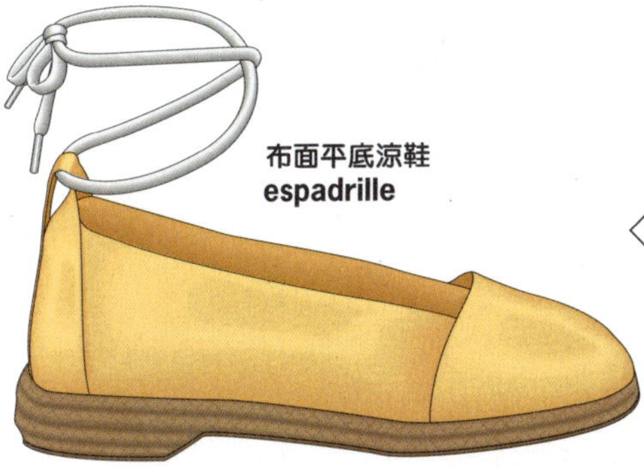

布面平底涼鞋
espadrille

平跟船鞋
loafer

涼鞋
sandal

"莫卡辛"鞋；軟幫鞋
moccasin

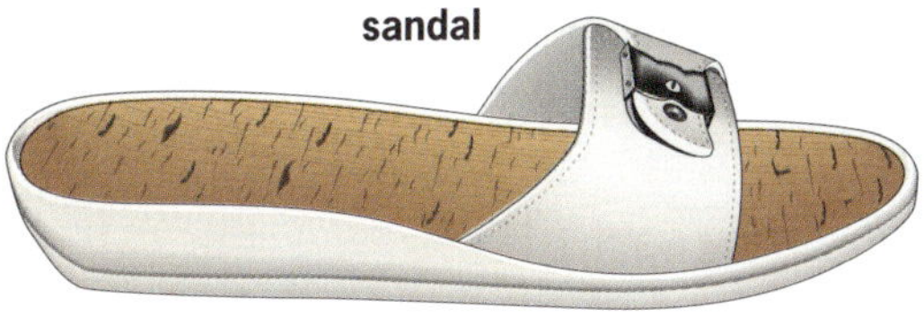

筒靴
boot

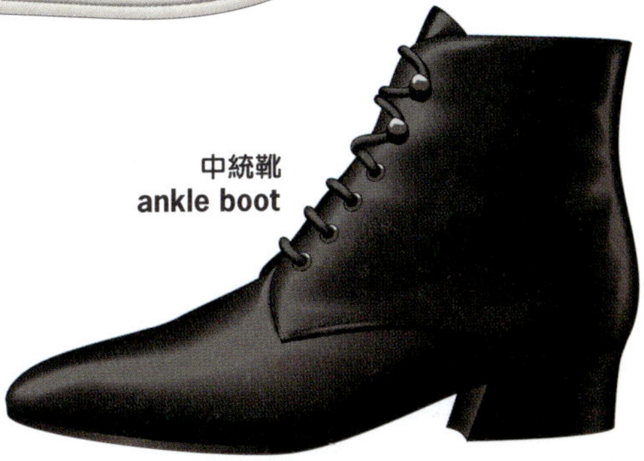

中統靴
ankle boot

服裝

運動服
SPORTSWEAR

健身服
EXERCISE WEAR

大圓領背心
tank top

女游泳衣
swimsuit

緊身連衣褲
leotard

徑賽服
TRACK SUIT

運動衫
sweatshirt

風衣
windbreaker / anorak

帶帽運動衫
hooded sweatshirt

褲子
pants /
waterproof
trousers

長運動褲
sweatpants / jogging bottoms

健身服
EXERCISE WEAR

無底緊身衣
footless tights

暖腿套
leg-warmer

游泳褲
swimming trunks

拳擊短褲
boxer shorts

跑鞋
running shoe / trainer

后幫
ounter

鞋領
collar

鞋幫后側部
quarter

襯里
lining

鞋舌
tongue

鞋側面突出部
nose of the quarter

鞋帶孔
eyelet

鞋面
vamp

后跟
el

縫合
stitching

中底
midsole

氣囊
air unit

鞋帶箍
tag

鞋帶
shoelace

外底
outsole

鞋釘
stud

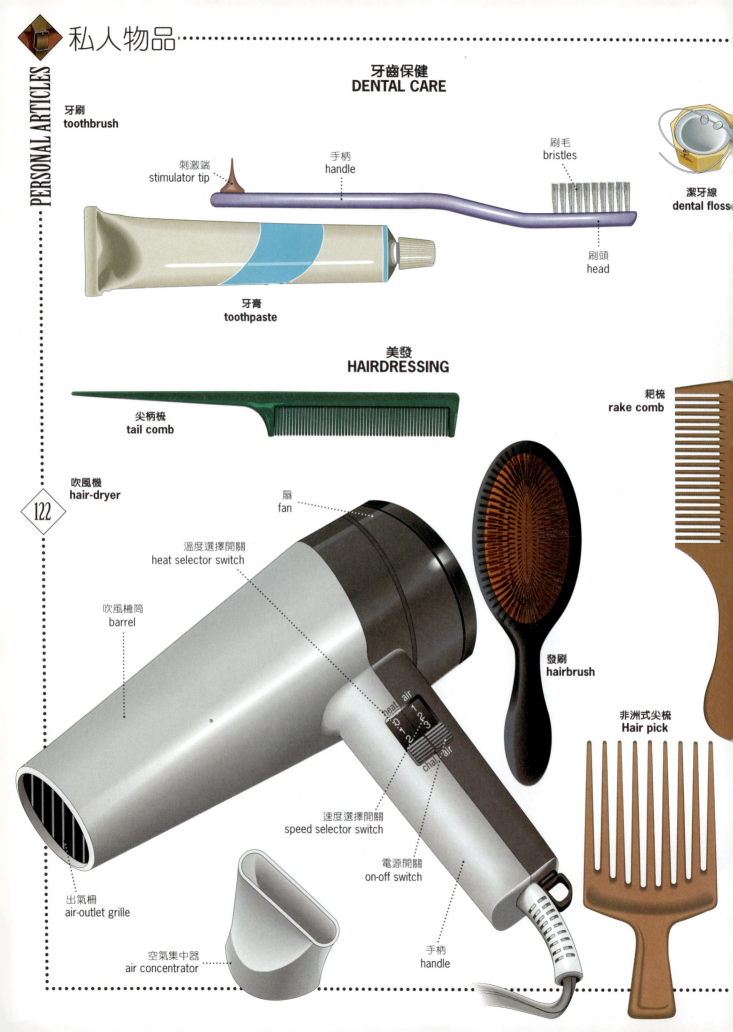

牙齒保健
DENTAL CARE

牙刷
toothbrush

刺激端
stimulator tip

手柄
handle

刷毛
bristles

潔牙線
dental floss

刷頭
head

牙膏
toothpaste

美髮
HAIRDRESSING

尖柄梳
tail comb

耙梳
rake comb

吹風機
hair-dryer

扇
fan

溫度選擇開關
heat selector switch

吹風機筒
barrel

發刷
hairbrush

非洲式尖梳
Hair pick

hot air

cold air

速度選擇開關
speed selector switch

電源開關
on-off switch

出氣柵
air-outlet grille

空氣集中器
air concentrator

手柄
handle

皮革制品
LEATHER GOODS

拉带皮包
rawstring bag

拉带
awstring

皮背包
knapsack

皮鑰匙套
key case

錢包
wallet

背帶
shoulder strap

眼鏡
GLASSES

眼鏡片
glass lens

鼻梁架
bridge

眼鏡橫梁
bar

女式錢包
purse

前袋
front pocket

眼鏡框
rim

鼻墊
nose pad

眼鏡腿
temple

123

傘
UMBRELLA

傘衣
canopy

傘尖
tip

分水面
spreader

環
ring

系傘帶
tie

伸縮傘
telescopic umbrella

傘柄
shank

傘套
cover

傘肋
rib

柄突
tab

手柄
handle

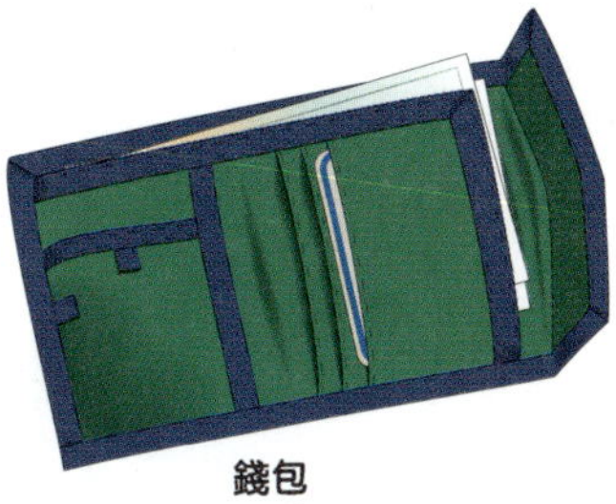

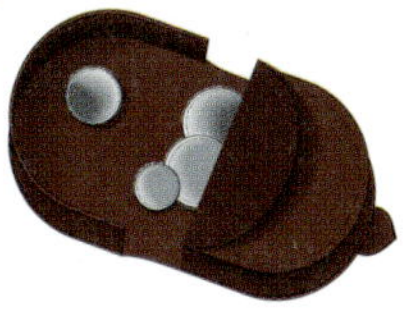

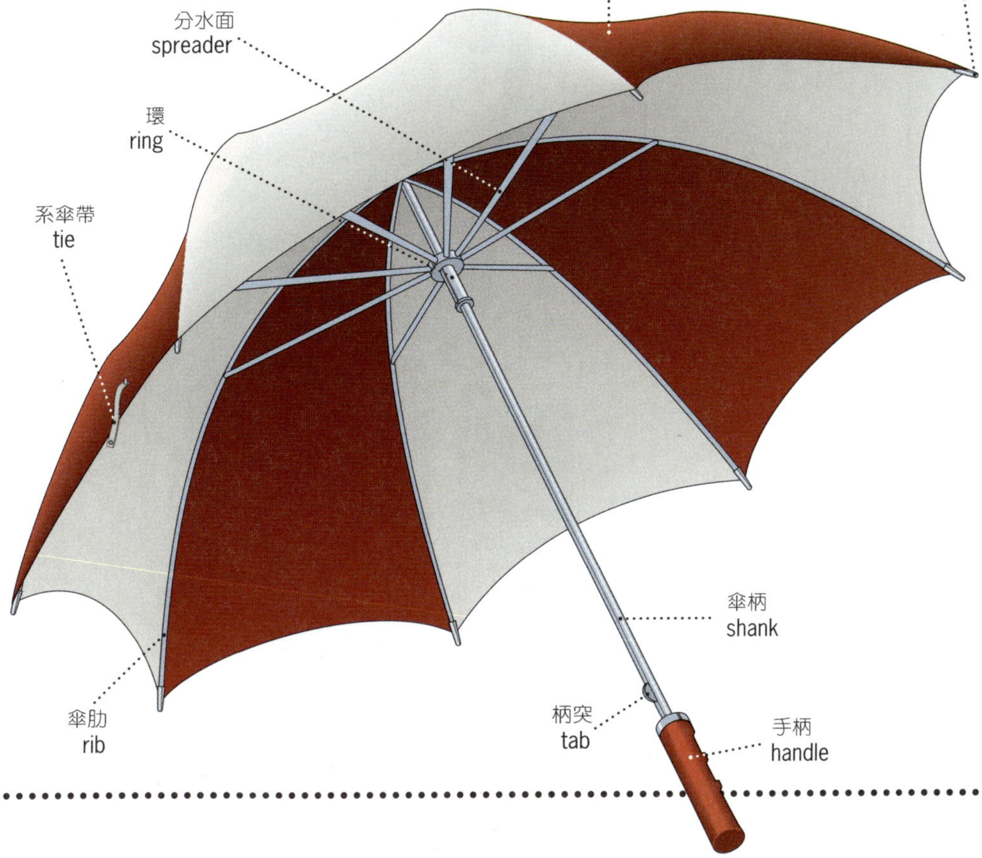

通信

電話機
telephone set

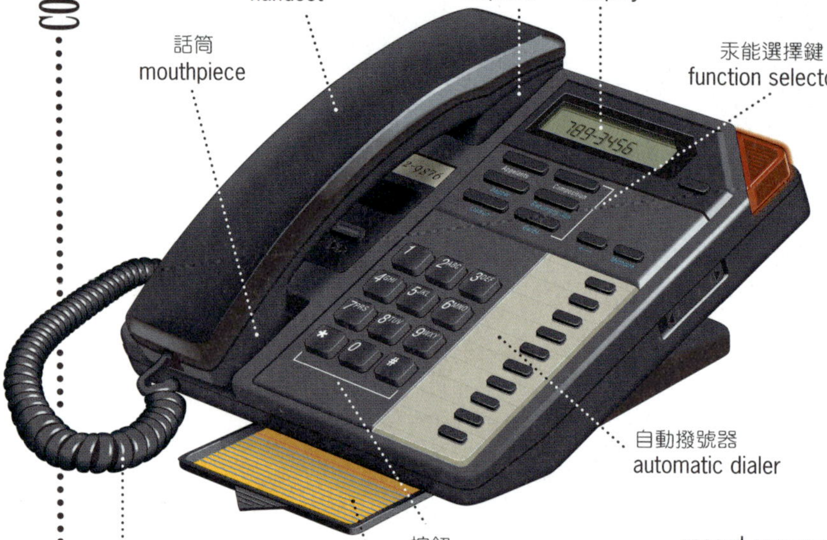

電話答錄
telephone answering machi

電話聽筒
handset

聽筒
earpiece

顯示屏
display

話筒
mouthpiece

乘能選擇鍵
function selectors

呼出播放磁帶盒
outgoing announcement cassette

引入播放磁帶盒
incoming message cassette

揚聲器
speaker

收聽
listen butt

789-3456

R3870

自動撥號器
automatic dialer

聽筒軟線
handset cord

按鈕
push buttons

錄音播放鍵
record announcement button

音量調節
volume control

放音機控制
cassette player contr

電話索引
telephone index

124

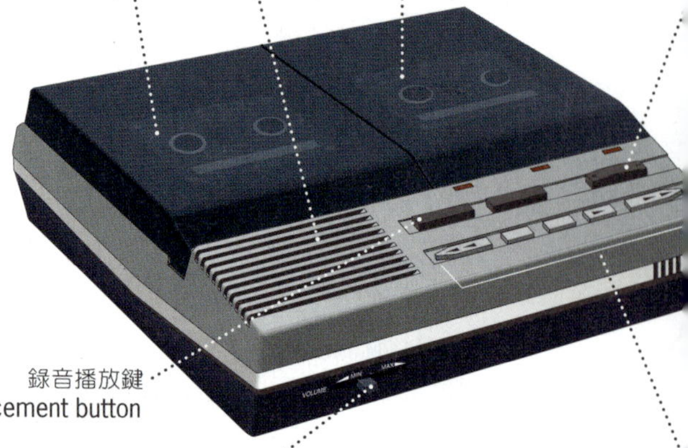

付費電話
pay phone

按鈕電話機
push-button telephone

投幣孔
coin slot

5
10
25
$

顯示屏
display

按鈕
push buttons

手機
portable cellular telephone

無繩電話
cordless telephone

電話聽筒
handset

讀卡機
card reader

123
456
789
*0#

333 1452

退幣盤
coin return tray

攝影
PHOTOGRAPHY

單鏡頭照相機（SLR）
single lens reflex (slr) camera

附件插座板
accessory shoe

附件插座板
film rewind button

直接接觸式閃光燈插座
hot-shoe contact

膠卷傳送鍵
film advance button

控制板
control panel

控制撥盤
control dial

曝光鍵
exposure button

膠卷卷動速率
film speed

遙控信號接收器
remote control terminal

照相機主體
camera body

對焦環
focus setting ring

快門線
shutter release button

物鏡
objective lens

電子閃光燈
electronic flash

閃光管
flashtube

光電管
photoelectric cell

安裝基腳
mounting foot

片孔
perforation

盒式膠卷
cassette film

牽引片
film leader

袖珍相機
compact camera

Polaroid® Land 照相機
Polaroid® Land camera

珍照相機
ocket camera

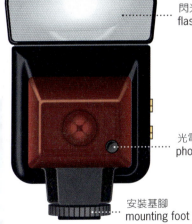

帶式膠卷
cartridge film

盒裝膠卷
film pack

125

電視
TELEVISION

電視機
television set

機殼
cabinet

屏幕
screen

遙控傳感器
remote control sensor

開關按鈕
on/off button

指示器
indicators

調整控制器
tuning controls

遙控器
remote control

電視模式
TV mode

錄像機模式
VCR mode

頻道選擇器
channel selector controls

預置鍵
preset buttons

錄像調節鍵
VCR controls

慢動作
slow-motion

錄像
record

暫停
pause

音量調節
volume control

電視/錄像轉換鍵
TV/video button

電視開關按鈕
TV on/off button

頻道瀏覽鍵
channel scan buttons

錄像開關按鈕
VCR on/off button

倒帶
rewind

快進
fast forward

播放
play

停止
stop

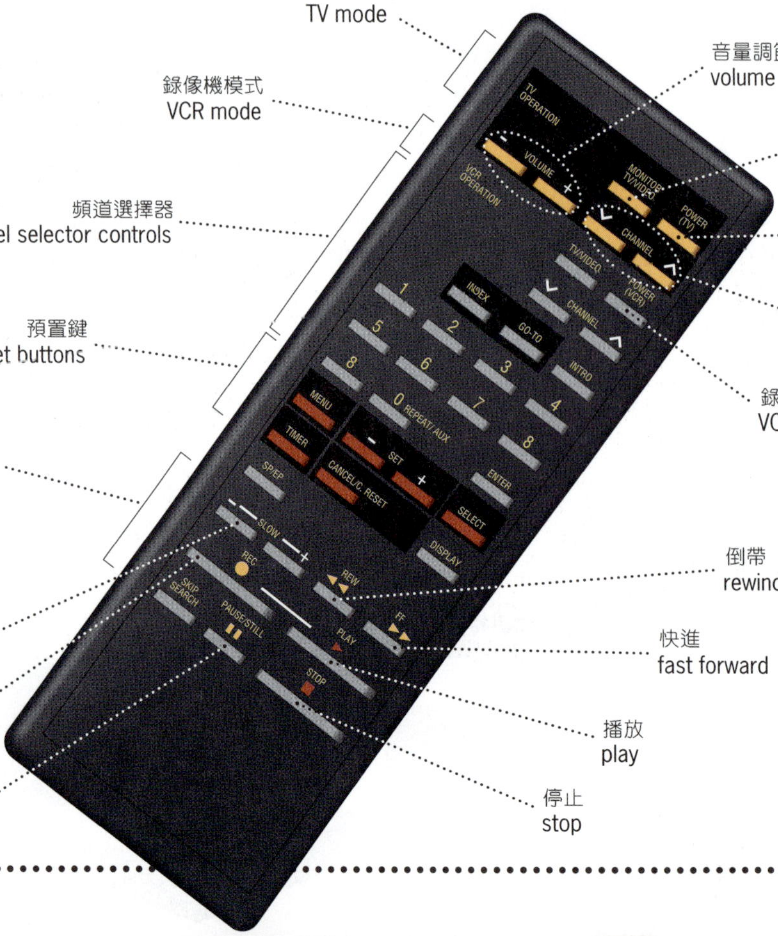

錄像設備
VIDEO

開關按鈕
on/off button

數據顯示屏
data display

預置鍵
preset buttons

盒式錄像機
videocassette recorder

磁帶彈出鍵
cassette eject switch

控制鍵
controls

盒式磁帶倉
cassette compartment

攝影機
video camera

附件插座板
accessory shoe

目鏡
eyepiece

電動變焦鍵
power zoom button

電子取景器
electronic viewfinder

磁帶彈出鍵
cassette eject switch

錄像帶操作鍵
videotape operation controls

取景器調節鍵
viewfinder adjustment keys

內置話筒
built-in microphone

電池
battery

變焦透鏡
zoom lens

拍攝調節鍵
shooting adjustment keys

盒式磁帶倉
cassette compartment

電池彈出鍵
battery eject switch

數據顯示屏
data display

剪輯/檢索按鈕
edit/search buttons

立體音響系統
STEREO SYSTEM / HI-FI SYSTEM

系統構件
SYSTEM COMPONENTS

調諧器
tuner

調頻天線
FM antenna

調幅天線
AM antenna

唱盤
turntable

小型盤放音機
compact disc player

擴音器
amplifier

盒式錄音座
cassette tape deck

圖形均衡器
graphic equalizer

喇叭
loudspeakers

左聲道
left channel

右聲道
right channel

高頻揚聲器
tweeter

中頻揚聲器
midrange

低音喇叭
woofer

震動膜;錐形
diaphragm; cone

喇叭罩
speaker cover

耳機
headphon

耳機軟墊
ear cushion

耳機頭環
headband

調節帶
adjusting band

耳機
earphone

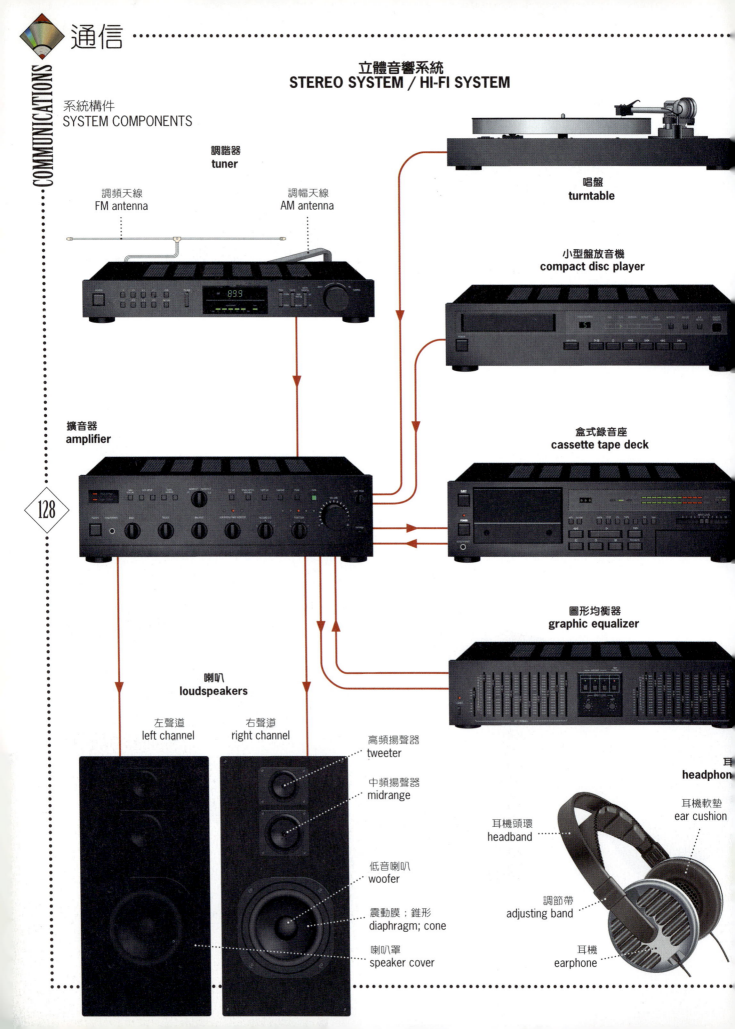

便攜式音響系統
PORTABLE SOUND SYSTEMS

開/關/音量調節鈕
on/off/volume control

便攜式光盤、調頻/調幅盒式收錄機
portable CD AM/FM cassette recorder

天線
antenna

模式選擇器
mode selectors

光盤播放器
compact disc player

手柄
handle

光盤
compact disc

立體聲控制器
stereo control

光盤播放控制器
disc player controls

耳機插座
headphone jack

調諧器
tuner

調諧旋鈕
tuning control

喇叭
speaker

盒式磁帶播放器
cassette player

盒式磁帶
cassette

磁帶播放控制器
cassette player controls

個人調幅/調頻盒式磁帶播放器；隨身聽
personal AM/FM cassette player; Walkman®

光盤
compact disc

電線
cable

耳機插頭
headphone plug

加壓部分
pressed area

129

耳機頭環
headband

開始讀盤處
reading start

開關按鈕
on/off button

音量調節
volume control

倒帶鍵
rewind button

調諧旋鈕
tuning control

播放鍵
play button

耳機
headphones

快進鍵
fast-forward button

技術質量証明帶
technical identification band

盒式磁帶
cassette

唱片
record

自動倒帶
auto reverse

盒式放音機
cassette player

螺旋進入槽
spiral-in groove

式磁帶
ssette

外殼
housing

調諧器
tuner

螺線
spiral

收帶盤
take-up reel

盤區
band

錄音帶
recording tape

脫尾槽
tail-out groove

磁帶導軌
tape guide

標簽
label

帶輪
de roller

卷帶窗
playing window

中心孔
center hole

汽車
CAR

車身
body

擋風玻璃
windshield / windscreen

擋風玻璃雨刷
windshield wiper / windscreen wiper

外后視鏡
outside mirror / wing mirror

洗滌器噴嘴
washer nozzle

發動機罩
hood / bonnet

前燈
headlight

散熱器護柵
grille

緩衝器
bumper

翼子板
fender / wing

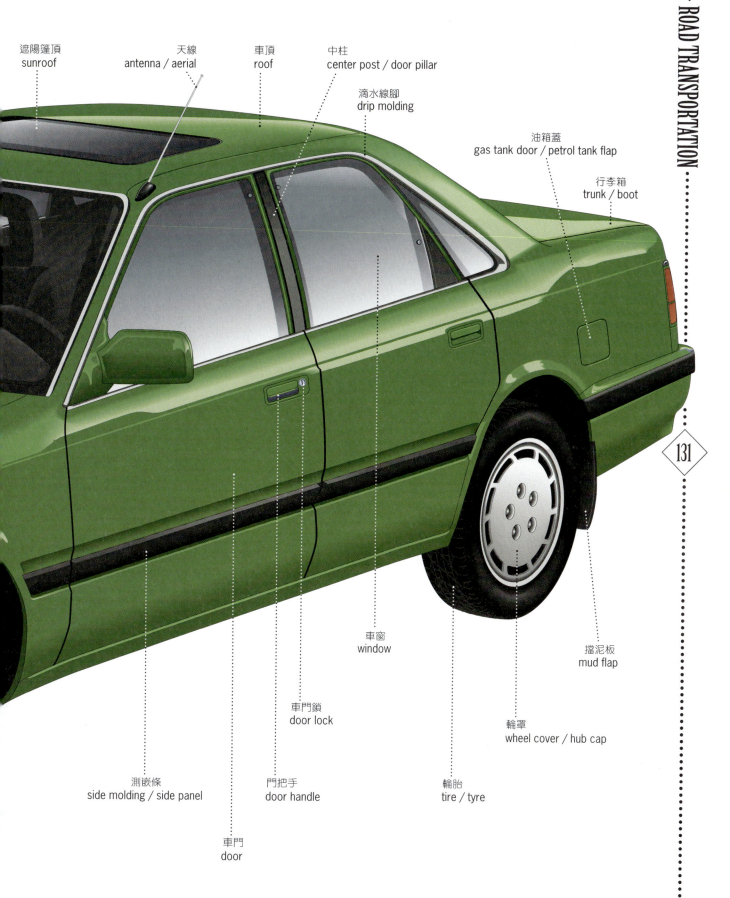

遮陽篷頂
sunroof

天線
antenna / aerial

車頂
roof

中柱
center post / door pillar

滴水線腳
drip molding

油箱蓋
gas tank door / petrol tank flap

行李箱
trunk / boot

車窗
window

擋泥板
mud flap

車門鎖
door lock

輪罩
wheel cover / hub cap

測嵌條
side molding / side panel

門把手
door handle

輪胎
tire / tyre

車門
door

車
CAR

儀表板
dashboard

雨刷開關
wiper switch

后視鏡
rearview mirror

梳妝鏡
vanity mirror

儀表盤
instrument panel

遮陽板
sun visor

點火開關
ignition switch

鍾表
clock

喇叭
horn

氣孔
air vent

方向盤
steering wheel

手套箱
glove compartme...

前燈/轉彎指示燈
headlight/turn signal

加熱器調節鈕
heater control

離合器踏板
clutch pedal

放音系統
audio system

剎車踏板
brake pedal

油門踏板
accelerator pedal

手刹車
handbrake

座椅間儲藏小櫃
center console / centre console

變速桿
gearshift lever / gear lever; gears

132

儀表盤
instrument panel

警報燈
warning lights

轉彎信號指示燈
turn signal indicator /
indicator light

油量表
fuel gauge

遠光指示燈
high beam indicator light /
main beam indicator light

溫度表
temperature gauge

旋轉計數器
rev(olution) counter

里程表
odometer / milometer

短距離里程表
trip odometer /
trip milometer

速度計
speedometer

車燈
CAR LIGHTS

前燈
front lights

短焦距光燈
w beam / dipped headlights

轉彎信號燈
turn signal / indicator

側燈
side light

遠光燈
high beam /
main beam headlights

霧燈
fog light / fog lamp

牌照燈
license plate light /
number plate light

制動燈
brake light

后燈
rear lights

轉彎信號燈
turn signal / indicator

尾燈
tail light / rear light

側燈
side light

制動燈
brake light

倒車燈
backup light / reversing light

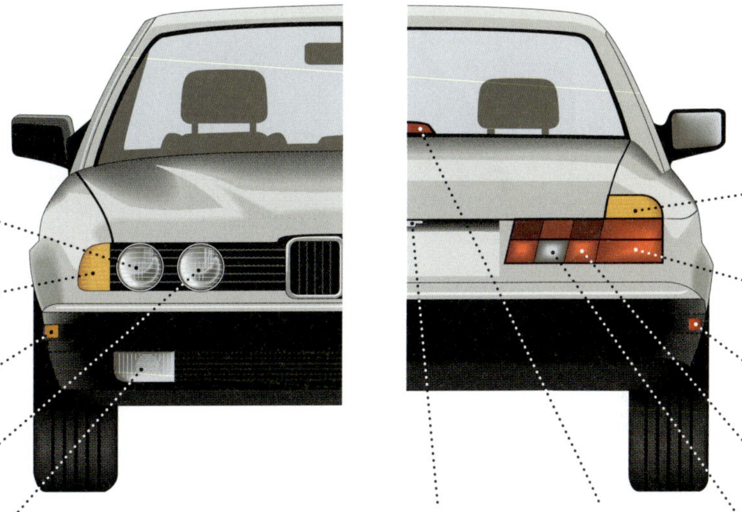

車身的類型
TYPES OF CAR BODIES

跑車
sports car

雙門小轎車
two-door sedan / coupe

倉門式后背車身小客車
hatchback

敞篷車
convertible

敞篷小型載貨卡車
pickup truck

旅行車
station wagon / estate car

四門轎車
four-door sedan / four-door saloon

小型貨車
minivan / estate wagon

多用汽車
multipurpose vehicle

豪華轎車
limousine

133

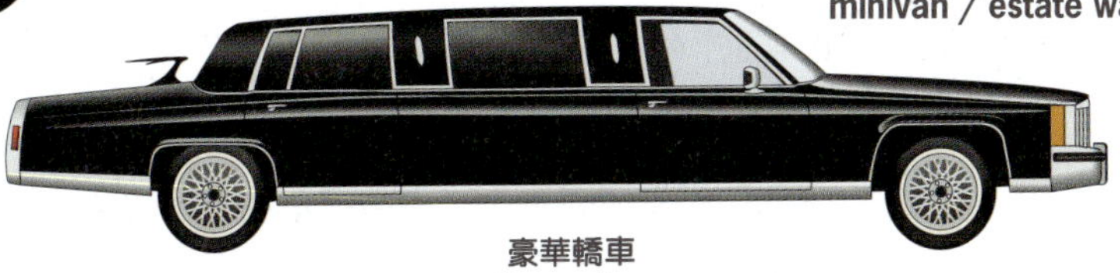

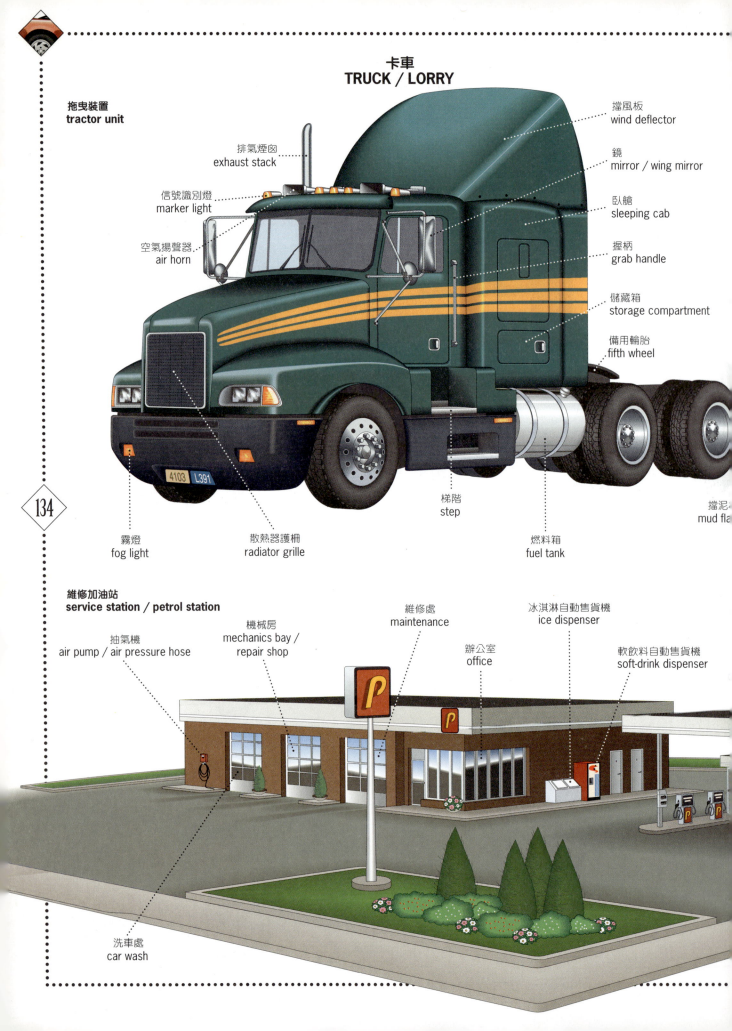

卡車
TRUCK / LORRY

拖曳裝置
tractor unit

排氣煙囪
exhaust stack

信號識別燈
marker light

空氣揚聲器
air horn

擋風板
wind deflector

鏡
mirror / wing mirror

臥艙
sleeping cab

握柄
grab handle

儲藏箱
storage compartment

備用輪胎
fifth wheel

擋泥
mud fla

梯階
step

燃料箱
fuel tank

霧燈
fog light

散熱器護柵
radiator grille

維修加油站
service station / petrol station

抽氣機
air pump / air pressure hose

機械房
mechanics bay /
repair shop

維修處
maintenance

辦公室
office

冰淇淋自動售貨機
ice dispenser

軟飲料自動售貨機
soft-drink dispenser

洗車處
car wash

摩托車
MOTORCYCLE

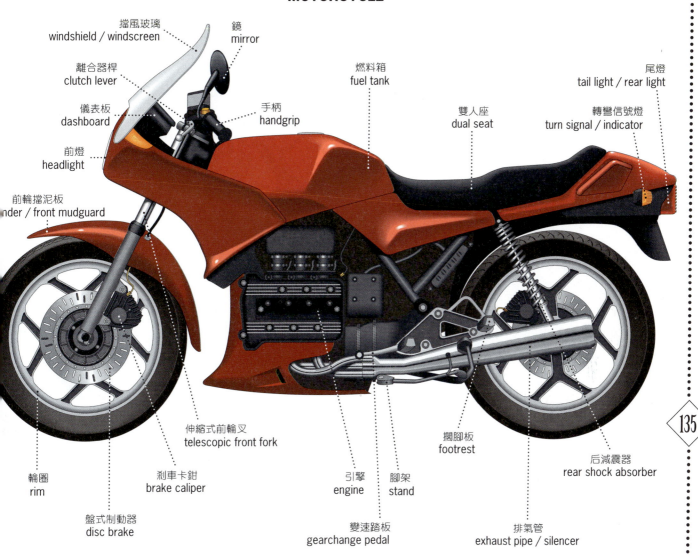

擋風玻璃
windshield / windscreen

鏡
mirror

離合器桿
clutch lever

儀表板
dashboard

前燈
headlight

手柄
handgrip

燃料箱
fuel tank

雙人座
dual seat

尾燈
tail light / rear light

轉彎信號燈
turn signal / indicator

前輪擋泥板
nder / front mudguard

伸縮式前輪叉
telescopic front fork

輪圈
rim

盤式制動器
disc brake

刹車卡鉗
brake caliper

引擎
engine

腳架
stand

變速踏板
gearchange pedal

擱腳板
footrest

排氣管
exhaust pipe / silencer

后減震器
rear shock absorber

用電話間
osk

加油泵
gasoline pump / petrol pump

油泵島
pump island / forecourt

保護頭盔
protective helmet / crash helmet

圓罩
bubble

遮陽板
visor

護頜
chin protector

自行車
BICYCLE

車凳
saddle

車凳桿
seat post

托架
carrier

發生器
generator / dynamo

反射鏡
reflector

后車燈
rear light

后刹車
rear brake

輪胎打氣泵
tire pump / tyre pump

車架
frame

水壺夾
water bottle clip

前變速器
front derailleur

水壺
water bottle

滑輪
chain wheel

曲柄
crank

腳箍
toe clip

腳踏板
pedal

擋泥板
mudguard

鏈條導板
chain guide

后變速器
rear derailleur

主動鏈
drive chain

自行車包
bicycle bag / pannier bag

閘線
brake cable

把手桿
stem

制動槓桿
brake lever

籠頭
handlebars

前剎車
front brake

前燈
headlamp

前叉
fork

輪軸
hub

輪胎
tire / tyre

輪圈
rim

輪輻
spoke

變速桿
gear lever

輪胎氣門嘴
tire valve / tyre valve

保護頭盔
protective helmet

山地車
mountain bike

內燃電力傳動機車
DIESEL-ELECTRIC LOCOMOTIVE

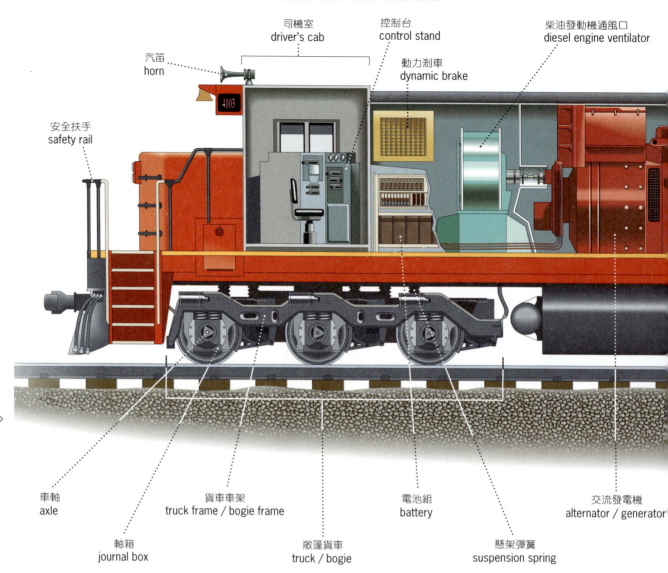

司機室
driver's cab

控制台
control stand

柴油發動機通風口
diesel engine ventilator

動力剎車
dynamic brake

汽笛
horn

安全扶手
safety rail

車軸
axle

貨車車架
truck frame / bogie frame

電池組
battery

交流發電機
alternator / generator

軸箱
journal box

敞篷貨車
truck / bogie

懸架彈簧
suspension spring

貨車車廂類型
TYPES OF FREIGHT CARS

牲畜車廂
livestock car / livestock van

底卸式車廂
hopper car / hopper wagon

棚車
box car / bogie wagon

汽車車廂
automobile car / bogie car-transporter wagon

集裝箱車廂
container car / container flat wagon

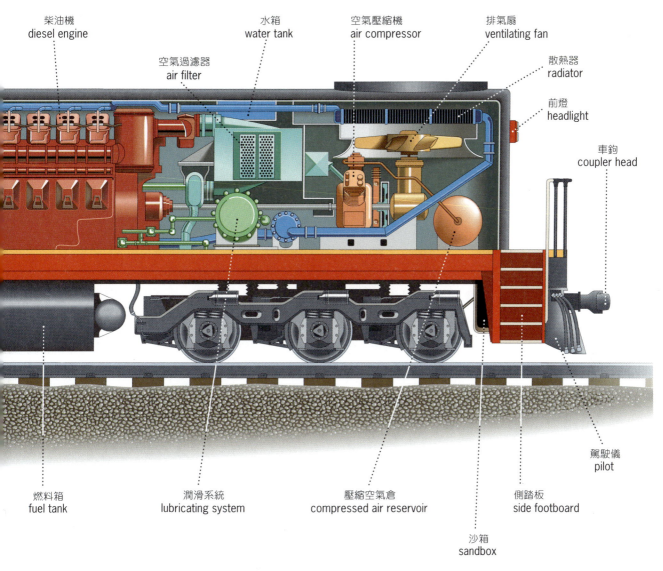

柴油機
diesel engine

空氣過濾器
air filter

水箱
water tank

空氣壓縮機
air compressor

排氣扇
ventilating fan

散熱器
radiator

前燈
headlight

車鉤
coupler head

燃料箱
fuel tank

潤滑系統
lubricating system

壓縮空氣倉
compressed air reservoir

沙箱
sandbox

側踏板
side footboard

駕駛儀
pilot

間壁平板貨車
bulkhead flat car / bulkhead flat wagon

罐車車廂
tank car / bogie tank wagon

平板貨車
flat car / bogie flat wagon

中央凹陷平板貨車
depressed center flat car / bogie well wagon

無蓋貨車
gondola car / bogie open wagon

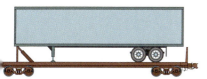

背負式運輸車廂
piggyback car / piggyback flat wagon

冷藏車廂
refrigerator car / refrigerator van

貨車守車
caboose / brake van

公路轍叉
HIGHWAY CROSSING / LEVEL CROSSING

公路轍叉鈴
highway crossing bell /
level crossing bell

道口標記
crossbuck sign / level crossing sign

天線桿
mast

遮陽板
visor

警戒燈
flashing light; warning light

信號背景板
signal background plate

2

軌道數標記
number of tracks sign

門臂燈
gate arm lamp

平衡錘
counterweight

門臂
gate arm

門臂架
gate arm support

道口閘門機械裝置
crossing gate mechanism

底座
base

高速火車
HIGH-SPEED TRAIN

吊線
catenary

導電弓
pantograph

駕駛室
driver's cab

前燈
headlight

電力車廂
power car

前燈
headlight

夜航標位燈
position light

客車車廂
passenger

駕駛儀
pilot

道渣
ballast

枕木墊板
tie plate / soleplate

枕木
tie / sleeper

鐵軌
rail

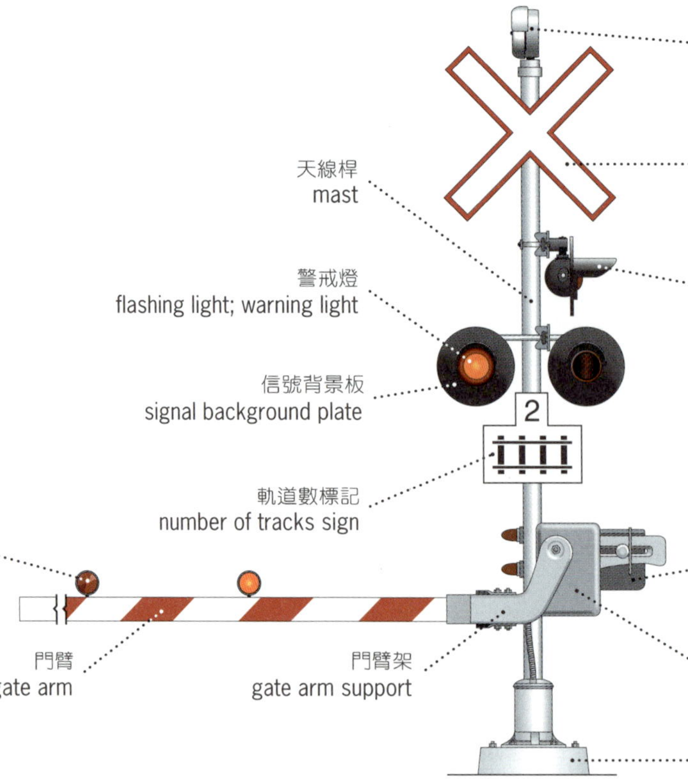

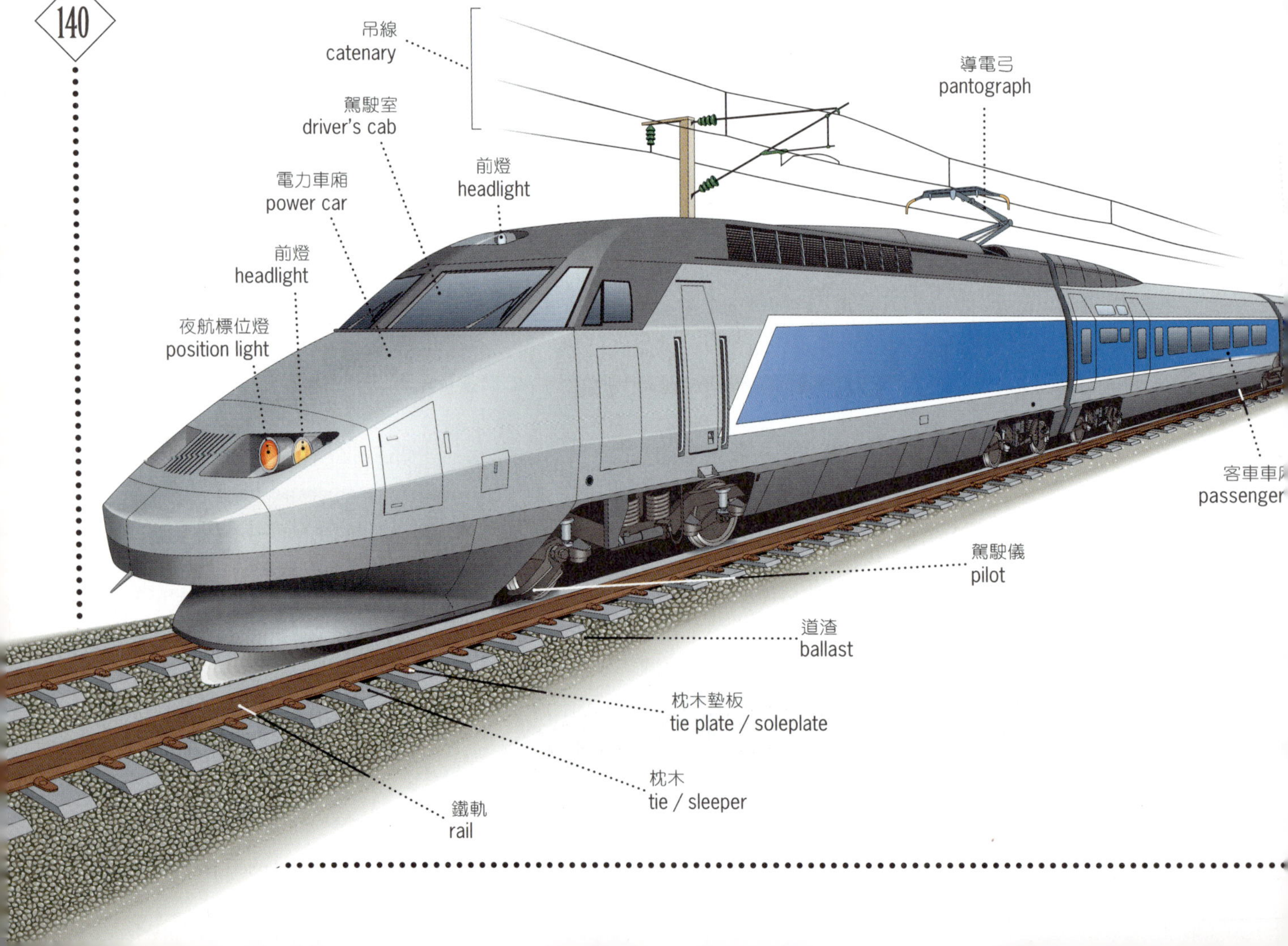

四桅帆船
FOUR-MASTED BARK / FOUR MASTED BAROQUE

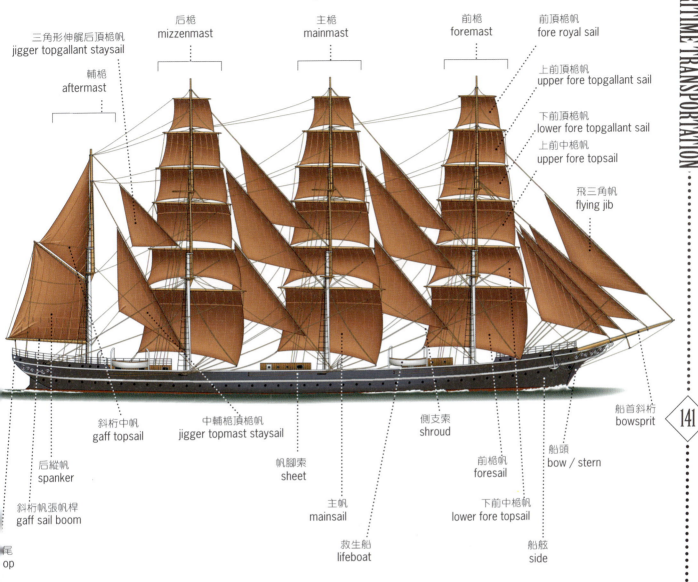

三角形伸艉后頂桅帆
jigger topgallant staysail

輔桅
aftermast

后桅
mizzenmast

主桅
mainmast

前桅
foremast

前頂桅帆
fore royal sail

上前頂桅帆
upper fore topgallant sail

下前頂桅帆
lower fore topgallant sail

上前中桅帆
upper fore topsail

飛三角帆
flying jib

斜桁中帆
gaff topsail

中輔桅頂桅帆
jigger topmast staysail

側支索
shroud

船首斜桁
bowsprit

后縱帆
spanker

帆腳索
sheet

前桅帆
foresail

船頭
bow / stern

斜桁帆張帆桿
gaff sail boom

主帆
mainsail

下前中桅帆
lower fore topsail

船舷
side

尾
op

救生船
lifeboat

氣墊船
HOVERCRAFT

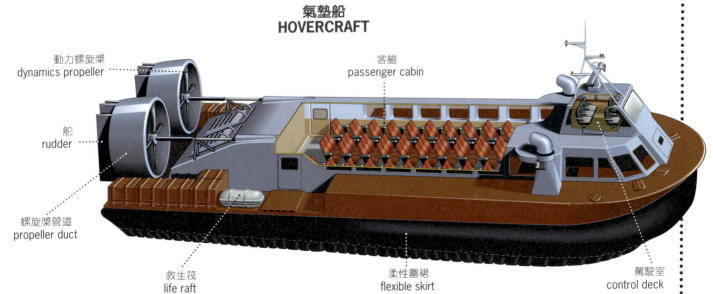

動力螺旋槳
dynamics propeller

客艙
passenger cabin

舵
rudder

螺旋槳管道
propeller duct

救生筏
life raft

柔性圍裙
flexible skirt

駕駛室
control deck

游輪
CRUISE LINER

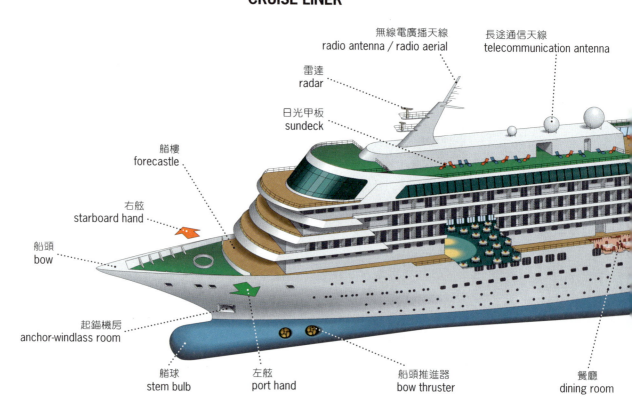

無線電廣播天線
radio antenna / radio aerial

長途通信天線
telecommunication antenna

雷達
radar

日光甲板
sundeck

艏樓
forecastle

右舷
starboard hand

船頭
bow

起錨機房
anchor-windlass room

艏球
stem bulb

左舷
port hand

船頭推進器
bow thruster

餐廳
dining room

港口
HARBOR

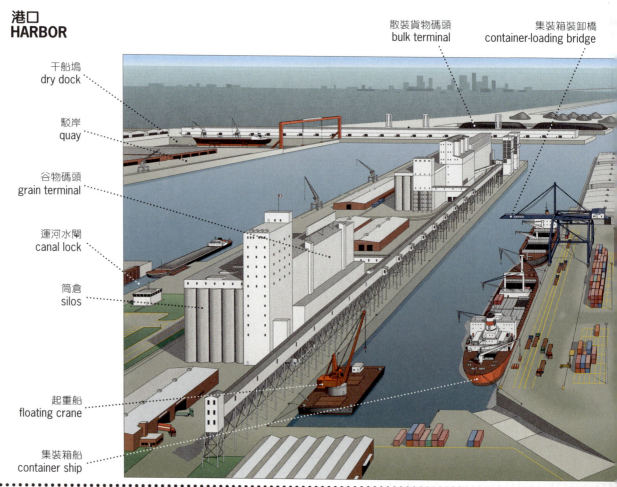

散裝貨物碼頭
bulk terminal

集裝箱裝卸橋
container-loading bridge

干船塢
dry dock

駁岸
quay

谷物碼頭
grain terminal

運河水閘
canal lock

筒倉
silos

起重船
floating crane

集裝箱船
container ship

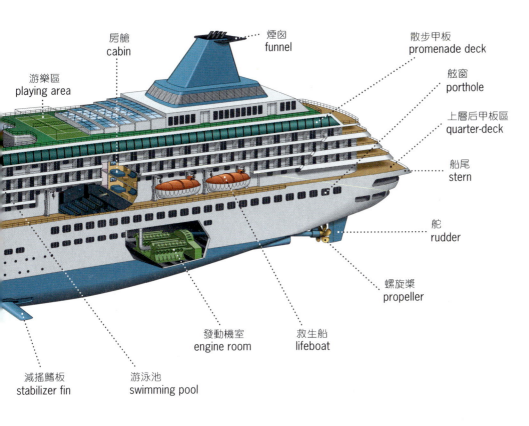

房艙
cabin

游樂區
playing area

煙囪
funnel

散步甲板
promenade deck

舷窗
porthole

上層后甲板區
quarter-deck

船尾
stern

舵
rudder

螺旋槳
propeller

發動機室
engine room

救生船
lifeboat

游泳池
swimming pool

減搖鰭板
stabilizer fin

143

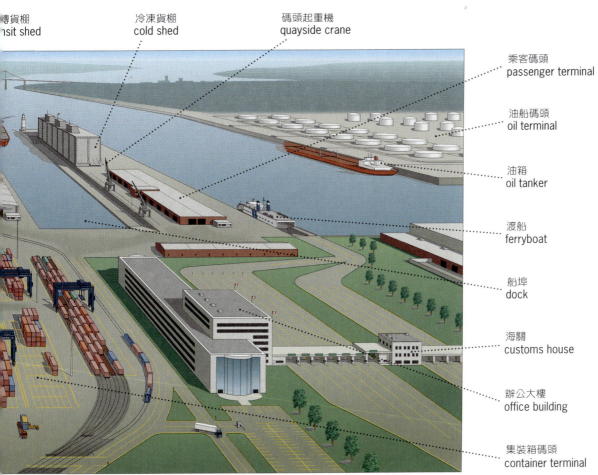

中轉貨棚
transit shed

冷凍貨棚
cold shed

碼頭起重機
quayside crane

乘客碼頭
passenger terminal

油船碼頭
oil terminal

油箱
oil tanker

渡船
ferryboat

船埠
dock

海關
customs house

辦公大樓
office building

集裝箱碼頭
container terminal

飛機
PLANE

機翼類型
TYPES OF WING SHAPES

直翼
straight wing

活動几何翼
variable geometry wing

后掠翼
swept-back wing

錐形翼
tapered wing

三角翼
delta wing

遠程噴氣式飛機
long-range jet

垂直尾翼
fin

方向舵
rudder

尾翼面
tail assembly

副翼
aileron

后緣
trailing edge

擾流器
spoiler

后緣阻力板
trailing edge flap

尾部
tail

機身
fuselage

水平安定面
horizontal stabilizer / tailplane

升降舵
elevator

小翼
winglet

機翼
wing

主起落架
main landing gear

航行燈
navigation light

前緣縫翼
wing slat

機翼前緣
leading edge

渦輪噴氣發動機
turbojet engine

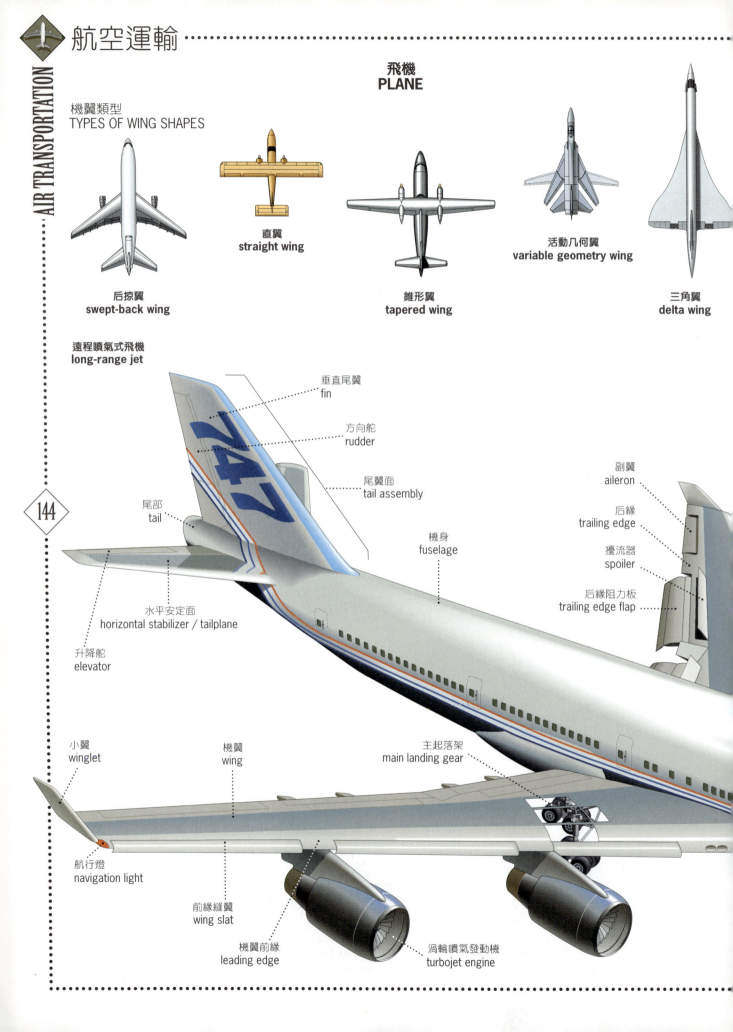

直升飛機
HELICOPTER

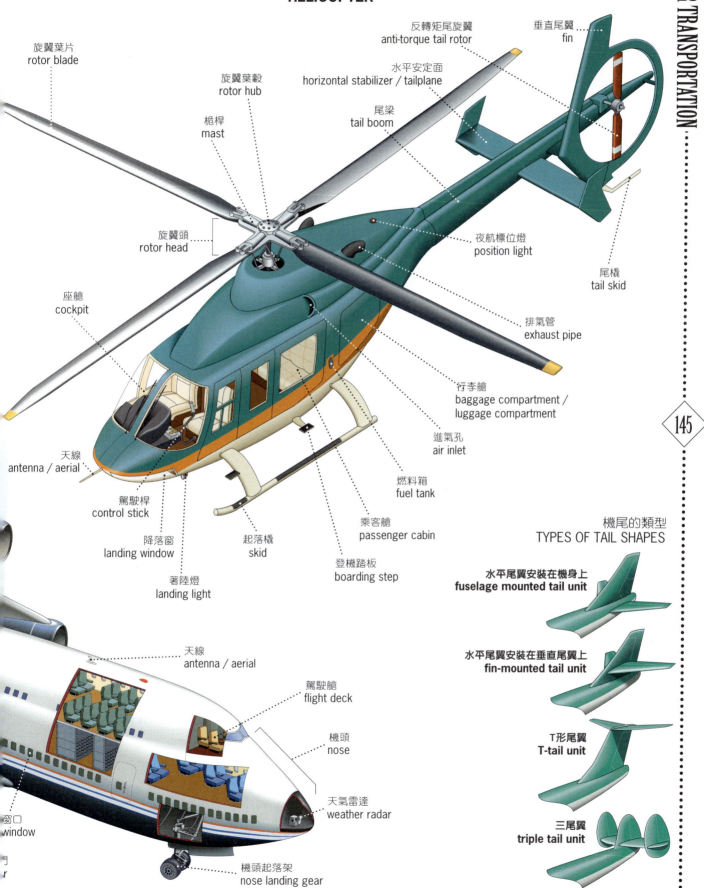

反轉矩尾旋翼
anti-torque tail rotor

水平安定面
horizontal stabilizer / tailplane

尾梁
tail boom

垂直尾翼
fin

旋翼葉片
rotor blade

旋翼葉轂
rotor hub

桅桿
mast

旋翼頭
rotor head

夜航標位燈
position light

尾橇
tail skid

座艙
cockpit

排氣管
exhaust pipe

行李艙
baggage compartment /
luggage compartment

進氣孔
air inlet

天線
antenna / aerial

駕駛桿
control stick

降落窗
landing window

著陸燈
landing light

起落橇
skid

乘客艙
passenger cabin

燃料箱
fuel tank

登機踏板
boarding step

天線
antenna / aerial

駕駛艙
flight deck

機頭
nose

天氣雷達
weather radar

窗口
window

機頭起落架
nose landing gear

145

機尾的類型
TYPES OF TAIL SHAPES

水平尾翼安裝在機身上
fuselage mounted tail unit

水平尾翼安裝在垂直尾翼上
fin-mounted tail unit

T形尾翼
T-tail unit

三尾翼
triple tail unit

機場
AIRPORT

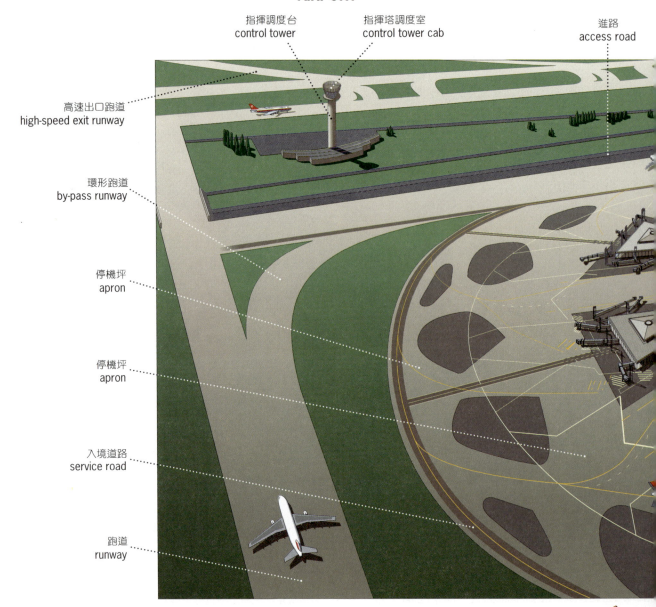

指揮調度台
control tower

指揮塔調度室
control tower cab

進路
access road

高速出口跑道
high-speed exit runway

環形跑道
by-pass runway

停機坪
apron

停機坪
apron

入境道路
service road

跑道
runway

機場地面設施
AIRPORT GROUND EQUIPMENT

牽引桿
tow bar

牽引車
tow tractor

集裝箱/貨板裝卸設備
container/pallet loader

登機車
universal step

行李傳送帶
baggage conveyor

機輪防滑墊塊
wheel chock

飛機維修棚
maintenance hangar

停車場
parking area

候機大廳
passenger terminal

登機人行道
boarding walkway

輻射狀登機處
radial passenger loading area

套管式走廊
telescopic corridor

服務區
service area

跑道線
runway line

行李拖車
baggage trailer

牽引車
tow tractor

食品供應車
catering vehicle

189   189

送客車
passenger transfer vehicle

航天飛機
SPACE SHUTTLE

起飛時的航天飛機
space shuttle at takeoff

外燃料箱
external tank

推進器降落傘
booster parachute

固體火箭推進器
solid rocket booster

航天飛機
shuttle

發動機噴管
nozzle

軌道上的航天飛機
space shuttle in orbit

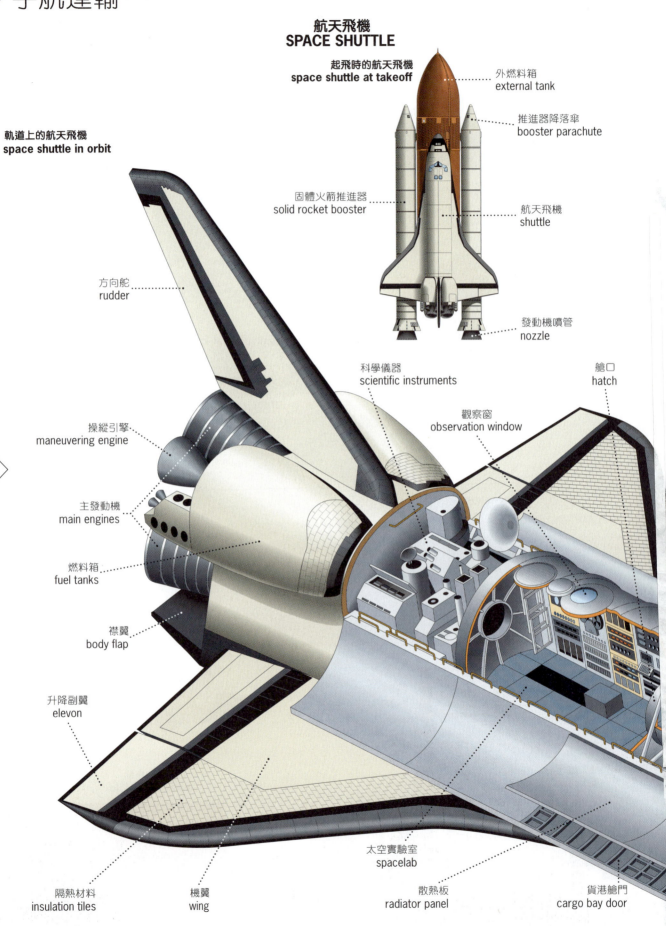

方向舵
rudder

操縱引擎
maneuvering engine

主發動機
main engines

燃料箱
fuel tanks

襟翼
body flap

升降副翼
elevon

科學儀器
scientific instruments

觀察窗
observation window

艙口
hatch

隔熱材料
insulation tiles

機翼
wing

太空實驗室
spacelab

散熱板
radiator panel

貨港艙門
cargo bay door

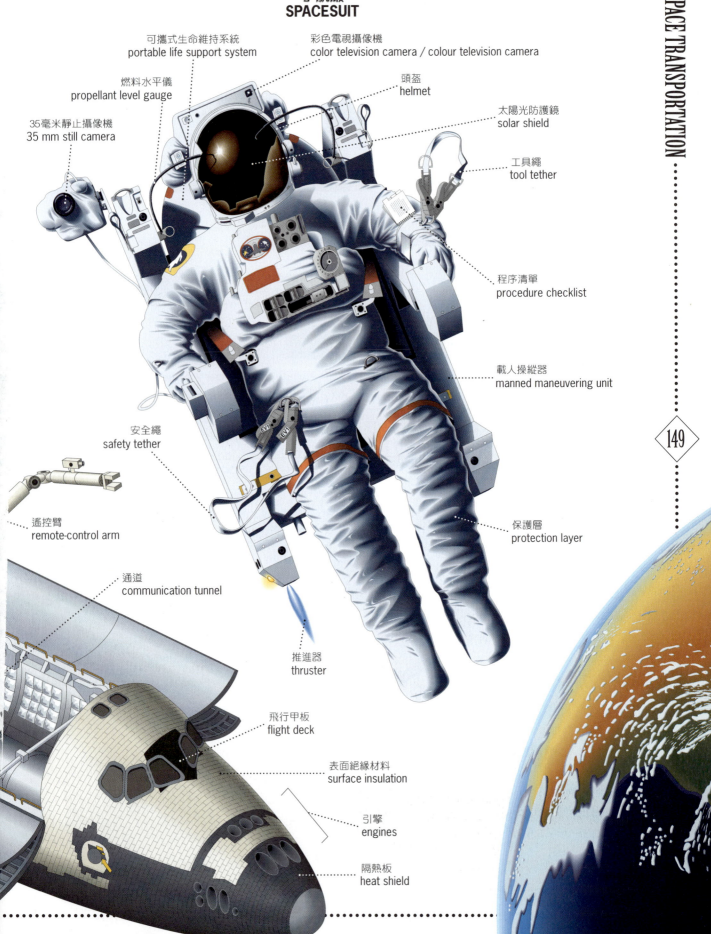

宇航服
SPACESUIT

可攜式生命維持系統
portable life support system

彩色電視攝像機
color television camera / colour television camera

燃料水平儀
propellant level gauge

頭盔
helmet

太陽光防護鏡
solar shield

35毫米靜止攝像機
35 mm still camera

工具繩
tool tether

程序清單
procedure checklist

載人操縱器
manned maneuvering unit

安全繩
safety tether

保護層
protection layer

遙控臂
remote-control arm

通道
communication tunnel

推進器
thruster

飛行甲板
flight deck

表面絕緣材料
surface insulation

引擎
engines

隔熱板
heat shield

學習用具
SCHOOL SUPPLIES

鉛筆
pencil

圓珠筆
ballpoint pen

活動鉛筆
mechanical pencil

筆形橡皮擦
stick eraser

自來水筆
fountain pen

橡皮套
eraser holder

記號筆
marker

橡皮擦
eraser / rubber

固體膠棒
glue stick

螢光筆
highlighter pen

起釘器
staple remover

書夾
fold back clip

回形針
paper clips

圖釘和撳釘
thumb tacks and pushpins / drawing pins

釘書機
stapler

卷筆機
pencil sharpener

釘書釘
staples

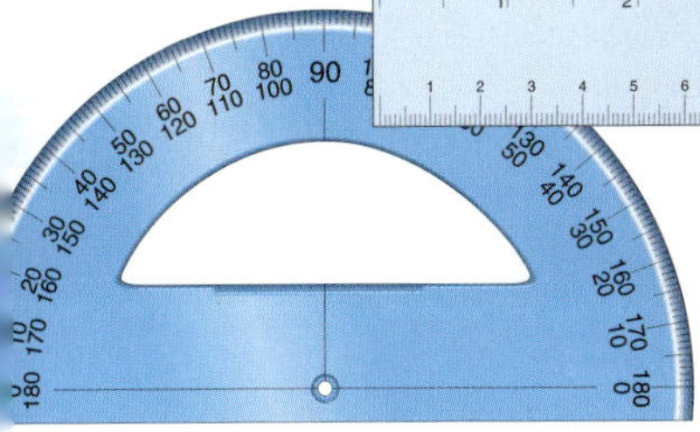

直尺
ruler

量角器
protractor

四眼活頁夾
ring binder

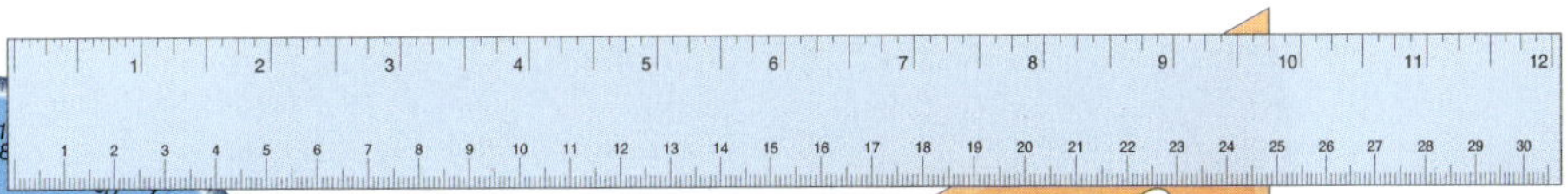

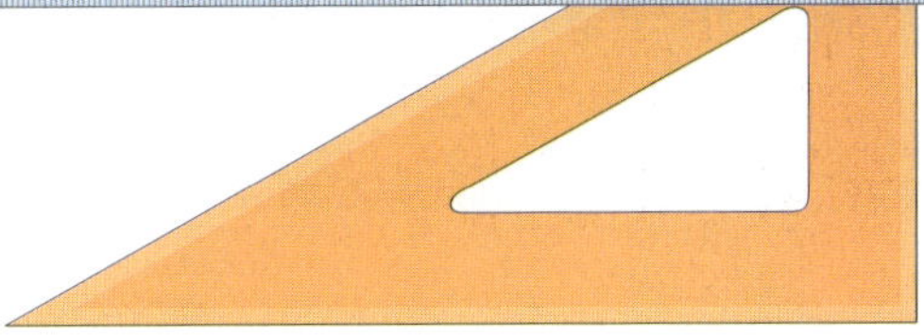

三角板
set square

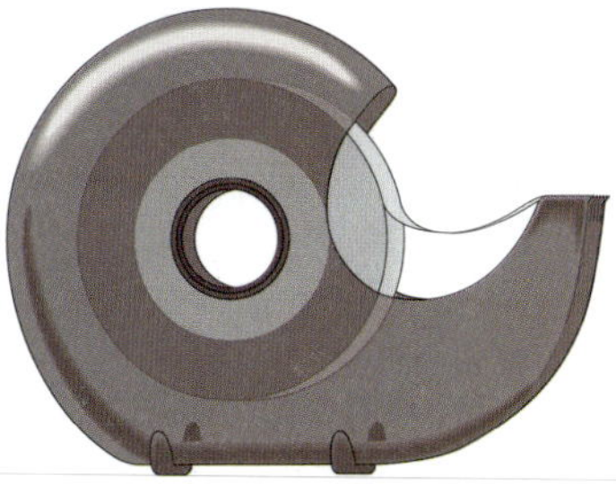

修正膠布
tape dispenser

螺旋裝訂筆記本
spiral bound notebook

活頁紙
loose-leaf paper

筆記本
notebook

記事手冊
notepad

公文包
briefcase

背包
ckpack / satchel

151

學校設備
SCHOOL EQUIPMENT

黑板
blackboard

152

高射投影器
overhead projector

鏡子
mirror

投影機
projection head

光學鏡片
optical lens

光學鏡台
optical stage

地球儀
globe of Earth

子午線托
meridian band

球體
globe

基座
base

旋轉軸
axis of rotation

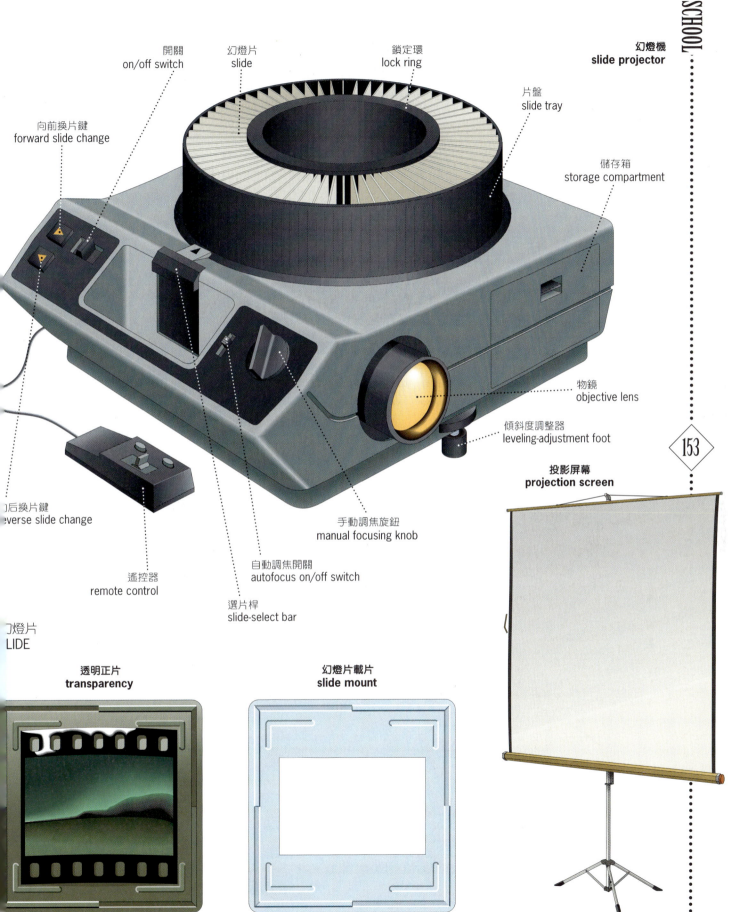

幻燈機
slide projector

開關
on/off switch

幻燈片
slide

鎖定環
lock ring

片盤
slide tray

向前換片鍵
forward slide change

儲存箱
storage compartment

物鏡
objective lens

傾斜度調整器
leveling-adjustment foot

投影屏幕
projection screen

后換片鍵
everse slide change

手動調焦旋鈕
manual focusing knob

遙控器
remote control

自動調焦開關
autofocus on/off switch

選片桿
slide-select bar

燈片
LIDE

透明正片
transparency

幻燈片載片
slide mount

學校設備
SCHOOL EQUIPMENT

袖珍計算器
pocket calculator

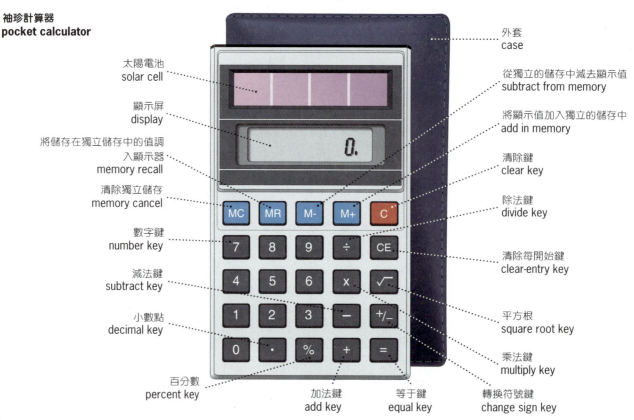

太陽電池
solar cell

顯示屏
display

將儲存在獨立儲存中的值調入顯示器
memory recall

清除獨立儲存
memory cancel

數字鍵
number key

減法鍵
subtract key

小數點
decimal key

百分數
percent key

加法鍵
add key

等于鍵
equal key

轉換符號鍵
change sign key

乘法鍵
multiply key

平方根
square root key

清除每開始鍵
clear-entry key

除法鍵
divide key

清除鍵
clear key

將顯示值加入獨立的儲存中
add in memory

從獨立的儲存中減去顯示值
subtract from memory

外套
case

個人電腦
personal computer

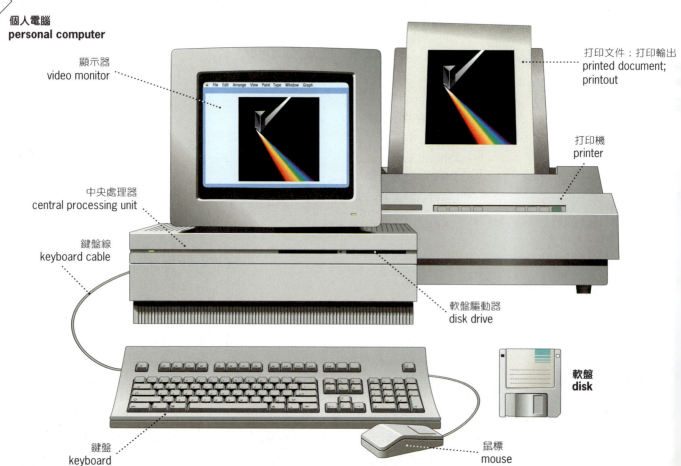

顯示器
video monitor

中央處理器
central processing unit

鍵盤線
keyboard cable

鍵盤
keyboard

鼠標
mouse

軟盤驅動器
disk drive

軟盤
disk

打印機
printer

打印文件；打印輸出
printed document; printout

放大鏡
magnifying glass

目鏡
eyepiece

活鏡筒
draw tube

粗調旋鈕
coarse adjustment knob

微調旋鈕
fine adjustment knob

顯微鏡
microscope

換鏡旋座
revolving nosepiece

物鏡
objective

試管
test tube

切片夾
stage clip

玻璃切片
glass slide

觀察台
stage

聚光鏡
condenser

反射鏡
mirror

顯微鏡臂
arm

155

基座
base

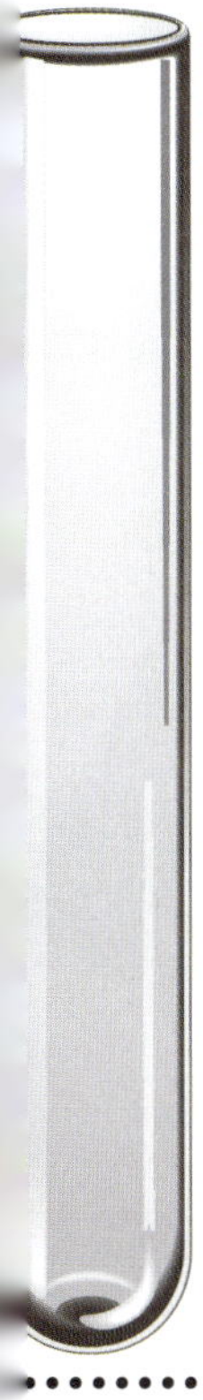

几何學
GEOMETRY

平面圖
PLANE SURFACES

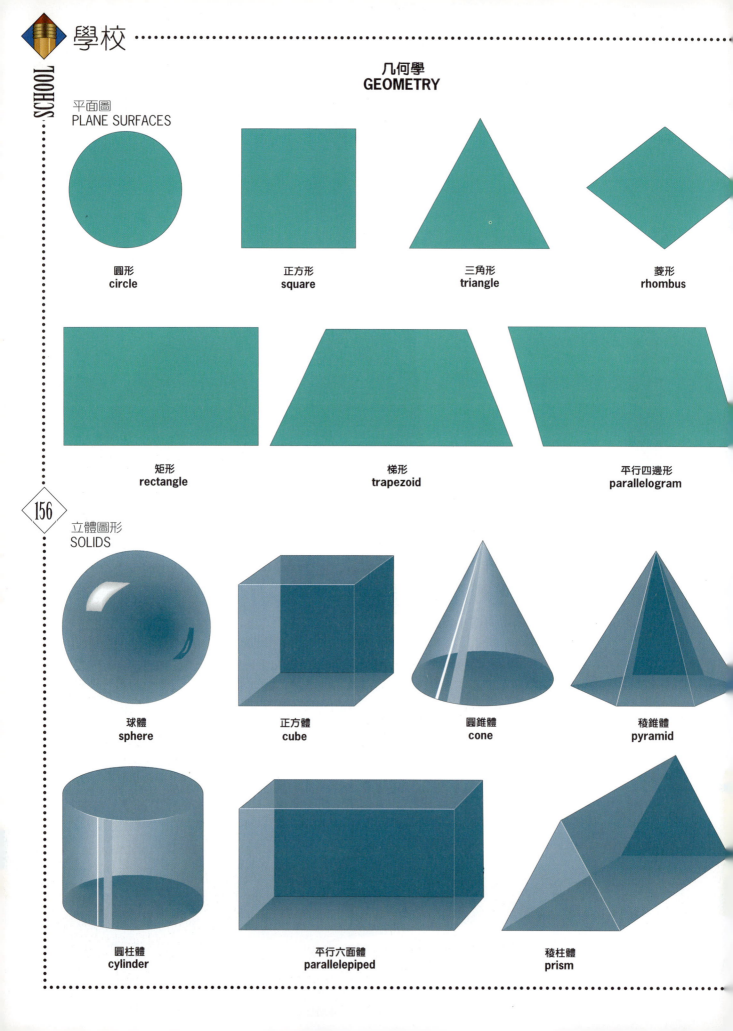

圓形
circle

正方形
square

三角形
triangle

菱形
rhombus

矩形
rectangle

梯形
trapezoid

平行四邊形
parallelogram

立體圖形
SOLIDS

球體
sphere

正方體
cube

圓錐體
cone

稜錐體
pyramid

圓柱體
cylinder

平行六面體
parallelepiped

稜柱體
prism

繪畫
DRAWING

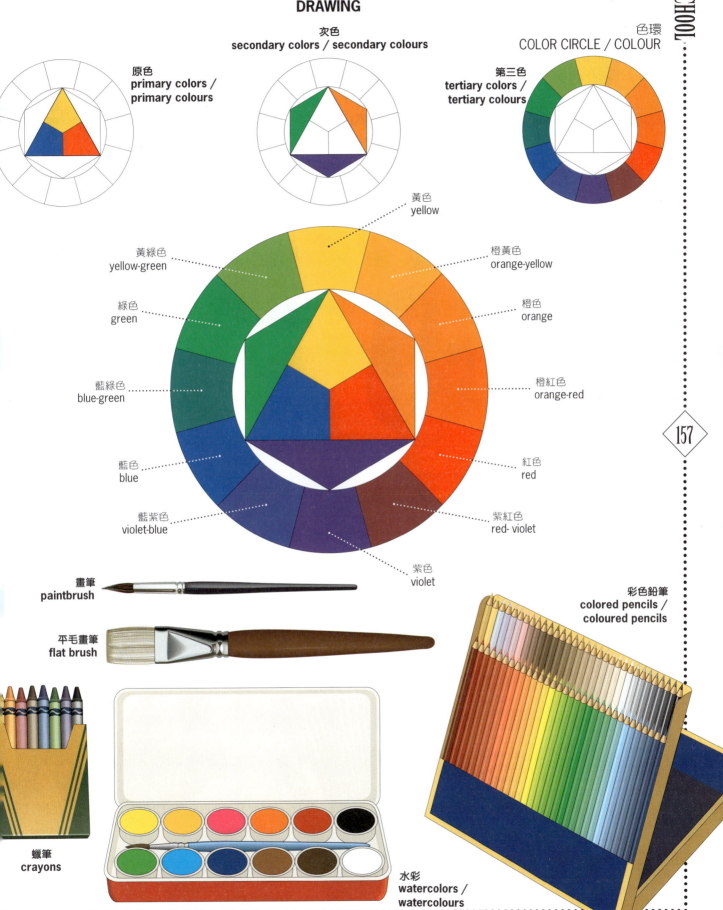

原色
**primary colors /
primary colours**

次色
secondary colors / secondary colours

色環
COLOR CIRCLE / COLOUR

第三色
**tertiary colors /
tertiary colours**

黃色
yellow

黃綠色
yellow-green

橙黃色
orange-yellow

綠色
green

橙色
orange

藍綠色
blue-green

橙紅色
orange-red

藍色
blue

紅色
red

藍紫色
violet-blue

紫紅色
red- violet

紫色
violet

畫筆
paintbrush

平毛畫筆
flat brush

彩色鉛筆
**colored pencils /
coloured pencils**

蠟筆
crayons

水彩
**watercolors /
watercolours**

傳統樂器
TRADITIONAL MUSICAL INSTRUMENTS

俄羅斯三角琴
balalaika

曼陀林
mandolin

齊特琴
zither

里拉琴
lyre

共鳴板
soundboard

三角琴身
triangular body

開放弦
open strings

旋律弦
melody strings

風
bagpip

班卓琴
banjo

排簫
panpipes

梨形琴身
pear-shaped body

圓形琴身
circular body

單音管
drone pipe

吹氣管
blowpipe; mouthpipe

口琴
harmonica

折式風箱
bellows

手風琴
accordion

最高聲部鍵盤
treble keyboard

最高聲部音栓
treble register

低音部鍵盤
bass keyboard

低音部音栓
bass register

風囊
windbag

調旋律管
chanter

鍵盤樂器
KEYBOARD INSTRUMENT

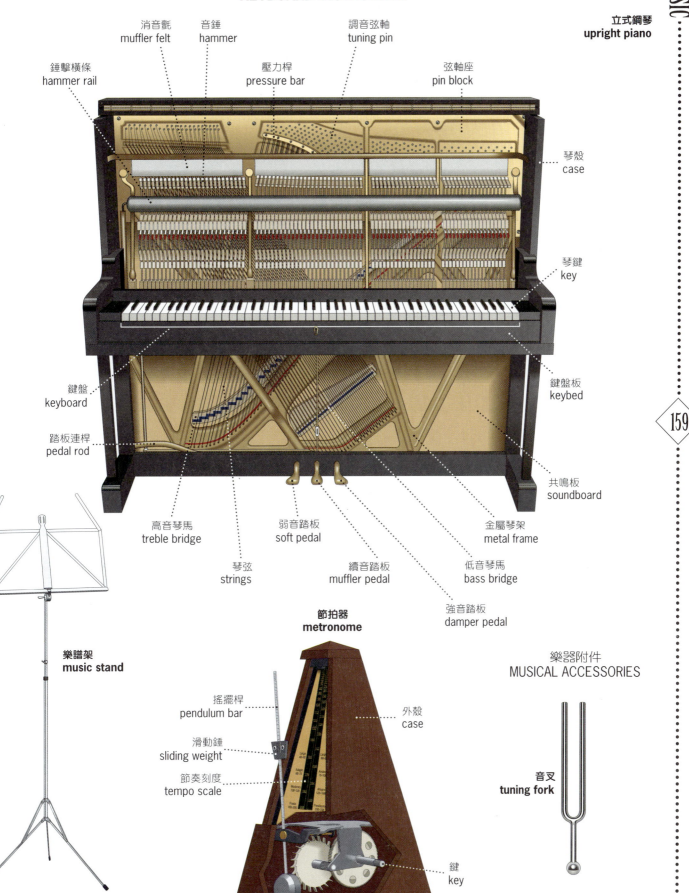

消音氈
muffler felt

音錘
hammer

調音弦軸
tuning pin

壓力桿
pressure bar

弦軸座
pin block

錘擊橫條
hammer rail

琴殼
case

琴鍵
key

鍵盤板
keybed

鍵盤
keyboard

踏板連桿
pedal rod

共鳴板
soundboard

高音琴馬
treble bridge

弱音踏板
soft pedal

金屬琴架
metal frame

琴弦
strings

續音踏板
muffler pedal

低音琴馬
bass bridge

強音踏板
damper pedal

節拍器
metronome

樂譜架
music stand

樂器附件
MUSICAL ACCESSORIES

搖擺桿
pendulum bar

外殼
case

滑動錘
sliding weight

節奏刻度
tempo scale

音叉
tuning fork

鍵
key

樂譜
MUSICAL NOTATION

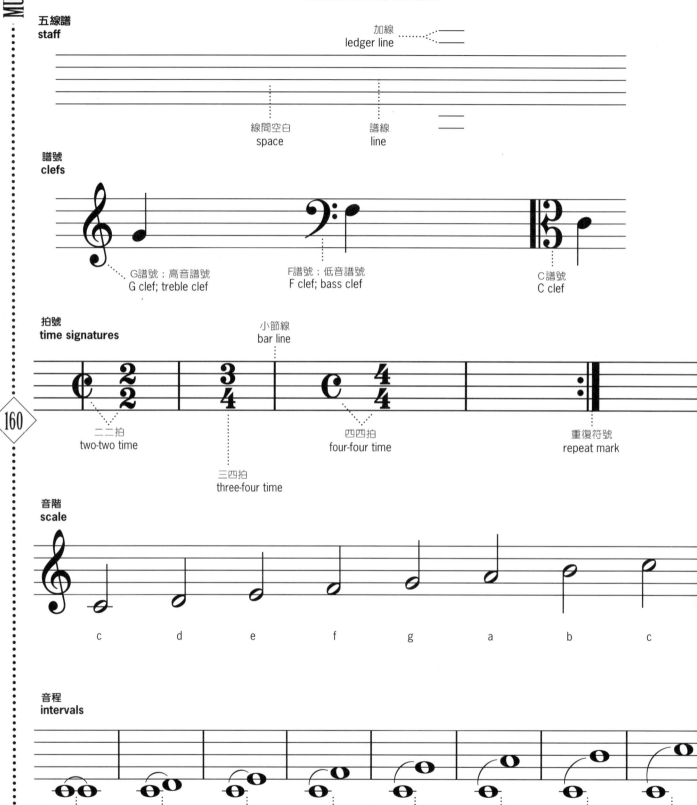

五線譜 staff

加線
ledger line

線間空白
space

譜線
line

譜號 clefs

G譜號；高音譜號
G clef; treble clef

F譜號；低音譜號
F clef; bass clef

C譜號
C clef

拍號 time signatures

小節線
bar line

二二拍
two-two time

三四拍
three-four time

四四拍
four-four time

重復符號
repeat mark

音階 scale

c　d　e　f　g　a　b　c

音程 intervals

同音
unison

二度音程
second

三度音程
third

四度音程
fourth

五度音程
fifth

六度音程
sixth

七度音程
seventh

八度音程
octave

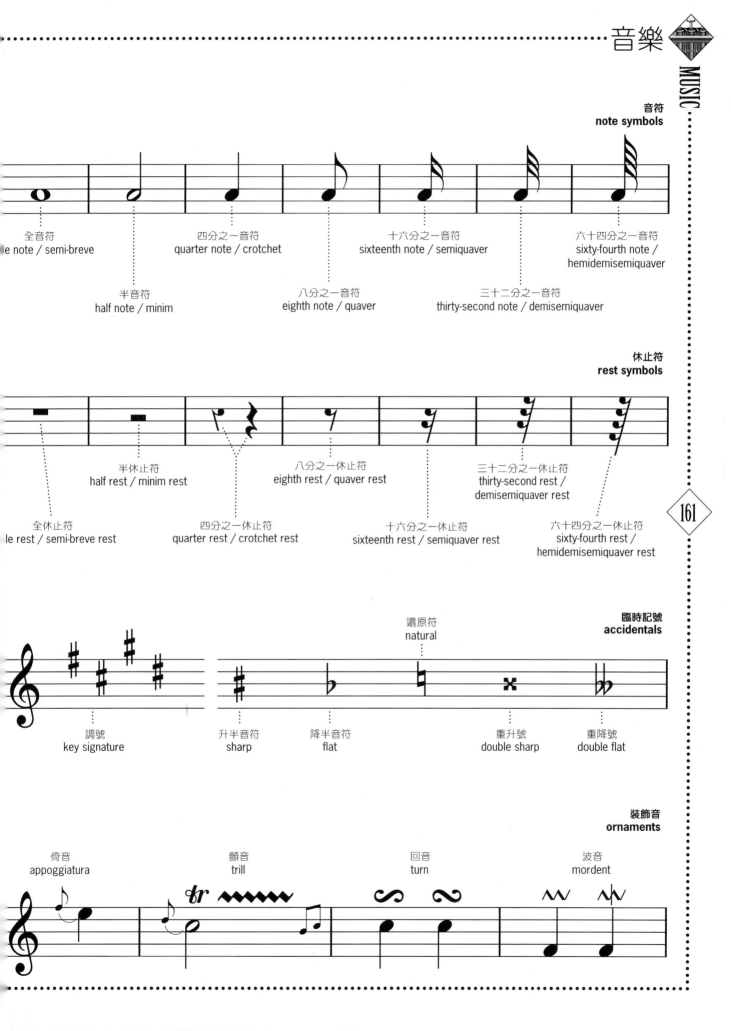

音符
note symbols

全音符
le note / semi-breve

半音符
half note / minim

四分之一音符
quarter note / crotchet

八分之一音符
eighth note / quaver

十六分之一音符
sixteenth note / semiquaver

三十二分之一音符
thirty-second note / demisemiquaver

六十四分之一音符
sixty-fourth note / hemidemisemiquaver

休止符
rest symbols

全休止符
le rest / semi-breve rest

半休止符
half rest / minim rest

四分之一休止符
quarter rest / crotchet rest

八分之一休止符
eighth rest / quaver rest

十六分之一休止符
sixteenth rest / semiquaver rest

三十二分之一休止符
thirty-second rest / demisemiquaver rest

六十四分之一休止符
sixty-fourth rest / hemidemisemiquaver rest

臨時記號
accidentals

還原符
natural

調號
key signature

升半音符
sharp

降半音符
flat

重升號
double sharp

重降號
double flat

裝飾音
ornaments

倚音
appoggiatura

顫音
trill

回音
turn

波音
mordent

弦樂器
STRINGED INSTRUMENTS

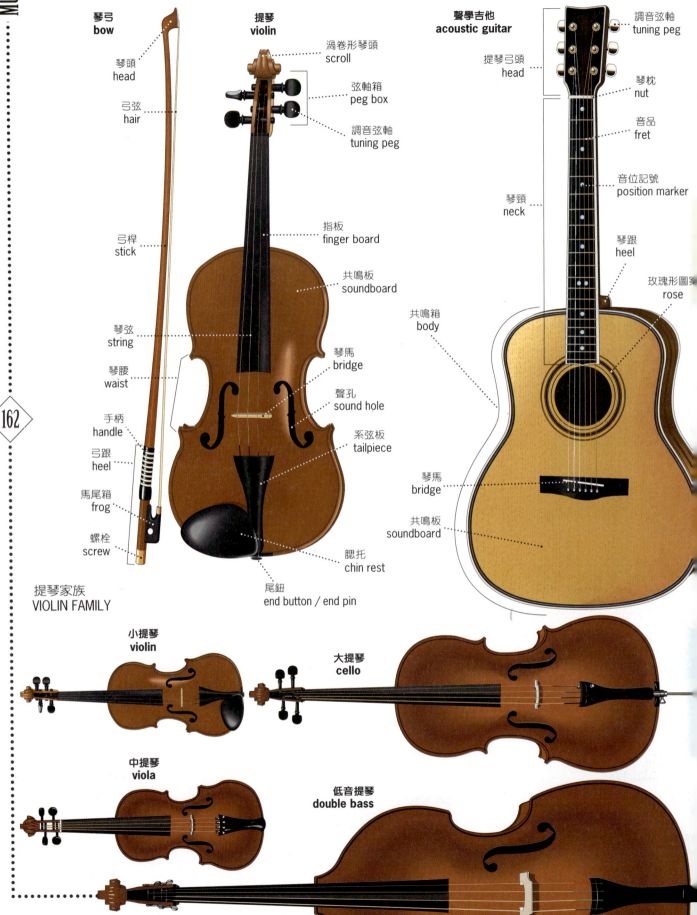

琴弓
bow

提琴
violin

聲學吉他
acoustic guitar

琴頭
head

弓弦
hair

弓桿
stick

琴弦
string

琴腰
waist

手柄
handle

弓跟
heel

馬尾箱
frog

螺栓
screw

渦卷形琴頭
scroll

弦軸箱
peg box

調音弦軸
tuning peg

指板
finger board

共鳴板
soundboard

琴馬
bridge

聲孔
sound hole

系弦板
tailpiece

腮托
chin rest

尾鈕
end button / end pin

調音弦軸
tuning peg

提琴弓頭
head

琴枕
nut

音品
fret

音位記號
position marker

琴頸
neck

琴跟
heel

玫瑰形圖案
rose

共鳴箱
body

琴馬
bridge

共鳴板
soundboard

162

提琴家族
VIOLIN FAMILY

小提琴
violin

大提琴
cello

中提琴
viola

低音提琴
double bass

電吉他
electric guitar

貝司
bass guitar

高音拾音器
treble pickup

琴馬組
bridge assembly

實心琴身
solid body

中音拾音器
midrange pickup

低音拾音器
bass pickup

音位記號
position marker

音品
fret

指板
finger board

調音弦軸
tuning peg

拾音鎖定器
pickguard

顫音臂
vibrato arm

拾音選擇器
pickup selector

音調調節器
tone controls

音量調節器
volume control

琴馬
nut

琴頸
neck

琴枕
head

輸出插孔
output jack

共鳴箱
body

琴馬
bridge

拾音器
pickups

帶釘
strap system

調音弦軸
tuning peg

琴枕
nut

音品
fret

低音音調調節器
bass tone control

高音音調調節器
treble tone control

穩定器
balancer

音量調節器
volume control

琴頸
neck

指點標記
position marker

指板
finger board

琴頭
head

管樂器
WIND INSTRUMENTS

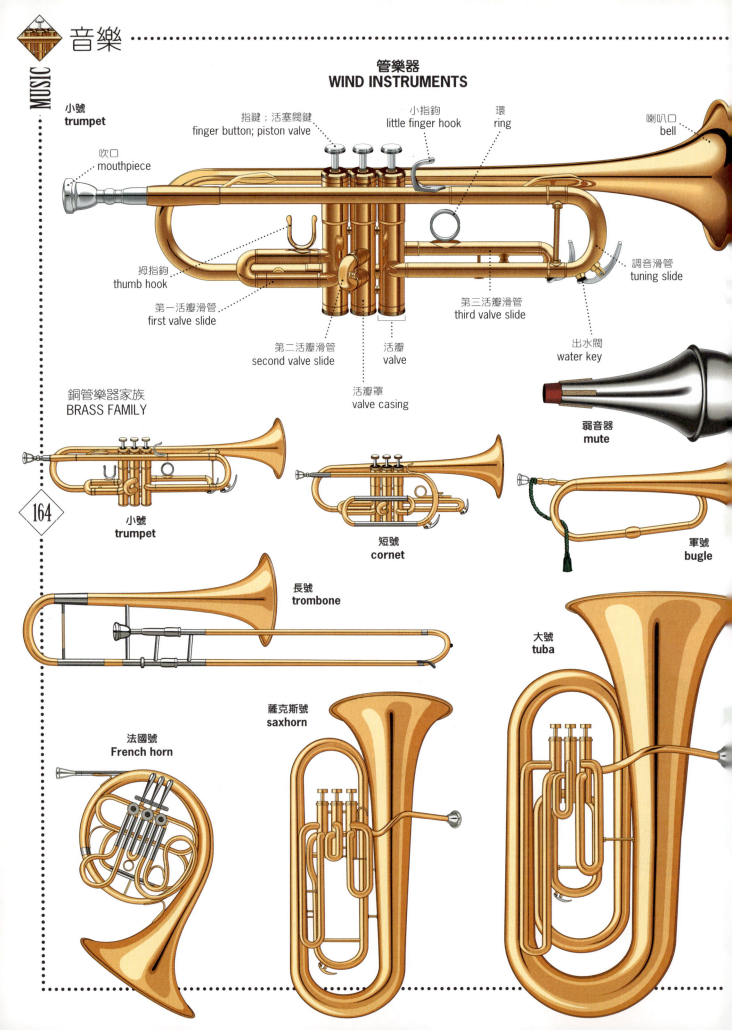

小號
trumpet

指鍵；活塞閥鍵
finger button; piston valve

小指鉤
little finger hook

環
ring

喇叭口
bell

吹口
mouthpiece

拇指鉤
thumb hook

第一活瓣滑管
first valve slide

第二活瓣滑管
second valve slide

活瓣
valve

第三活瓣滑管
third valve slide

調音滑管
tuning slide

出水閥
water key

活瓣罩
valve casing

銅管樂器家族
BRASS FAMILY

弱音器
mute

小號
trumpet

短號
cornet

軍號
bugle

長號
trombone

大號
tuba

薩克斯號
saxhorn

法國號
French horn

變音插管
crook

簧樂器
REEDS

綁帶
ligature

吹口
mouthpiece

簧片
reed

單簧管
single reed

雙簧管
double reed

高八度音裝置
octave mechanism

薩克斯管
saxophone

木管樂器家族
WOODWIND FAMILY

薩克斯管
saxophone

短笛
piccolo

喇叭口
bell

喇叭口拉條
bell brace

圓柱管
body

長笛
flute

八孔直笛
recorder

拇指托
thumb rest

鍵
key

雙簧管
oboe

單簧管
clarinet

中音單簧管
English horn /
cor anglais

巴松管
bassoon

打擊樂器
PERCUSSION INSTRUMENTS

鼓
drums

鈸
cymbal

鑼
tom-toms

查爾斯頓鈸
Charleston cymbal; hi-hat cymbal

鼓面
batter head

小軍鼓
snare drum

三角架
tripod stand

大鼓
bass drum

支架
stand

踏板
pedal

高音鼓
tenor drum

大頭錘
mallet

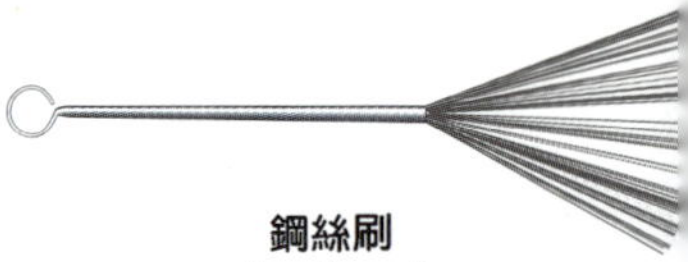

鋼絲刷
wire brush

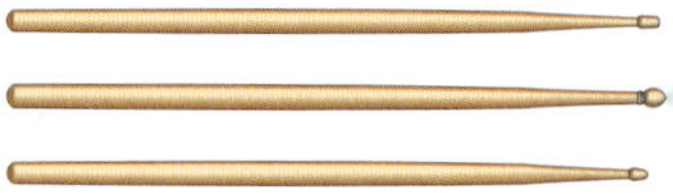

鼓槌
sticks

大頭錘
mallets

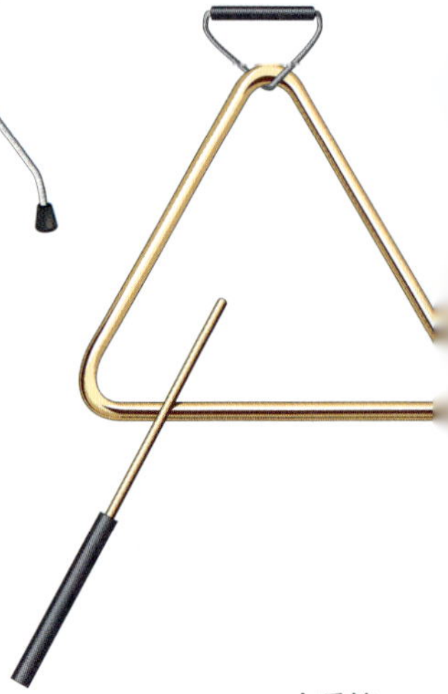

三角鐵
triangle

叉鈴
sistrum

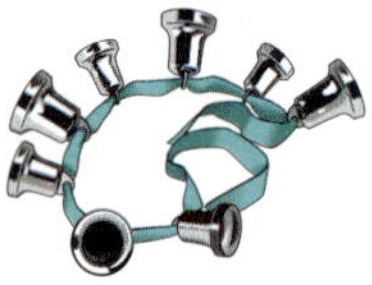

串鈴
set of bells

雪橇鈴
sleigh bells

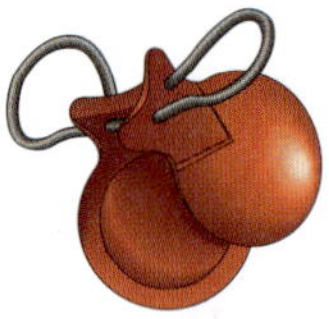

響板
castanets

小手鼓
bongos

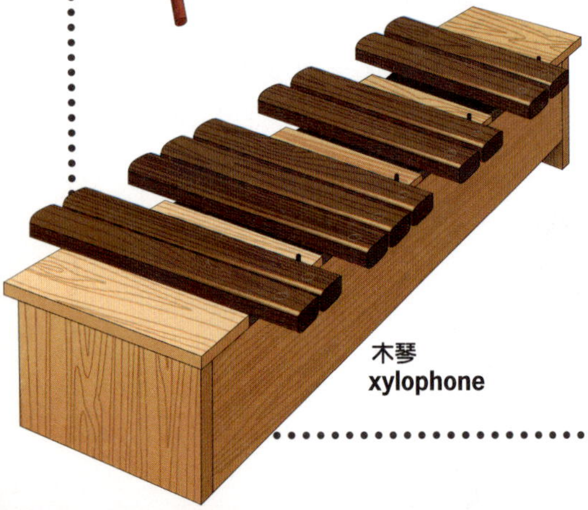

木琴
xylophone

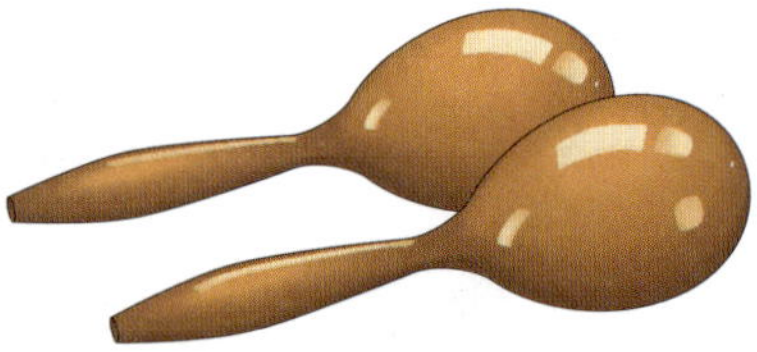

沙球
maracas

鈴鼓
tambourine

交響樂團
SYMPHONY ORCHESTRA

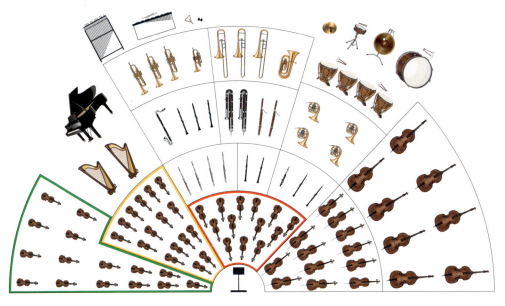

指揮台
conductor's podium

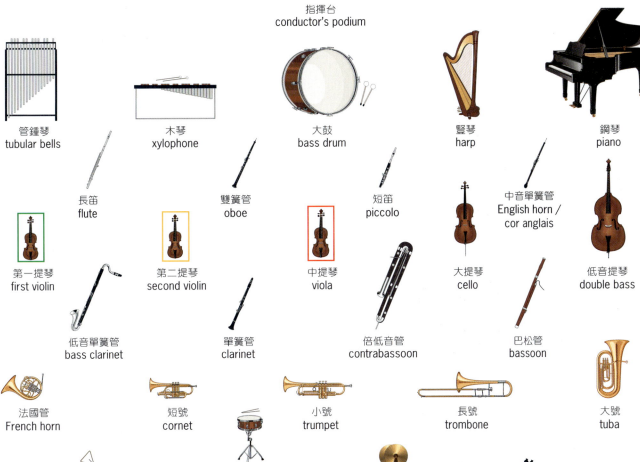

管鐘琴
tubular bells

木琴
xylophone

大鼓
bass drum

豎琴
harp

鋼琴
piano

長笛
flute

雙簧管
oboe

短笛
piccolo

中音單簧管
English horn /
cor anglais

第一提琴
first violin

第二提琴
second violin

中提琴
viola

大提琴
cello

低音提琴
double bass

低音單簧管
bass clarinet

單簧管
clarinet

倍低音管
contrabassoon

巴松管
bassoon

法國管
French horn

短號
cornet

小號
trumpet

長號
trombone

大號
tuba

三角鐵
triangle

小軍鼓
snare drum

鈸
cymbals

響板
castanets

定音鼓
kettledrum

鑼
gong

團隊運動

外場手/守場員手套
fielder's glove

網格
web

固定帶
strap

大拇指
thumb

鞋跟
heel

花邊
lace

手指
finger

手掌
palm

球型體
knob

把手
handle

球棒
ba

擊球區
hitting area

棒球
baseball

71-74毫米
71 – 74 mm

擊球手頭盔
batter's helmet

隊服
team shirt

擊球手套
batting glove

擊球
batt

內襯
undershirt

短褲
pants / trousers

型鐵
stirrup sock

釘鞋
spiked shoe

接球手
catcher

接球架
frame

護喉
throat protector

面罩
mask

接球手手套
catcher's glove

護胸
chest protector

護脛
shin guard

護趾
toe guard

護膝
knee pad

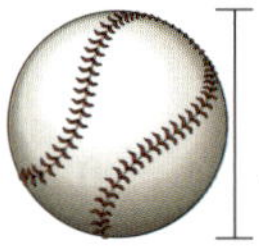

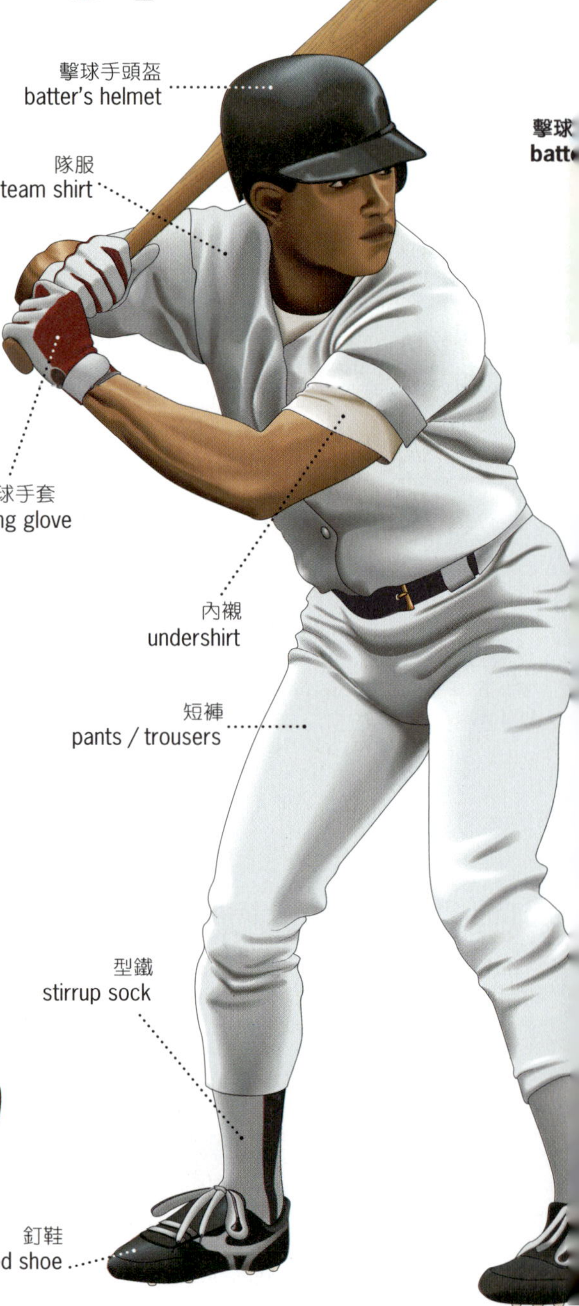

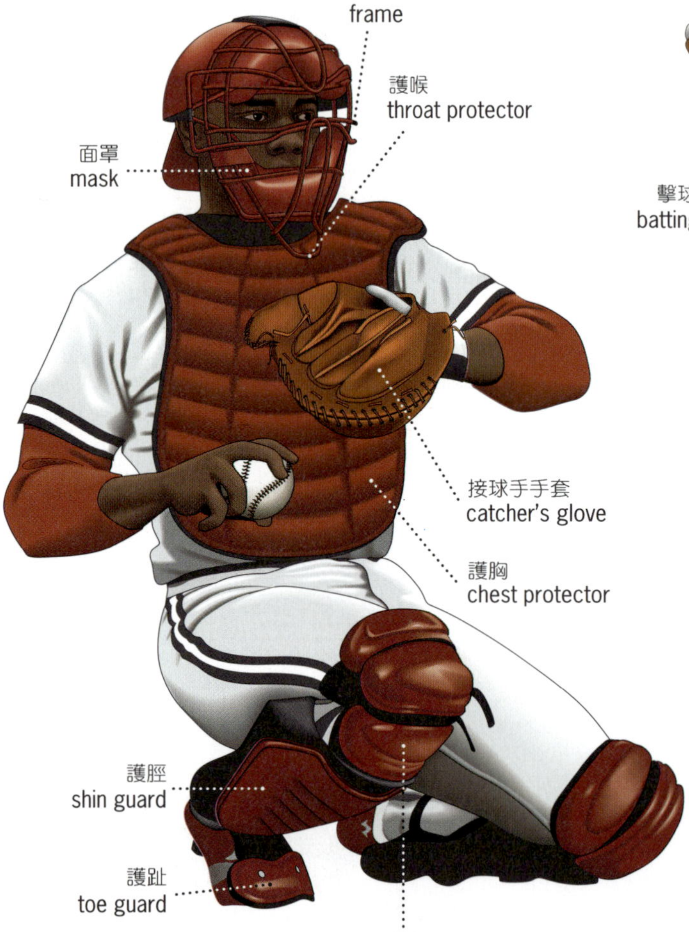

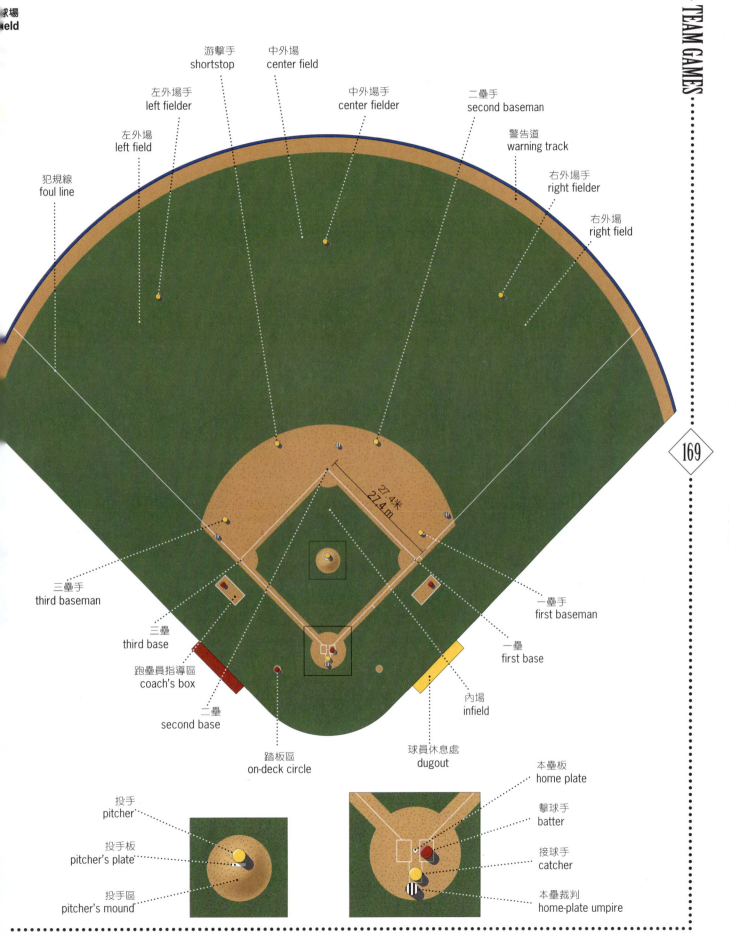

球場
field

游擊手
shortstop

中外場
center field

左外場手
left fielder

中外場手
center fielder

二壘手
second baseman

左外場
left field

警告道
warning track

右外場手
right fielder

犯規線
foul line

右外場
right field

27.4米
27.4 m

三壘手
third baseman

一壘手
first baseman

三壘
third base

一壘
first base

跑壘員指導區
coach's box

內場
infield

二壘
second base

踏板區
on-deck circle

球員休息處
dugout

本壘板
home plate

擊球手
batter

投手
pitcher

投手板
pitcher's plate

接球手
catcher

投手區
pitcher's mound

本壘裁判
home-plate umpire

美式足球（橄欖球）
AMERICAN FOOTBALL

美式足球運動員
American football player

頸帶
chin strap

頭盔
helmet

球員號碼
player's number

隊服
team shirt

護腕
wristband

橄欖球
footbal

279-286毫米
279 – 286 mm

防護裝
protective equipmer

頭盔
helmet

面罩
face mask

護肩
shoulder pad

護胸
chest protector

護臂
arm guard

護肋
rib pad

護肘
elbow pad

護臀
hip pad

護腰
lumbar pad

防護杯
protective cup

護股
thigh pad

護膝
knee pad

短褲
pants / trousers

球襪
sock

防滑鞋
cleated shoe

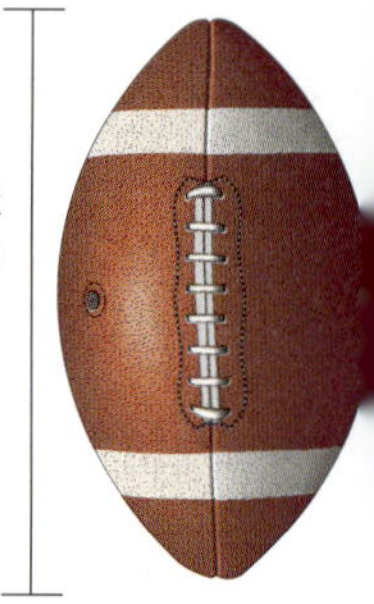

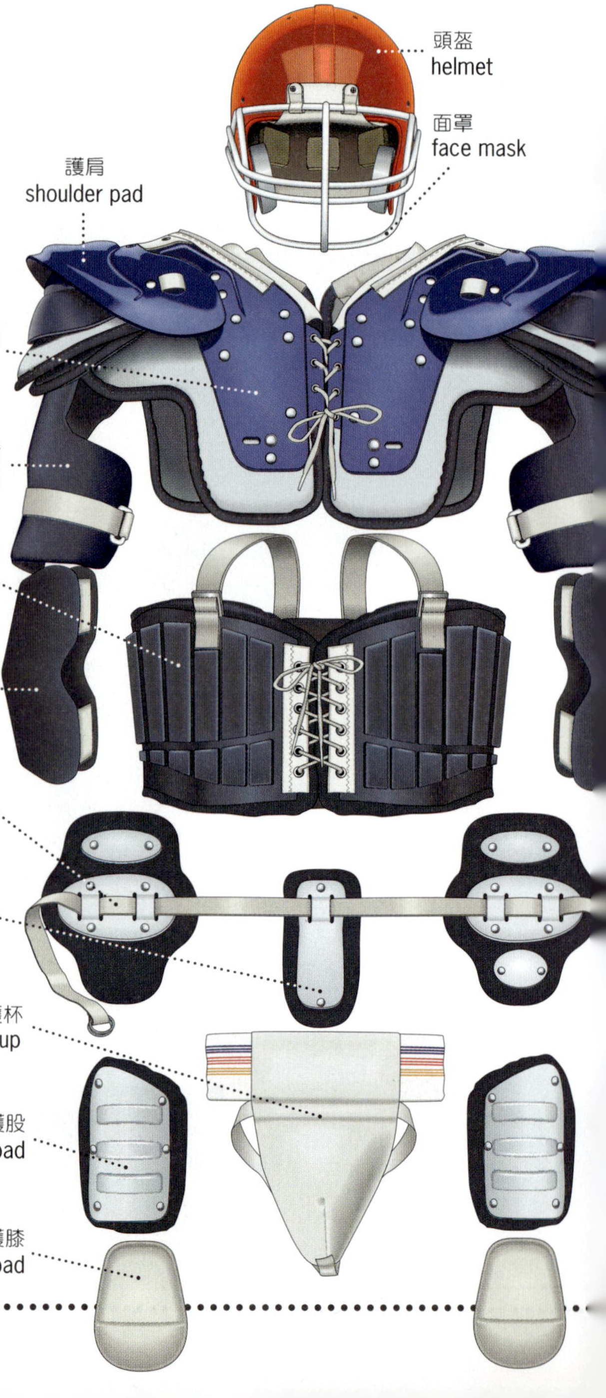

進攻
OFFENSE

爭球
scrimmage

防守
DEFENSE

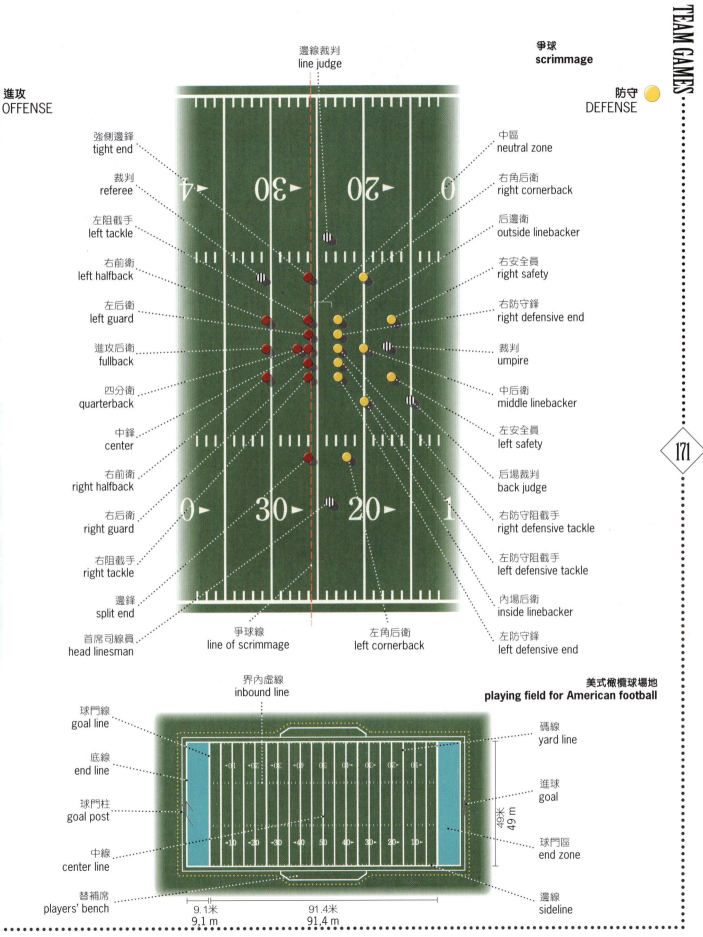

邊線裁判
line judge

強側邊鋒
tight end

裁判
referee

左阻截手
left tackle

右前衛
left halfback

左后衛
left guard

進攻后衛
fullback

四分衛
quarterback

中鋒
center

右前衛
right halfback

右后衛
right guard

右阻截手
right tackle

邊鋒
split end

首席司線員
head linesman

中區
neutral zone

右角后衛
right cornerback

后邊衛
outside linebacker

右安全員
right safety

右防守鋒
right defensive end

裁判
umpire

中后衛
middle linebacker

左安全員
left safety

后場裁判
back judge

右防守阻截手
right defensive tackle

左防守阻截手
left defensive tackle

內場后衛
inside linebacker

左防守鋒
left defensive end

爭球線
line of scrimmage

左角后衛
left cornerback

美式橄欖球場地
playing field for American football

界內虛線
inbound line

球門線
goal line

底線
end line

球門柱
goal post

中線
center line

替補席
players' bench

碼線
yard line

進球
goal

球門區
end zone

邊線
sideline

49米
49 m

9.1米
9.1 m

91.4米
91.4 m

足球（英式）
SOCCER

足球運動員
soccer player

足球
soccer ball

隊服
team shirt

218毫米
218 mm

172

運動短褲
shorts

護脛
shin guard

足球鞋
soccer shoe / football boot

可換鞋釘
interchangeable studs

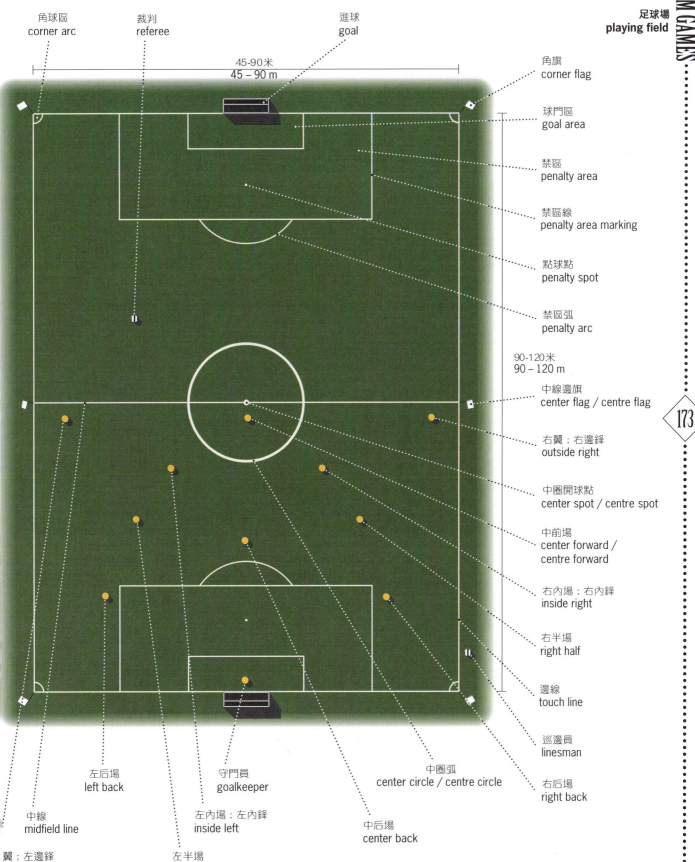

角球區
corner arc

裁判
referee

進球
goal

角旗
corner flag

球門區
goal area

禁區
penalty area

禁區線
penalty area marking

點球點
penalty spot

禁區弧
penalty arc

45-90米
45 – 90 m

90-120米
90 – 120 m

中線邊旗
center flag / centre flag

右翼；右邊鋒
outside right

中圈開球點
center spot / centre spot

中前場
center forward /
centre forward

右內場；右內鋒
inside right

右半場
right half

邊線
touch line

巡邊員
linesman

右后場
right back

左后場
left back

守門員
goalkeeper

中圈弧
center circle / centre circle

中線
midfield line

左內場；左內鋒
inside left

左半場
left half

中后場
center back

翼；左邊鋒
tside left

團隊運動

板球
CRICKET

板球選手
cricket player

板球棒
bat

手套
glove

三柱門
wicket

（三柱門上的）橫木
bail

（三柱門的）柱
stump

護墊
pad

板球鞋
cricket shoe

鞋釘
studs

三柱守門員
wicket-keeper

擊球員
batsman

守場員
fielders

板球場
pitch

裁判
umpire

球:
fie

投球手
bowler

裁判
umpire

擊球員
batsman

板球棒
bat

把手
handle

球棒
willow

板球
cricket ball

70-73毫米
70 – 73 mm

好球部位
groove

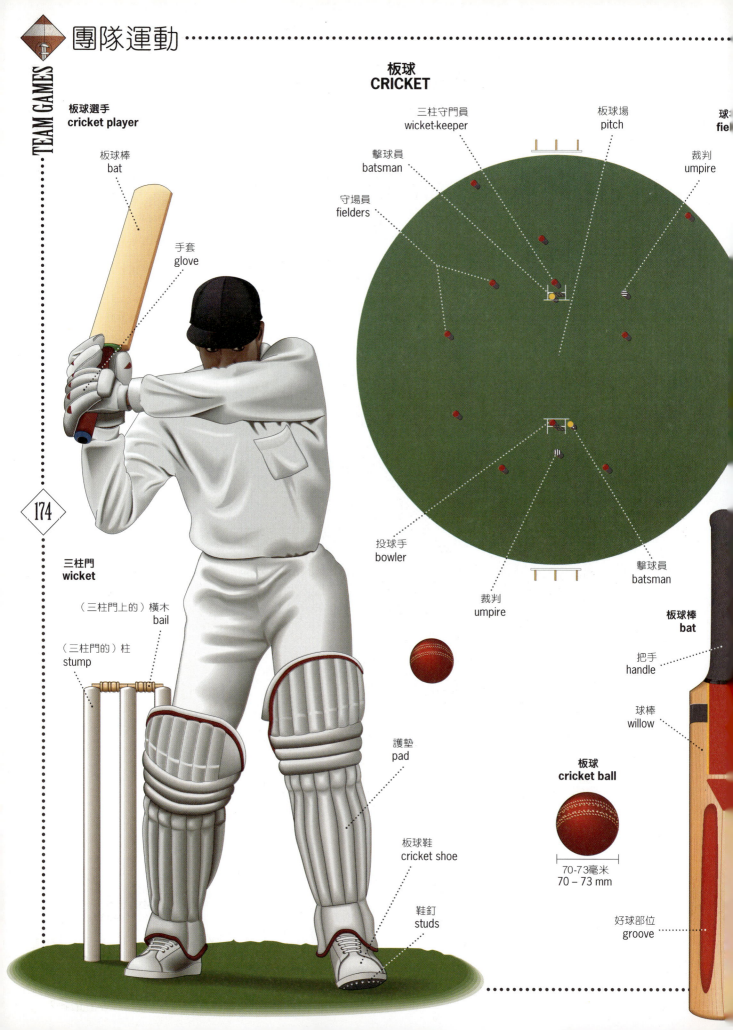

曲棍球
FIELD HOCKEY

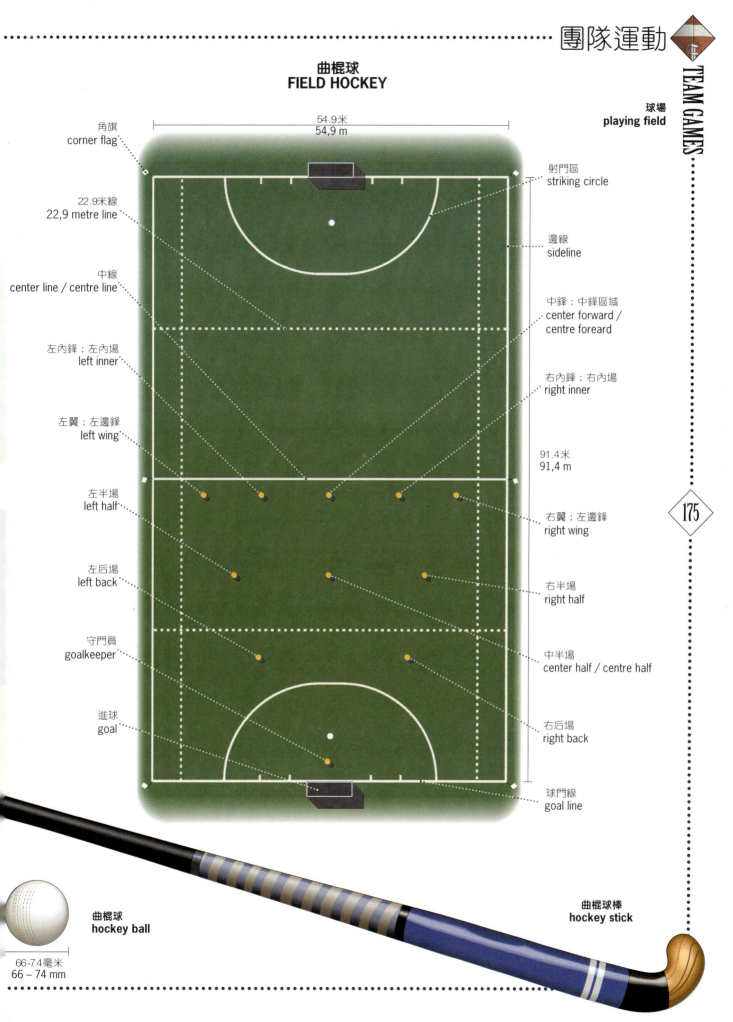

54.9米
54,9 m

角旗
corner flag

射門區
striking circle

22.9米線
22,9 metre line

邊線
sideline

中線
center line / centre line

中鋒；中鋒區域
center forward /
centre foreard

左內鋒；左內場
left inner

右內鋒；右內場
right inner

左翼；左邊鋒
left wing

91.4米
91,4 m

左半場
left half

右翼；左邊鋒
right wing

左后場
left back

右半場
right half

守門員
goalkeeper

中半場
center half / centre half

進球
goal

右后場
right back

球門線
goal line

曲棍球
hockey ball

曲棍球棒
hockey stick

66-74毫米
66 – 74 mm

冰球場
rink

冰球
ICE HOCKEY

冰
puc

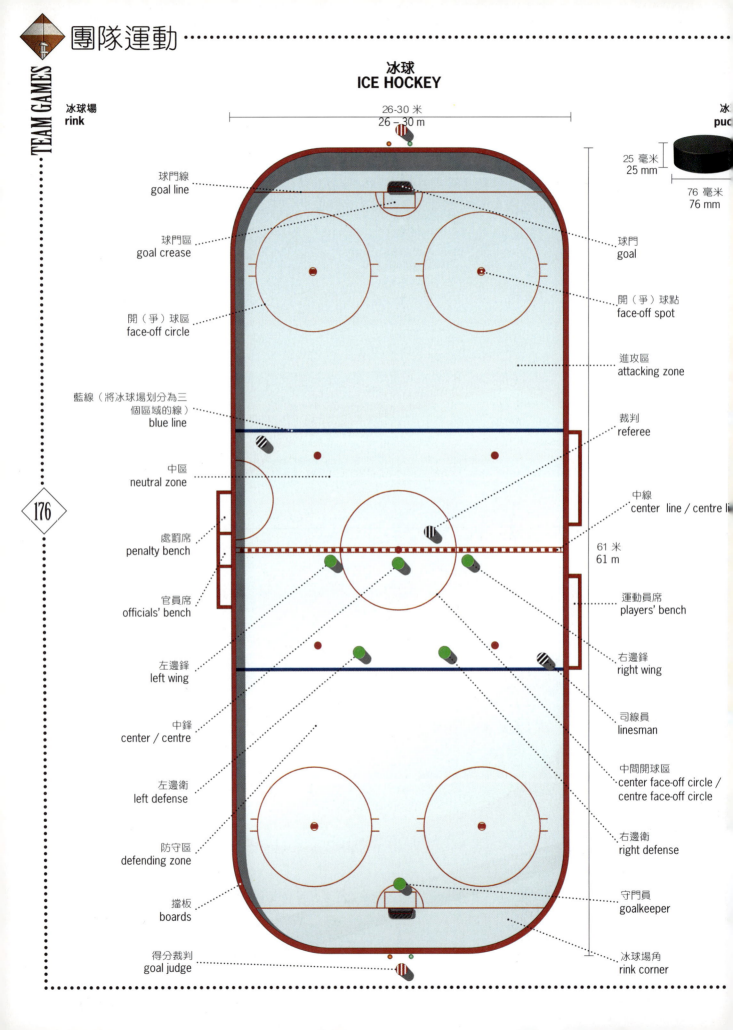

26-30 米
26 – 30 m

25 毫米
25 mm

76 毫米
76 mm

球門線
goal line

球門區
goal crease

開（爭）球區
face-off circle

藍線（將冰球場划分為三個區域的線）
blue line

中區
neutral zone

處罰席
penalty bench

官員席
officials' bench

左邊鋒
left wing

中鋒
center / centre

左邊衛
left defense

防守區
defending zone

擋板
boards

得分裁判
goal judge

球門
goal

開（爭）球點
face-off spot

進攻區
attacking zone

裁判
referee

中線
center line / centre li

61 米
61 m

運動員席
players' bench

右邊鋒
right wing

司線員
linesman

中間開球區
center face-off circle /
centre face-off circle

右邊衛
right defense

守門員
goalkeeper

冰球場角
rink corner

冰球棍
layer's stick

冰球棍上端
butt end

柄
shaft

頭盔
helmet

護肩
shoulder pad

防護帶
protective girdle

防護杯
protective cup

護脛
shin pad

冰球運動員
ice hockey player

護肘
elbow pad

冰球手套腕部；護腕
cuff

手套
glove

護膝
knee pad

冰鞋
skate

冰刀刃
blade

鞋后跟
el

守門員
goalkeeper

面罩
face mask

護臂
arm pad

護背
back pad

護喉
throat protector

護身
body pad

冰球褲
pants

守門員接球手套
catch glove

守門員護墊
goalkeeper's pad

溜冰鞋
skate

守門員的球棍
goalkeeper's stick

冰刀刃
blade

籃球
BASKETBALL

(籃)球場
court

15米
15 m

籃
basket

禁區
free-throw lane

運動員席
players' bench

左前鋒
left forward

計時員
timekeeper

時鐘操作員
clock operator

記錄員
scorer

左后衛
left guard

中圈
center circle / centre circle

禁區線
free-throw line

邊線
sideline

第二空間
second space

第一空間
first space

底線
end line

禁區/三秒區
restricted area

半圓區
semi-circle

裁判
referee

右前鋒
right forward

28米
28 m

中線
center line / centre line

罰球區
restricting circle

右后衛
right guard

裁判
referee

中鋒
center / centre

籃球
basketball

244毫米
244 mm

bask

籃板
backboard

籃圈
rim

籃網
net

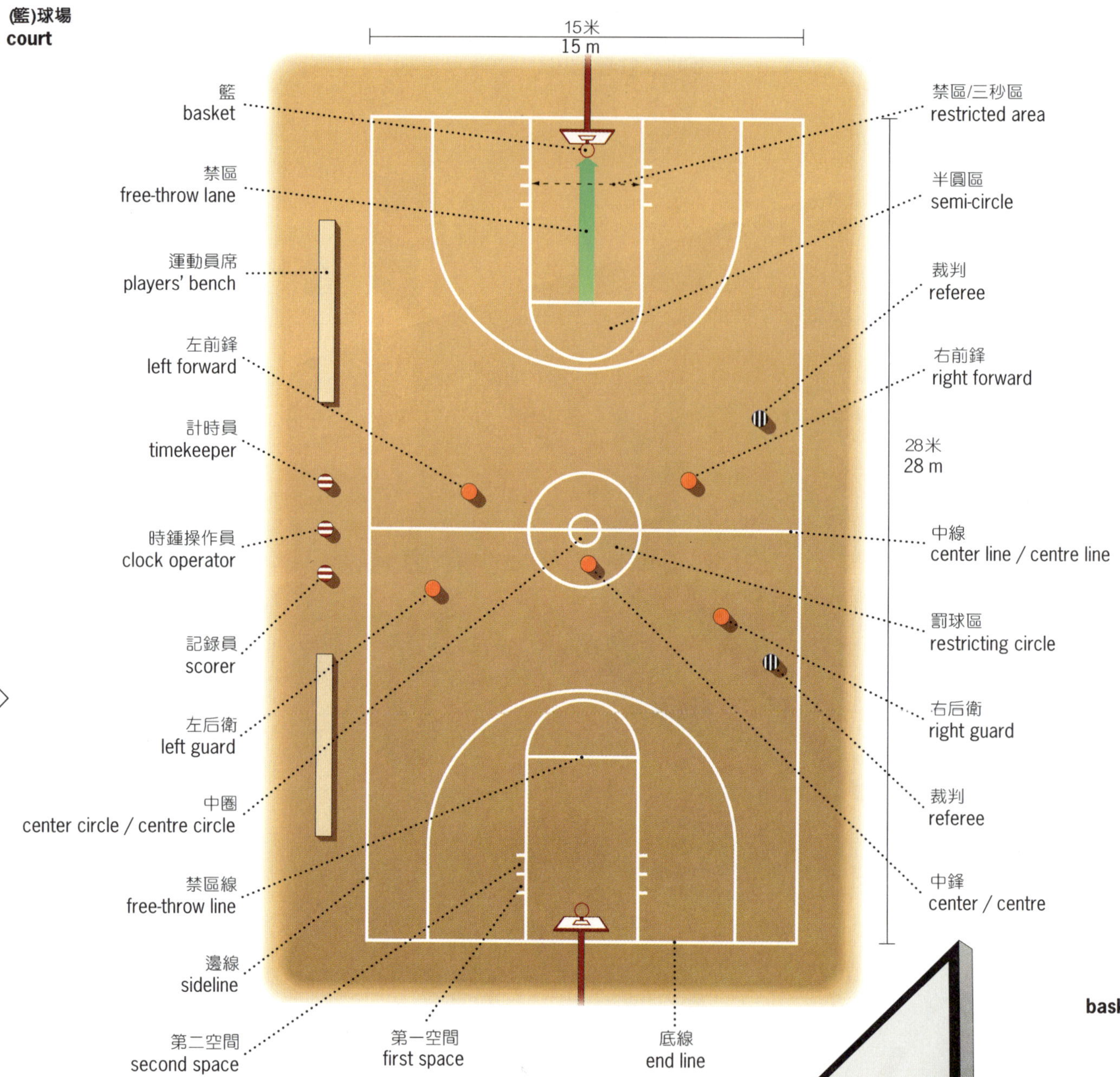

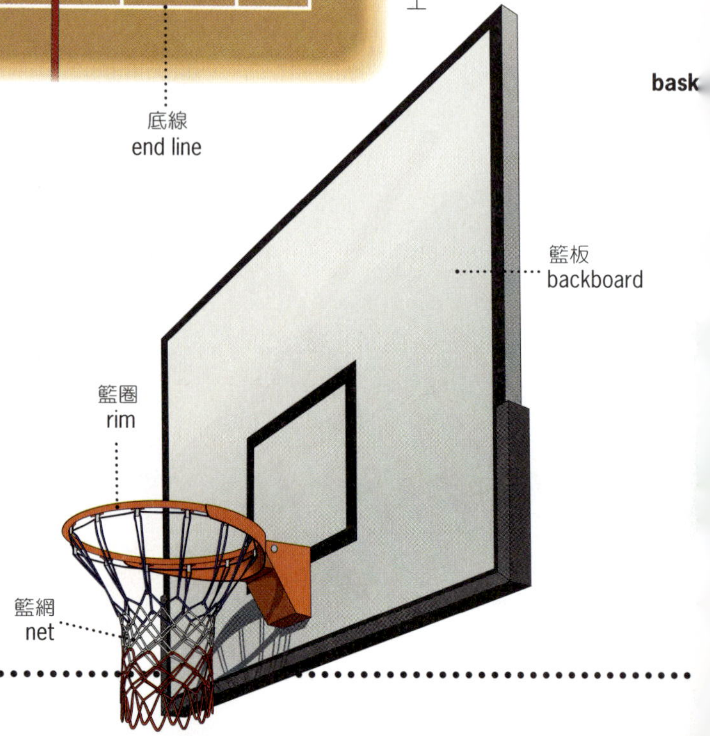

排球
VOLLEYBALL

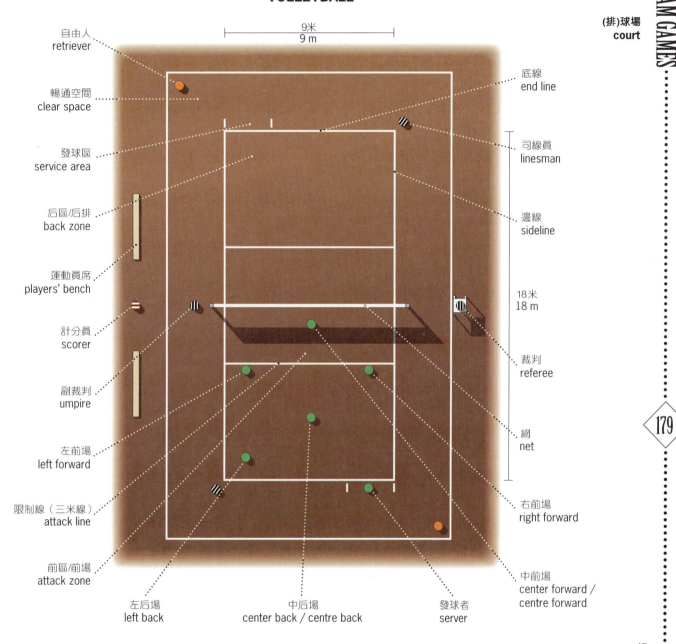

(排)球場
court

自由人
retriever

暢通空間
clear space

發球區
service area

后區/后排
back zone

運動員席
players' bench

計分員
scorer

副裁判
umpire

左前場
left forward

限制線（三米線）
attack line

前區/前場
attack zone

9米
9 m

底線
end line

司線員
linesman

邊線
sideline

18米
18 m

裁判
referee

網
net

右前場
right forward

中前場
center forward /
centre forward

左后場
left back

中后場
center back / centre back

發球者
server

179

網
net

排球
volleyball

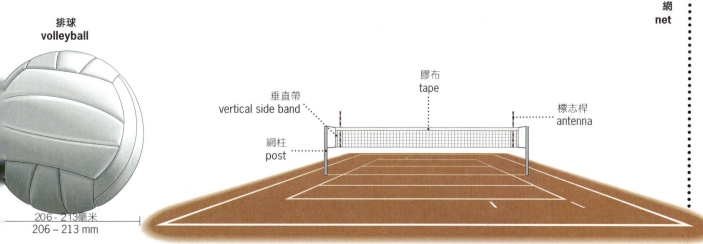

206 - 213毫米
206 – 213 mm

垂直帶
vertical side band

膠布
tape

標志桿
antenna

網柱
post

團隊運動

網球
TENNIS

8.23米
8,23 m

司線員
linesman

中點標志
center mark / centre ma

接球者
receiver

底線
baseline

后場
backcourt

發球線
service line

前場
forecourt

發球裁判
service judge

中區發球線
center service line /
centre service line

單打邊線
singles sideline

23.8米
23,8 m

裁判
umpire

網線裁判
net judge

左發球區
left service court

網
net

（單打和雙打之間的）狹長區
alley

右發球區
right service court

發球者
server

發球裁判
foot fault judge

球童
ball boy

雙打邊線
doubles sideline

11米
11 m

中間帶（位于球網中央）
center strap / centre strap

單打網柱
singles pole

網帶（位于球網上端）
net band

雙打網柱
doubles pole

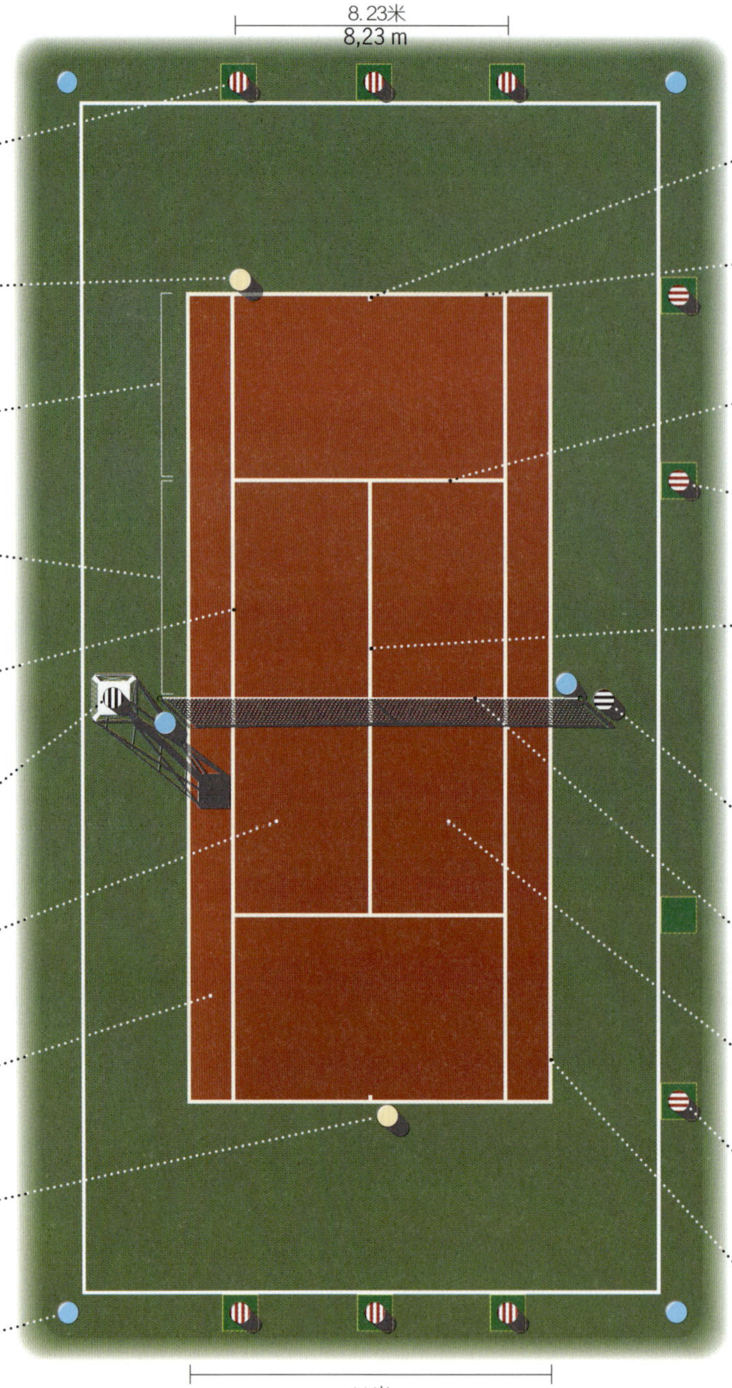

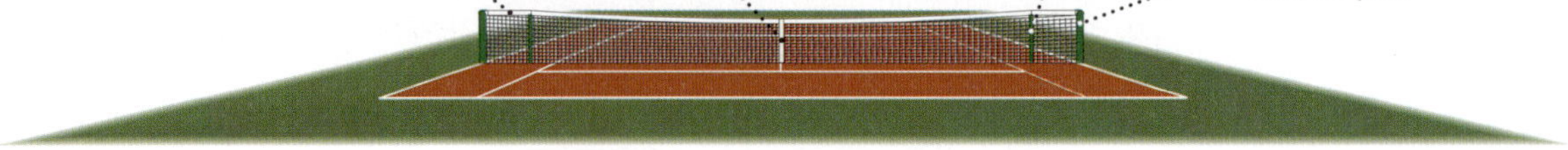

網球
tennis ball

64-68米
64 – 68 mm

網球手
tennis player

頭帶
headband

網球恤
polo shirt

護腕
wristband

網球裙
skirt

網球鞋
tennis shoe

網球襪
sock

網球拍
tennis racket

球拍上端
butt

拍柄把手
handle

拍柄
shaft

球拍頸部
throat

球拍肩部
shoulder

拍頭
head

拍架
frame

拍面
strings

游泳
SWIMMING

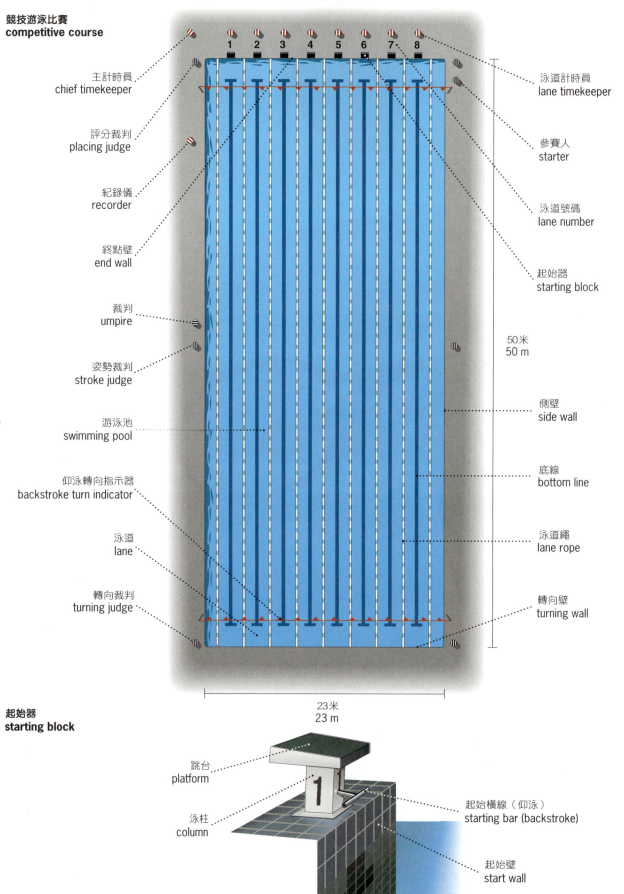

競技游泳比賽
competitive course

主計時員
chief timekeeper

評分裁判
placing judge

紀錄儀
recorder

終點壁
end wall

裁判
umpire

姿勢裁判
stroke judge

游泳池
swimming pool

仰泳轉向指示器
backstroke turn indicator

泳道
lane

轉向裁判
turning judge

泳道計時員
lane timekeeper

參賽人
starter

泳道號碼
lane number

起始器
starting block

50米
50 m

側壁
side wall

底線
bottom line

泳道繩
lane rope

轉向壁
turning wall

23米
23 m

起始器
starting block

跳台
platform

泳柱
column

起始橫線（仰泳）
starting bar (backstroke)

起始壁
start wall

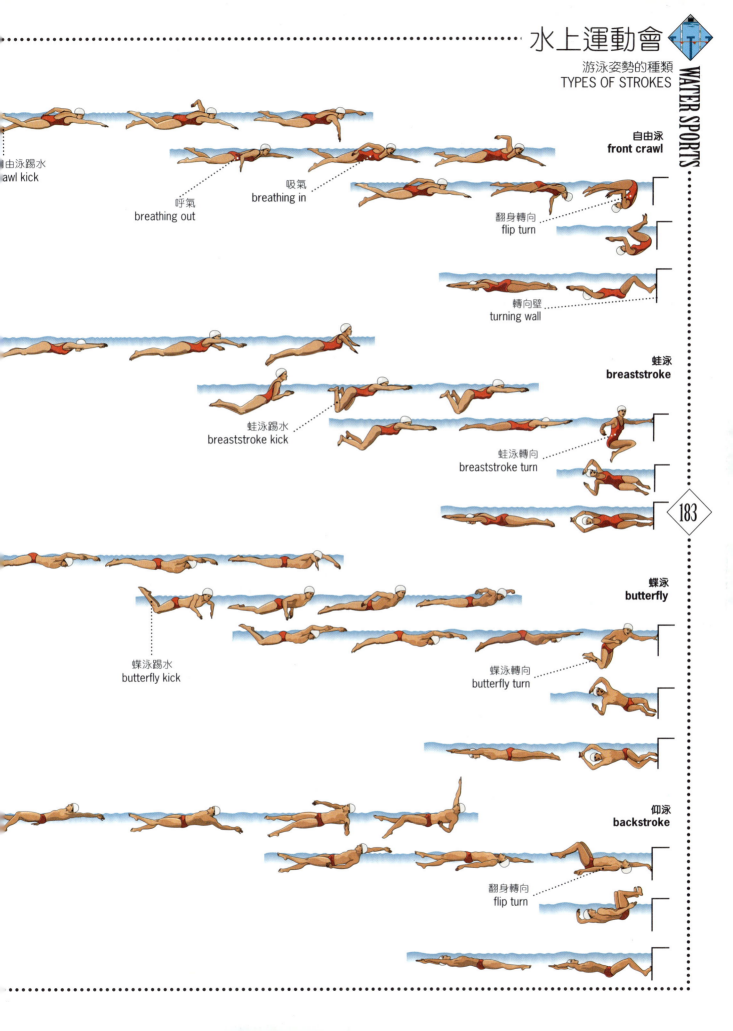

自由泳踢水
awl kick

呼氣
breathing out

吸氣
breathing in

自由泳
front crawl

翻身轉向
flip turn

轉向壁
turning wall

蛙泳
breaststroke

蛙泳踢水
breaststroke kick

蛙泳轉向
breaststroke turn

183

蝶泳
butterfly

蝶泳踢水
butterfly kick

蝶泳轉向
butterfly turn

仰泳
backstroke

翻身轉向
flip turn

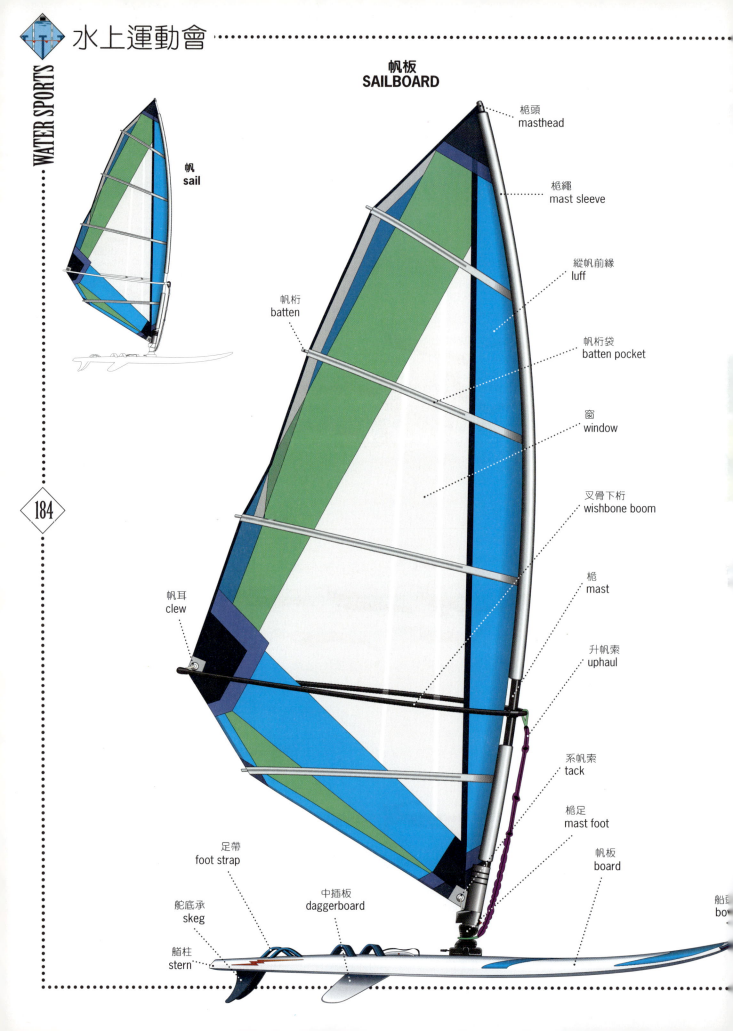

帆板
SAILBOARD

帆
sail

槓頭
masthead

槓繩
mast sleeve

縱帆前緣
luff

帆桁袋
batten pocket

窗
window

叉骨下桁
wishbone boom

槓
mast

升帆索
uphaul

系帆索
tack

槓足
mast foot

帆板
board

帆桁
batten

帆耳
clew

足帶
foot strap

中插板
daggerboard

舵底承
skeg

艉柱
stern

船□
bo□

滑冰
SKATING

內靴
inner boot

護靴
upper shell

旱冰鞋
n-line skate

可調節搭扣
adjusting buckle

鞋身
boot

速度滑冰鞋
speed skate

輪軸
axle

滑輪
wheel

滑輪板
truck

鞋根制動器
heel stop

冰球鞋
hockey skate

護腱
tendon guard

鞋身
boot

內包頭
toe box

冰刀尖
point

冰刀刃
blade

花樣滑冰鞋
igure skate

鞋鉤
hook

后拉線
backstay

鞋帶孔
eyelet

鞋身
boot

冰刀柱
stanchion

后端
edge

冰刀刃
blade

鞋舌
tongue

鞋帶
lace

鞋底
sole

前端
toe pick

冰刀護罩
skate guard

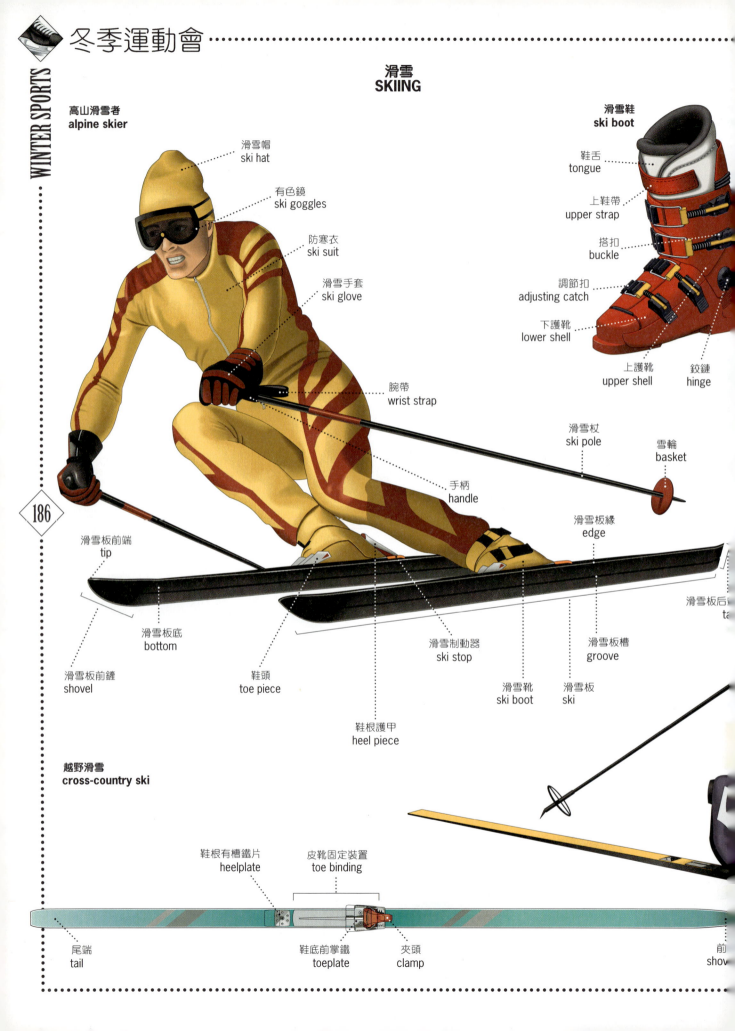

滑雪
SKIING

高山滑雪者
alpine skier

滑雪鞋
ski boot

滑雪帽
ski hat

有色鏡
ski goggles

防寒衣
ski suit

滑雪手套
ski glove

鞋舌
tongue

上鞋帶
upper strap

搭扣
buckle

調節扣
adjusting catch

下護靴
lower shell

上護靴
upper shell

鉸鏈
hinge

腕帶
wrist strap

滑雪杖
ski pole

雪輪
basket

手柄
handle

滑雪板緣
edge

186

滑雪板前端
tip

滑雪板底
bottom

滑雪制動器
ski stop

滑雪板槽
groove

滑雪板后
ta

滑雪板前鏟
shovel

鞋頭
toe piece

滑雪靴
ski boot

滑雪板
ski

鞋根護甲
heel piece

越野滑雪
cross-country ski

鞋根有槽鐵片
heelplate

皮靴固定裝置
toe binding

尾端
tail

鞋底前掌鐵
toeplate

夾頭
clamp

前
shov

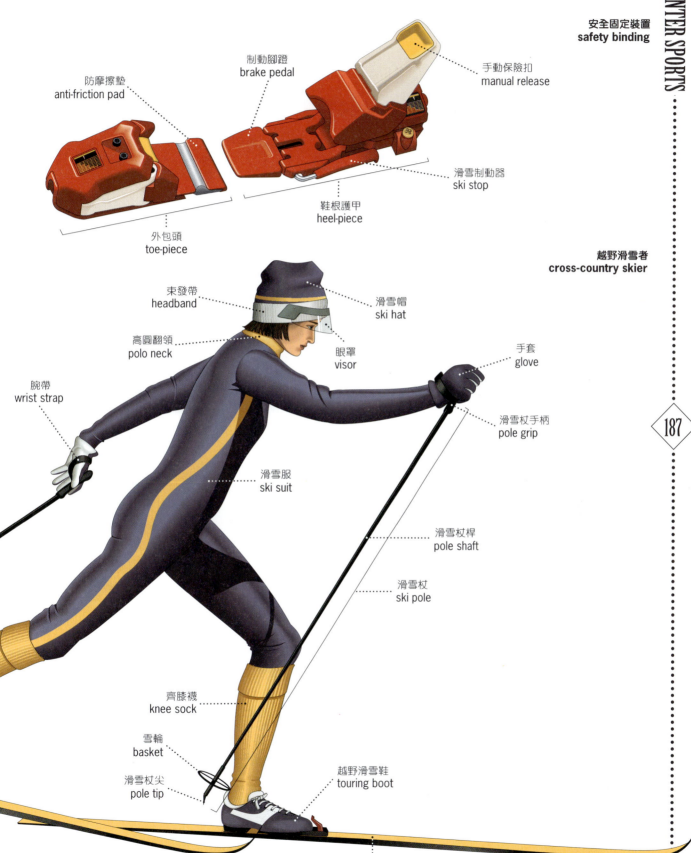

安全固定裝置
safety binding

制動腳蹬
brake pedal

手動保險扣
manual release

防摩擦墊
anti-friction pad

滑雪制動器
ski stop

鞋根護甲
heel-piece

外包頭
toe-piece

越野滑雪者
cross-country skier

束髮帶
headband

滑雪帽
ski hat

高圓翻領
polo neck

眼罩
visor

手套
glove

腕帶
wrist strap

滑雪杖手柄
pole grip

滑雪服
ski suit

滑雪杖桿
pole shaft

滑雪杖
ski pole

齊膝襪
knee sock

雪輪
basket

越野滑雪鞋
touring boot

滑雪杖尖
pole tip

越野滑雪板
cross-country ski

体操 ··

體操
GYMNASTICS

鞍馬
pommel horse

鞍馬
horse

基底
base

環上
saddle

鞍頸
neck

鞍臀
croup

鞍環
pommel

牢固件
fastening system

跳馬
vaulting horse

平衡
balance bea

跳板
springboard

蹦床
trampoline

彈性床
bed

安全墊
safety pad

床腿
leg

床架
frame

彈簧
spring

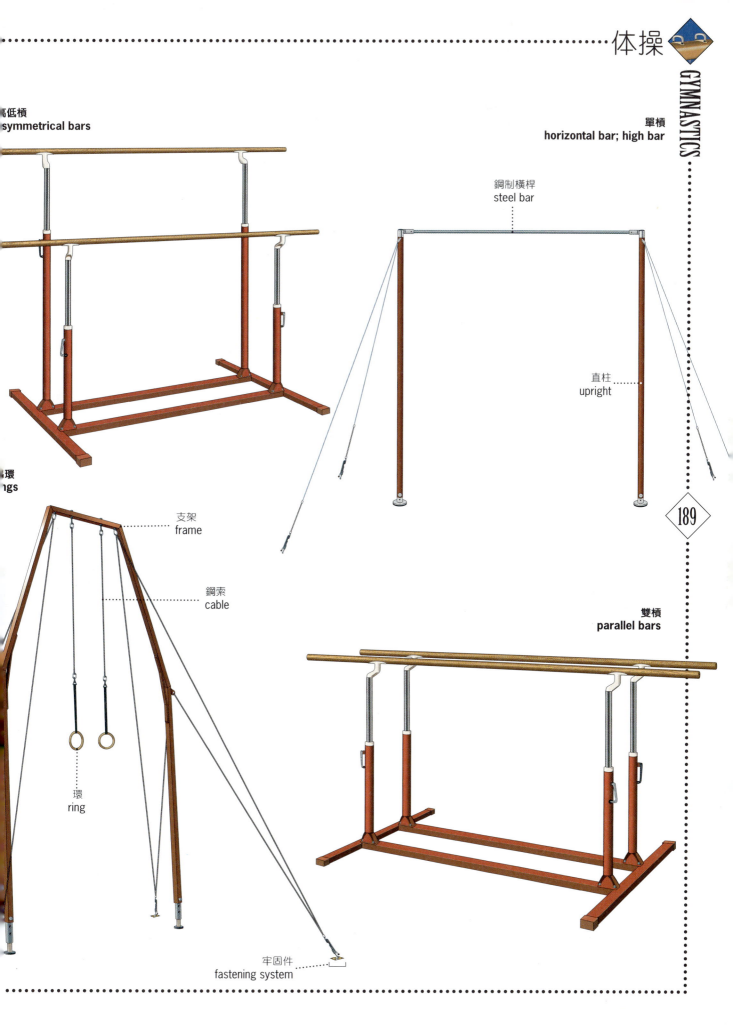

高低槓
asymmetrical bars

單槓
horizontal bar; high bar

鋼制橫桿
steel bar

直柱
upright

環
rings

支架
frame

鋼索
cable

環
ring

雙槓
parallel bars

牢固件
fastening system

帳篷
TENTS

雙人帳篷
two-person tent

防雨帆布外頂
rainfly / flysheet

門
door

雨篷
awning

支索
guy line /
guy rope

拉緊裝置
strainer

拉鏈
zipper / zip

內部帳篷
inner tent

椿
stake / tent p

帳篷的主要類型
MAJOR TYPES OF TENTS

大篷車車篷
wagon tent

大型帳篷
wall tent

小型帳篷
pup tent / ridge tent

圓頂帳篷
dome tent

自動跳出式帳篷
pop-up tent

家用帳篷
family tent

單人帳篷
one-person tent

臥具
SLEEPING EQUIPMENT

床和床墊
BEDS AND MATTRESSES

泡沫墊
foam pad

自動充氣墊
self-inflating mattress

充氣設備
inflator

充氣/壓縮裝置
inflator-deflator

折疊式帆布床
folding cot / camp bed

睡袋
SLEEPING BAGS

氣墊
ir mattress / air bed

木乃伊式睡袋
mummy

半木乃伊式睡袋
semi-mummy

矩形睡袋
rectangular

野營用具
CAMPING EQUIPMENT

瑞士軍刀
Swiss army knife

剪刀
scissors

直尺
ruler

刮鱗器
fish scaler

指甲挫
file

放大鏡
magnifier

十字螺絲刀
cross-tip screwdriver

小刀片
small blade

螺絲刀
screwdriver

啟瓶器
bottle opener

指甲槽
nail nick

螺絲刀
screwdriver

大刀片
large blade

鑽子
awl

螺絲起子
corkscrew

罐頭起子
can opener / tin opener

皮套
leather sheath

七首
knife

手電筒
**flashlight /
pocket toch**

刀鞘
sheath

斧頭
hatchet / axe

碟子
plate

廚具
COOKING SET

咖啡壺
coffee pot

煎鍋
frying pan

杯子
cup

旅行水壺
canteen

手柄
handle

深平底鍋
saucepan

背包
backpack / rucksack

頂帶
top flap

背帶
shoulder strap

側收縮帶
side compression strap

骨架
internal frame

腰帶
waist belt

搭扣
tightening buckle

背帶環
strap loop

前收縮帶
front compression strap

急救箱
first aid kit

磁羅盤
magnetic compass

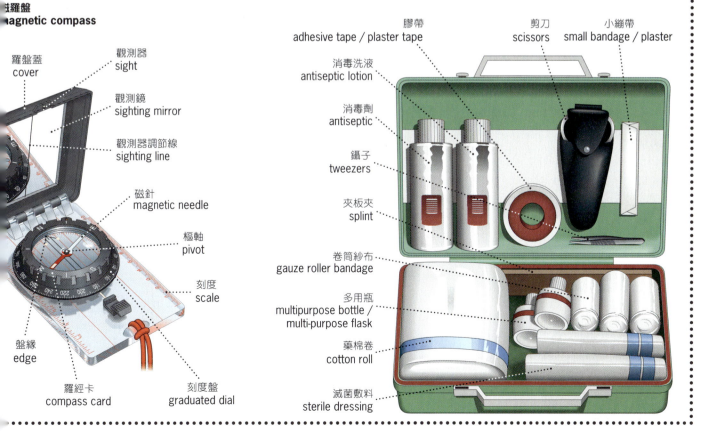

羅盤蓋
cover

觀測器
sight

觀測鏡
sighting mirror

觀測器調節線
sighting line

磁針
magnetic needle

樞軸
pivot

刻度
scale

盤緣
edge

羅經卡
compass card

刻度盤
graduated dial

膠帶
adhesive tape / plaster tape

剪刀
scissors

小繃帶
small bandage / plaster

消毒洗液
antiseptic lotion

消毒劑
antiseptic

鑷子
tweezers

夾板夾
splint

卷筒紗布
gauze roller bandage

多用瓶
multipurpose bottle /
multi-purpose flask

藥棉卷
cotton roll

滅菌敷料
sterile dressing

撲克牌游戲
CARD GAMES

紅桃
heart

方塊
diamond

梅花
club

黑桃
spade

小丑
Joker

"A"/愛司
Ace

"K"/老K
King

"Q"/王后
Queen

"J"/傑克
Jack

骰子
DICE

撲克牌式擲骰
poker die

普通骰子
ordinary die

多米諾骨
DOMINOE

（擲出的）一對同點骰子
doublet

雙六
double-six

一邊空白的骰子
blank

點數
pip

兩邊空白的骰子
double-blank

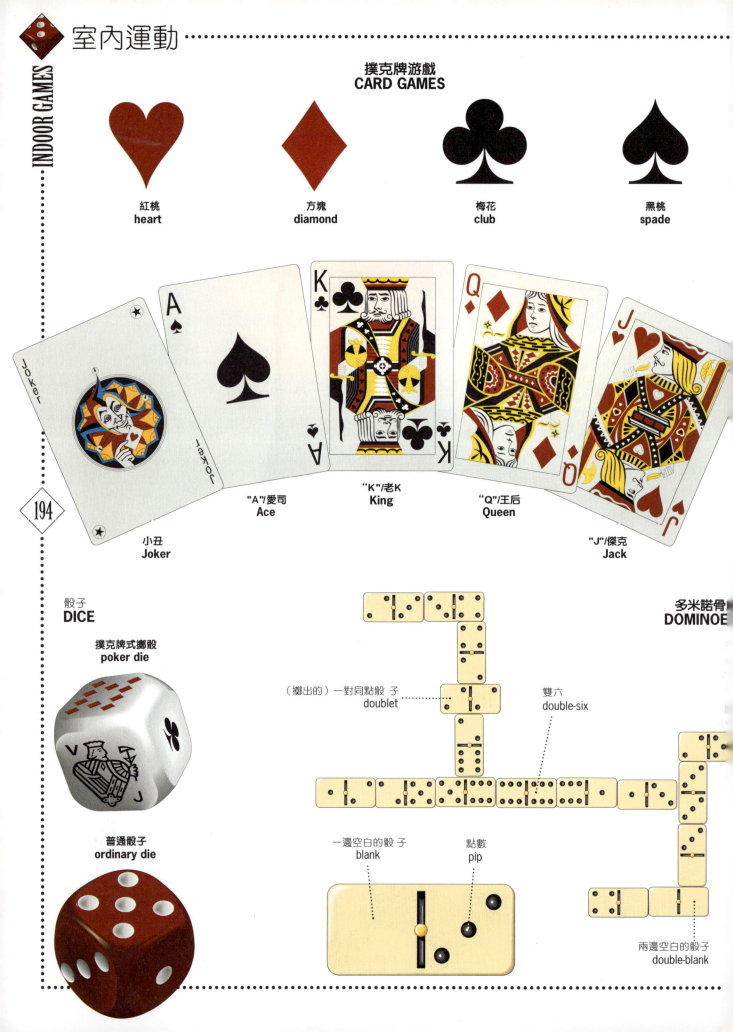

國際象棋
CHESS

棋盤
chessboard

后翼
Queen's side

王翼
King's side

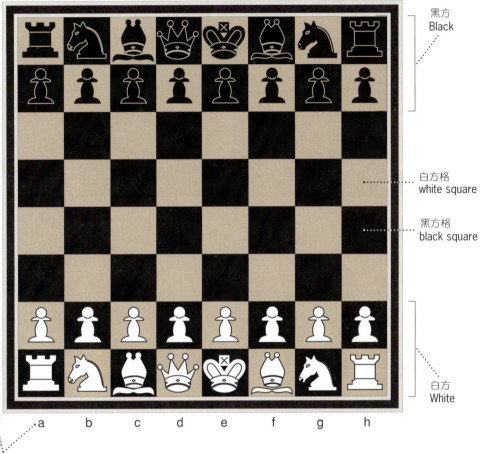

黑方
Black

白方格
white square

黑方格
black square

白方
White

a　b　c　d　e　f　g　h

棋譜記法
chess notation

棋子移動法
types of movements

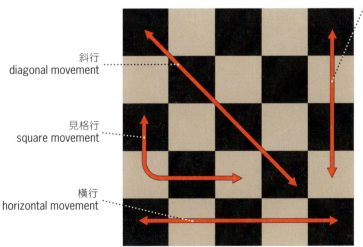

縱行
vertical movement

斜行
diagonal movement

見格行
square movement

橫行
horizontal movement

卒
Pawn

馬
Knight

象
Bishop

車
Rook

后
Queen

王
King

195

室內運動

15子游戲
BACKGAMMON

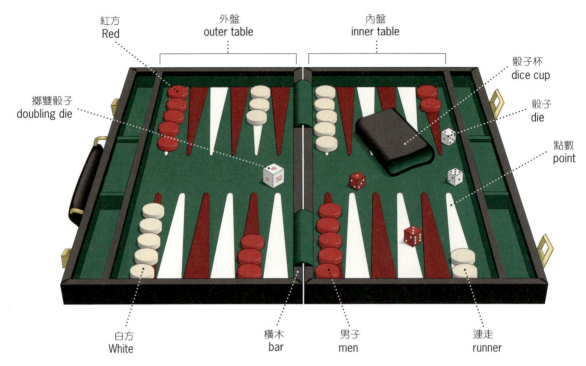

紅方
Red

外盤
outer table

內盤
inner table

骰子杯
dice cup

擲雙骰子
doubling die

骰子
die

點數
point

白方
White

橫木
bar

男子
men

連走
runner

西洋跳棋
CHECKERS / DRAUGHTS

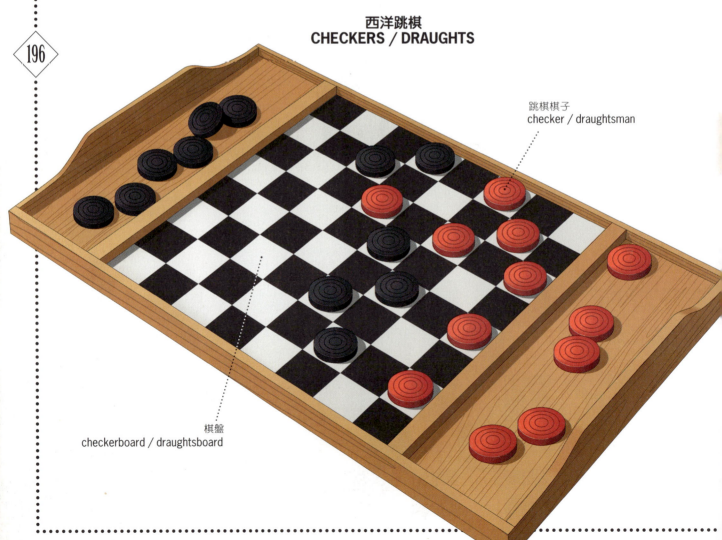

跳棋棋子
checker / draughtsman

棋盤
checkerboard / draughtsboard

錄像娛樂系統
VIDEO ENTERTAINMENT SYSTEM

圖像顯示
visual display

盒式游戲磁盤
game cartridge

控制桌面
control deck

控制桿
control pad

功能鍵
function button

飛鏢
dart

鏢尾
flight

箭頭
shaft

箭桿
barrel

得分
point

投鏢游戲
GAME OF DARTS

鏢板
dartboard

扇形分數
segment score number

二倍圈
double ring

三倍圈
triple ring

靶心
bull's-eye

25分圈
25 ring

時間的計算
MEASURE OF TIME

跑表
stopwatch

吊環
ring

開始鍵
start button

復位鍵
reset button

停止鍵
stop button

秒針
second hand

分針
minute hand

1/10秒針
1/10th second hand

表殼
case

25
20
15
10
5

min

1/10 SEC

55 5
50 10
45 15
40 20
35 25
30

模擬指針表
analog watch

表面
dial

廚房定時鐘
kitchen timer

煮蛋計時器（沙漏）
egg timer

數字式電子表
digital watch

指針
gnomon

日
sund

針影
shadow

鍾面
dial

液晶顯示屏
liquid crystal display

溫度的測量
MEASURE OF TEMPERATURE

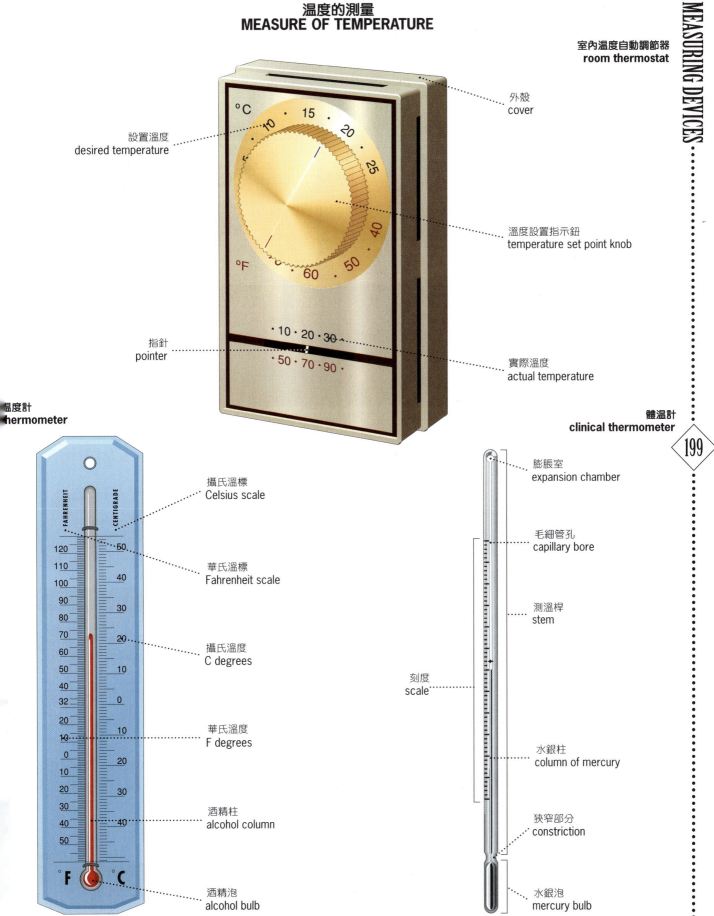

室內溫度自動調節器
room thermostat

外殼
cover

設置溫度
desired temperature

°C

°F

溫度設置指示鈕
temperature set point knob

指針
pointer

實際溫度
actual temperature

溫度計
thermometer

攝氏溫標
Celsius scale

華氏溫標
Fahrenheit scale

攝氏溫度
C degrees

華氏溫度
F degrees

酒精柱
alcohol column

酒精泡
alcohol bulb

FAHRENHEIT   CENTIGRADE

F   C

體溫計
clinical thermometer

膨脹室
expansion chamber

毛細管孔
capillary bore

測溫桿
stem

刻度
scale

水銀柱
column of mercury

狹窄部分
constriction

水銀泡
mercury bulb

重量的測量
MEASURE OF WEIGHT

等臂天平
balance

刻度盤
dial

指針
pointer

砝碼
weight

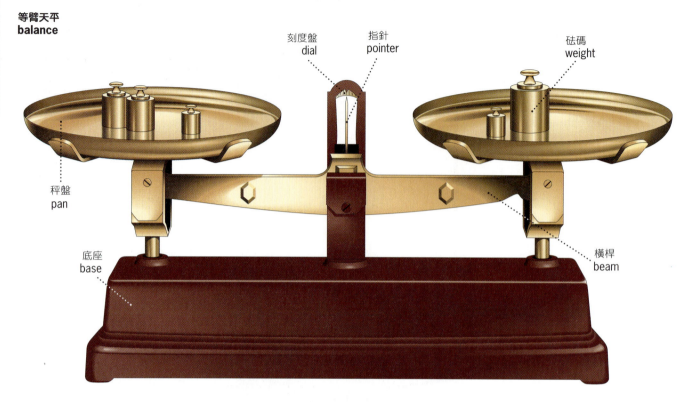

秤盤
pan

底座
base

橫桿
beam

桿秤
steelyard

滑動秤砣
sliding weight

刻度
notch

游標尺
vernier scale

秤盤
pan

橫桿
beam

刻度尺
graduated scale

底座
base

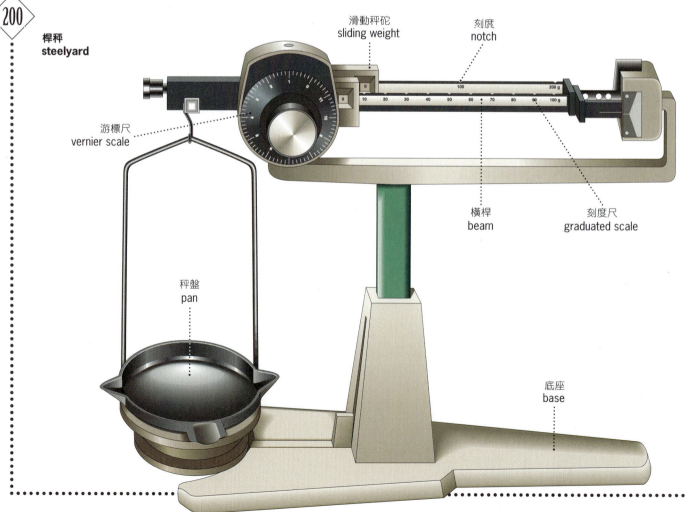

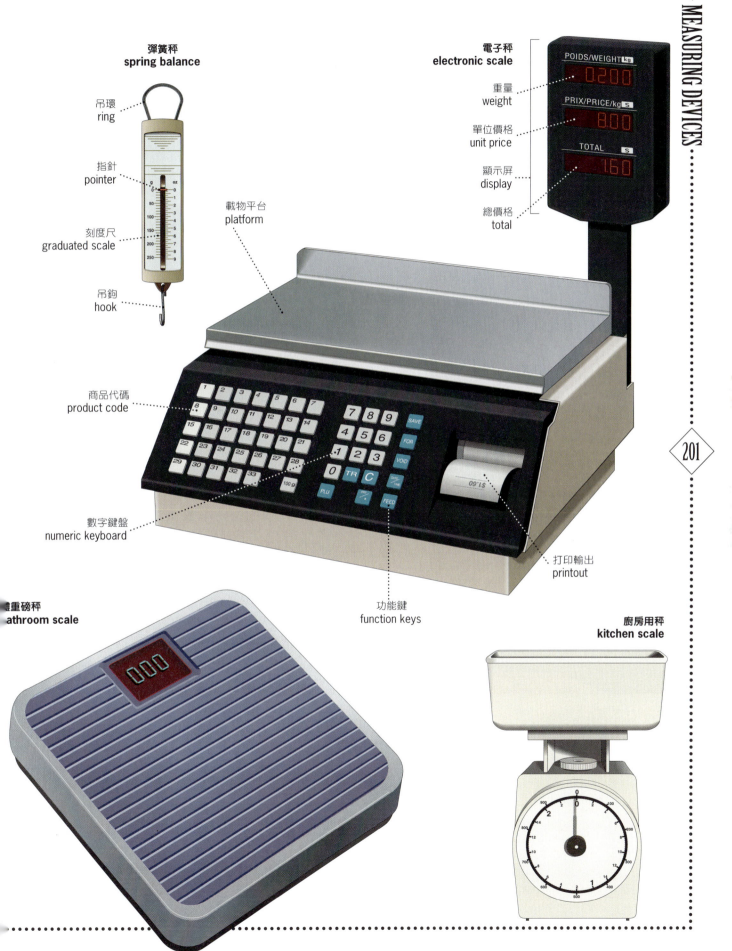

彈簧秤
spring balance

吊環
ring

指針
pointer

刻度尺
graduated scale

吊鉤
hook

載物平台
platform

電子秤
electronic scale

POIDS/WEIGHT kg
0200

重量
weight

PRIX/PRICE/kg $
8.00

單位價格
unit price

TOTAL $
160

顯示屏
display

總價格
total

商品代碼
product code

數字鍵盤
numeric keyboard

功能鍵
function keys

打印輸出
printout

體重磅秤
athroom scale

000

廚房用秤
kitchen scale

原油
OIL

勘探
PROSPECTING

地面勘探
surface prospecting

鑽探
DRILLING

鑽機
drilling rig

地面輸送
GROUND TRANSPOR

管道
pipeline

油罐拖車
tank trailer / road traile

近海勘探
offshore prospecting / offshore drilling

生產平台
production platform

海上輸
MARITIME TRANSPOR

衝擊波
shock wave

測震記錄
seismographic recording

集油層
petroleum trap

炸藥裝置
blasting charge

海底管道
submarine pipeline

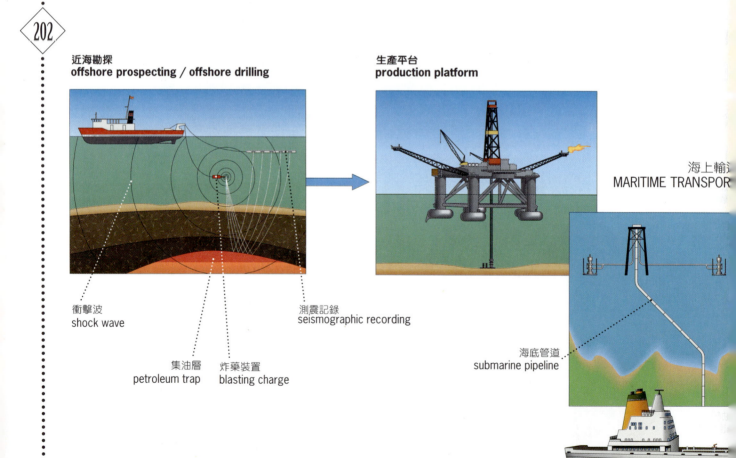

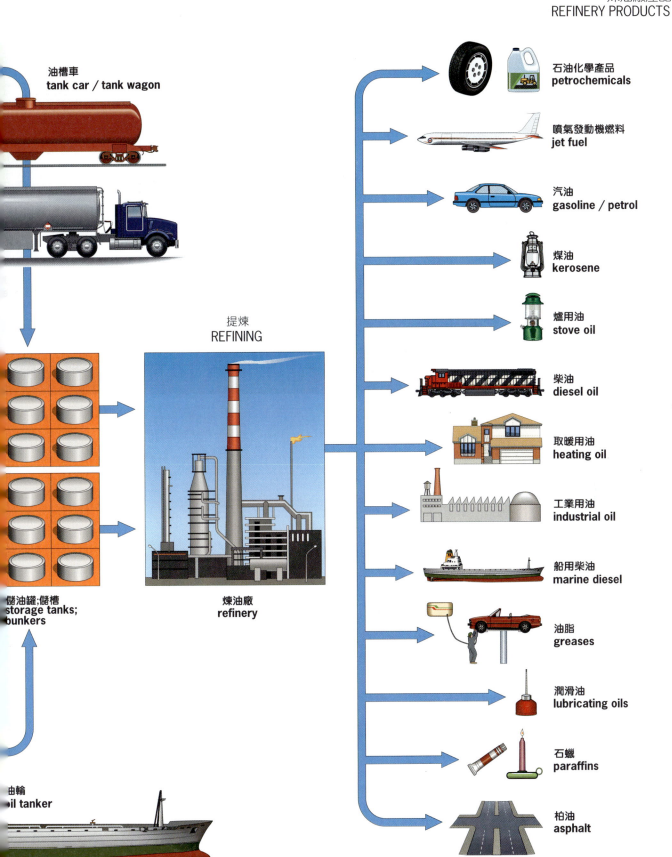

油槽車
tank car / tank wagon

提煉
REFINING

儲油罐;儲槽
storage tanks;
bunkers

煉油廠
refinery

油輪
oil tanker

石油化學產品
petrochemicals

噴氣發動機燃料
jet fuel

汽油
gasoline / petrol

煤油
kerosene

爐用油
stove oil

柴油
diesel oil

取暖用油
heating oil

工業用油
industrial oil

船用柴油
marine diesel

油脂
greases

潤滑油
lubricating oils

石蠟
paraffins

柏油
asphalt

水力能源
HYDROELECTRIC ENERGY

水力綜合示意圖
hydroelectric complex

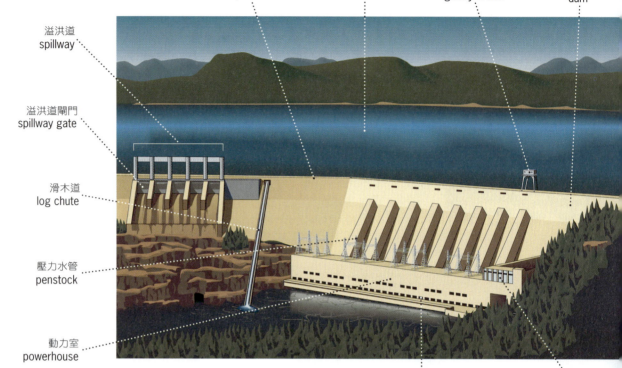

溢洪道
spillway

溢洪道閘門
spillway gate

滑木道
log chute

壓力水管
penstock

動力室
powerhouse

壩頂
top of dam

水庫
reservoir

龍門起重機
gantry crane

大壩
dam

主機房
machine hall

控制室
control room

水力發電站橫截面示意圖
cross section of hydroelectric power station

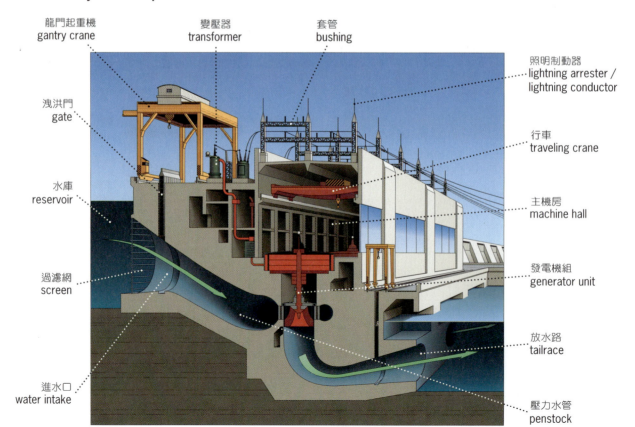

龍門起重機
gantry crane

變壓器
transformer

套管
bushing

洩洪門
gate

水庫
reservoir

過濾網
screen

進水口
water intake

照明制動器
lightning arrester /
lightning conductor

行車
traveling crane

主機房
machine hall

發電機組
generator unit

放水路
tailrace

壓力水管
penstock

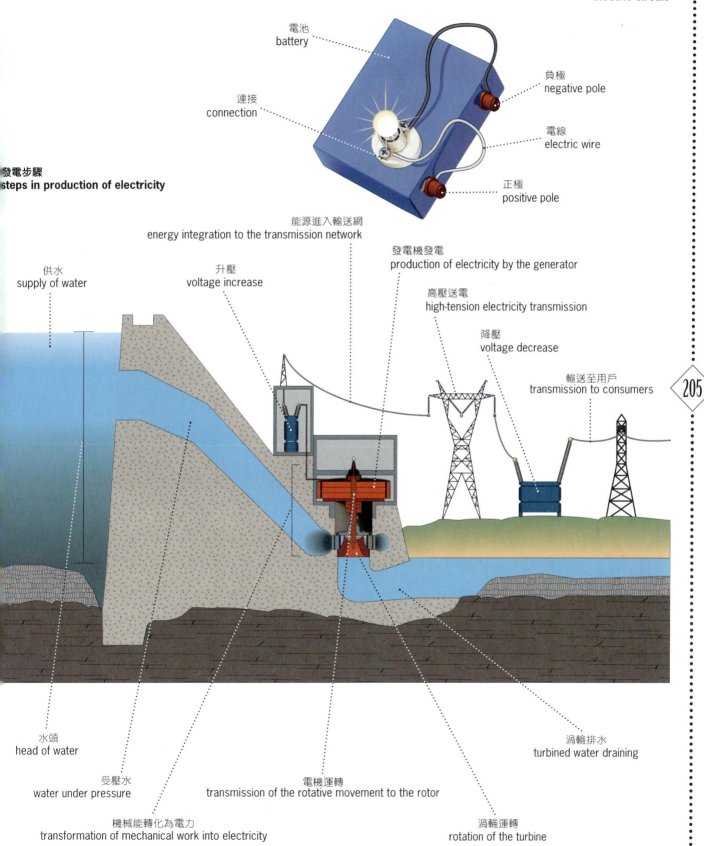

能源

ENERGY

電路
electric circuit

電池
battery

連接
connection

負極
negative pole

電線
electric wire

正極
positive pole

發電步驟
steps in production of electricity

能源進入輸送網
energy integration to the transmission network

發電機發電
production of electricity by the generator

高壓送電
high-tension electricity transmission

供水
supply of water

升壓
voltage increase

降壓
voltage decrease

輸送至用戶
transmission to consumers

205

水頭
head of water

渦輪排水
turbined water draining

受壓水
water under pressure

電機運轉
transmission of the rotative movement to the rotor

機械能轉化為電力
transformation of mechanical work into electricity

渦輪運轉
rotation of the turbine

核能
NUCLEAR ENERGY

核能發電站
nuclear power station

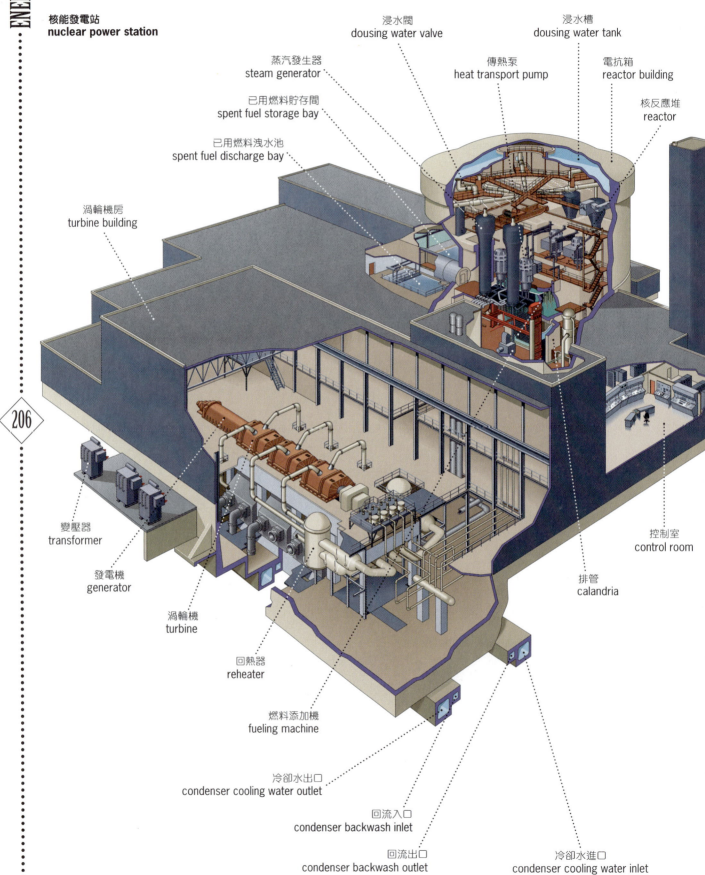

浸水閥
dousing water valve

浸水槽
dousing water tank

蒸汽發生器
steam generator

傳熱泵
heat transport pump

電抗箱
reactor building

已用燃料貯存間
spent fuel storage bay

核反應堆
reactor

已用燃料洩水池
spent fuel discharge bay

渦輪機房
turbine building

變壓器
transformer

發電機
generator

渦輪機
turbine

回熱器
reheater

燃料添加機
fueling machine

冷卻水出口
condenser cooling water outlet

回流入口
condenser backwash inlet

回流出口
condenser backwash outlet

冷卻水進口
condenser cooling water inlet

控制室
control room

排管
calandria

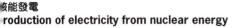

核能發電
production of electricity from nuclear energy

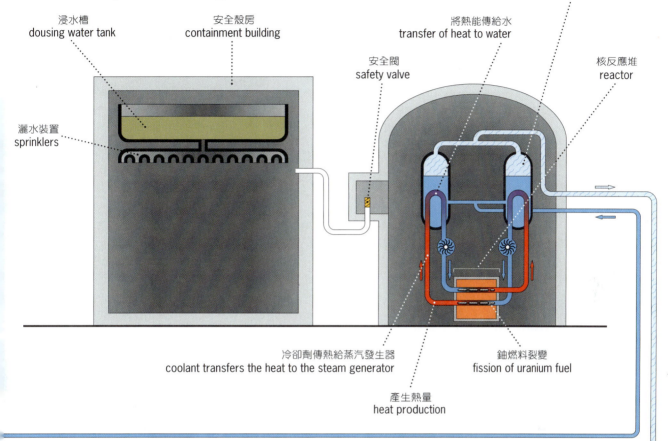

浸水槽
dousing water tank

安全殼房
containment building

水轉化為蒸汽
water turns into steam

將熱能傳給水
transfer of heat to water

核反應堆
reactor

安全閥
safety valve

灑水裝置
sprinklers

冷卻劑傳熱給蒸汽發生器
coolant transfers the heat to the steam generator

鈾燃料裂變
fission of uranium fuel

產生熱量
heat production

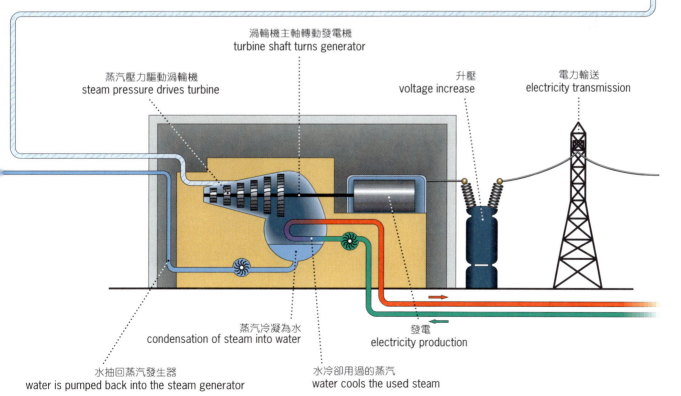

渦輪機主軸轉動發電機
turbine shaft turns generator

蒸汽壓力驅動渦輪機
steam pressure drives turbine

升壓
voltage increase

電力輸送
electricity transmission

蒸汽冷凝為水
condensation of steam into water

發電
electricity production

水抽回蒸汽發生器
water is pumped back into the steam generator

水冷卻用過的蒸汽
water cools the used steam

太陽能
SOLAR ENERGY

太陽能電池板
solar panel

太陽能電
solar ce

電池板外框
frame

太陽輻射
solar radiation

電
electric circu

玻璃
glass

白熾燈泡;電燈泡
incandescent lamp; light bulb

保險絲
fuse

端子箱
terminal box

二極管
diode

正電接頭
positive contact

負電接頭
negative contact

電池
battery

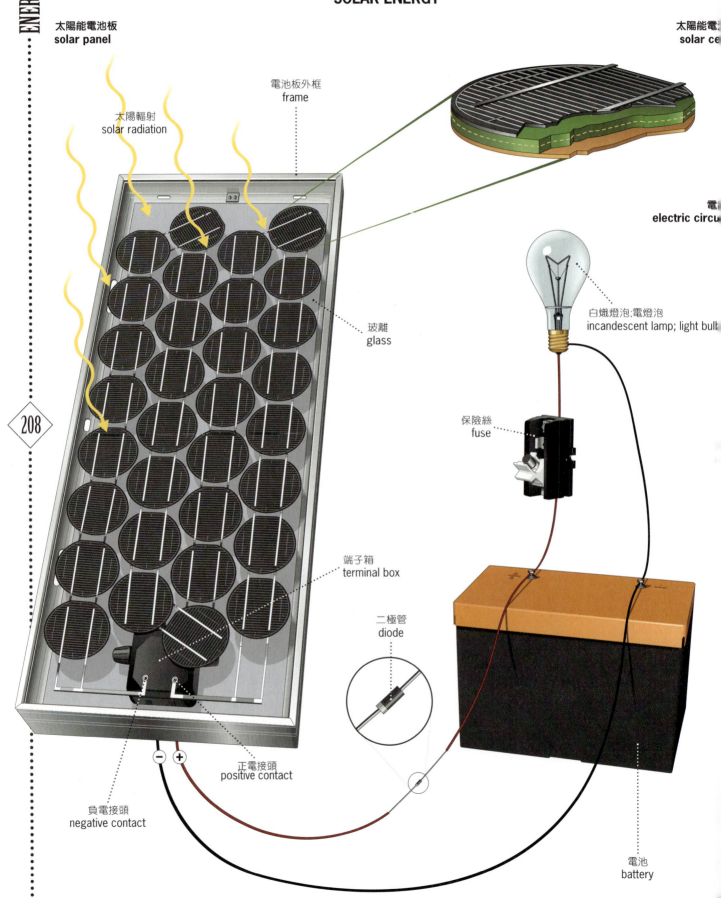

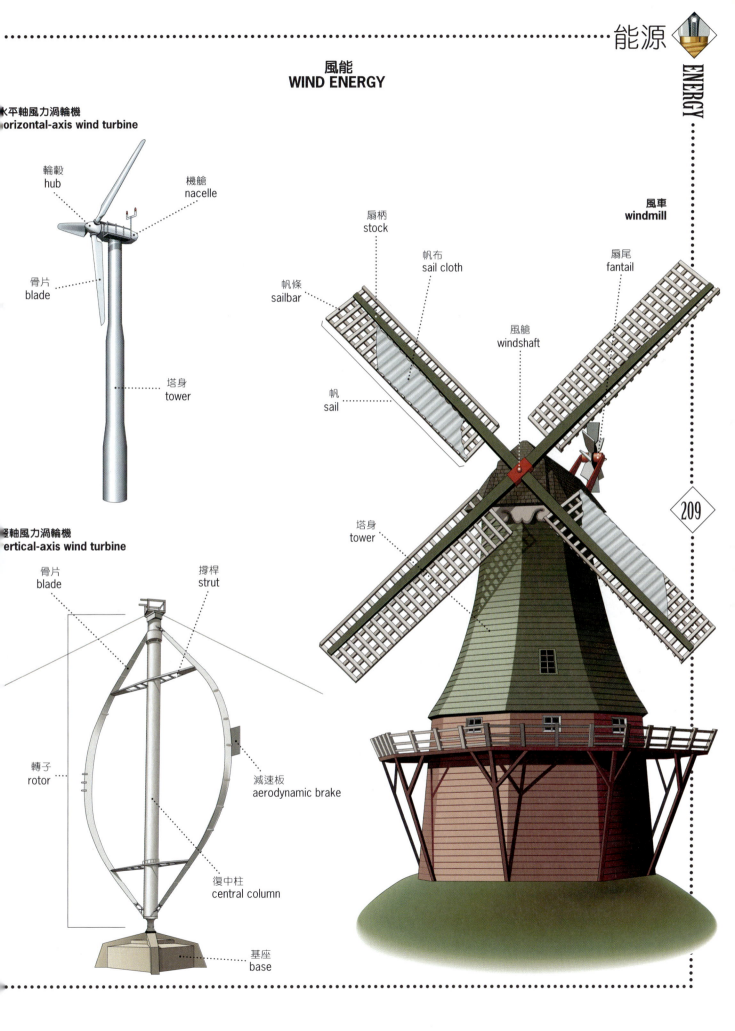
風能
WIND ENERGY

水平軸風力渦輪機
orizontal-axis wind turbine

輪轂
hub

機艙
nacelle

骨片
blade

塔身
tower

豎軸風力渦輪機
vertical-axis wind turbine

骨片
blade

撐桿
strut

轉子
rotor

減速板
aerodynamic brake

復中柱
central column

基座
base

風車
windmill

扇柄
stock

帆布
sail cloth

帆條
sailbar

扇尾
fantail

風艙
windshaft

帆
sail

塔身
tower

防火
FIRE PREVENTION

消防軟管
fire hose

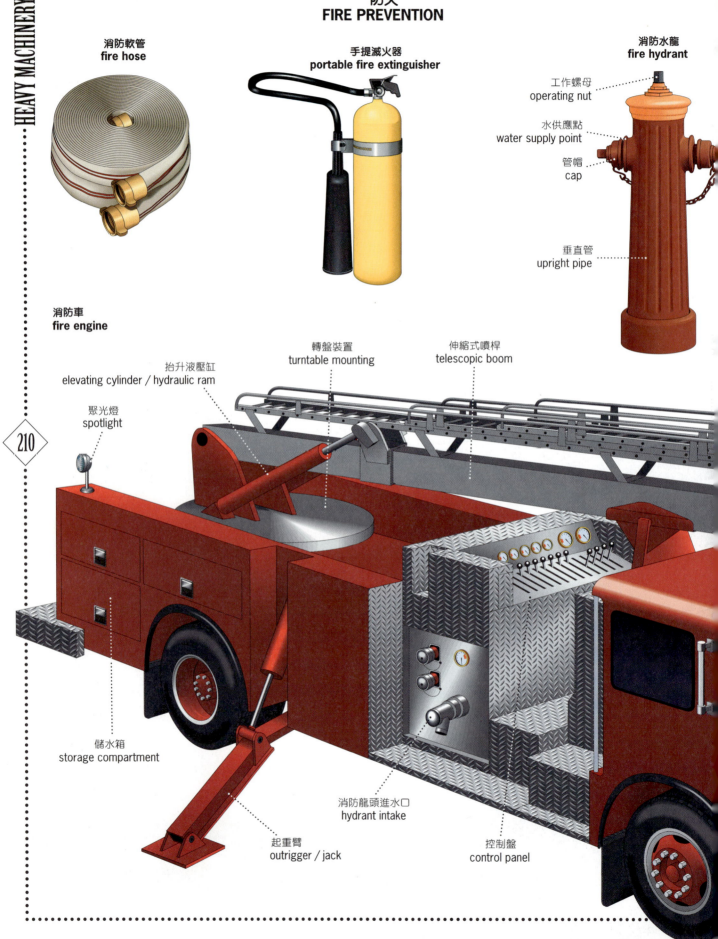

手提滅火器
portable fire extinguisher

消防水龍
fire hydrant

工作螺母
operating nut

水供應點
water supply point

管帽
cap

垂直管
upright pipe

消防車
fire engine

抬升液壓缸
elevating cylinder / hydraulic ram

轉盤裝置
turntable mounting

伸縮式噴桿
telescopic boom

聚光燈
spotlight

儲水箱
storage compartment

起重臂
outrigger / jack

消防龍頭進水口
hydrant intake

控制盤
control panel

吊桿
pike pole

消防人員
fire-fighter

空氣壓縮缸
compressed-air cylinder

消防輕便斧
fire-fighter's hatchet / fireman's axe

頭盔
helmet

全面罩
full face mask

自給式氧氣呼吸機
self-contained breathing apparatus

供氧管
air-supply tube

苔梯
ower ladder

閃光燈
flashing light

頂梯
top ladder

預警裝置
warning device

梯管噴嘴
ladder pipe nozzle

防火抗浸服
fireproof and waterproof garment

膠靴
rubber boot

重型車輛
HEAVY VEHICLES

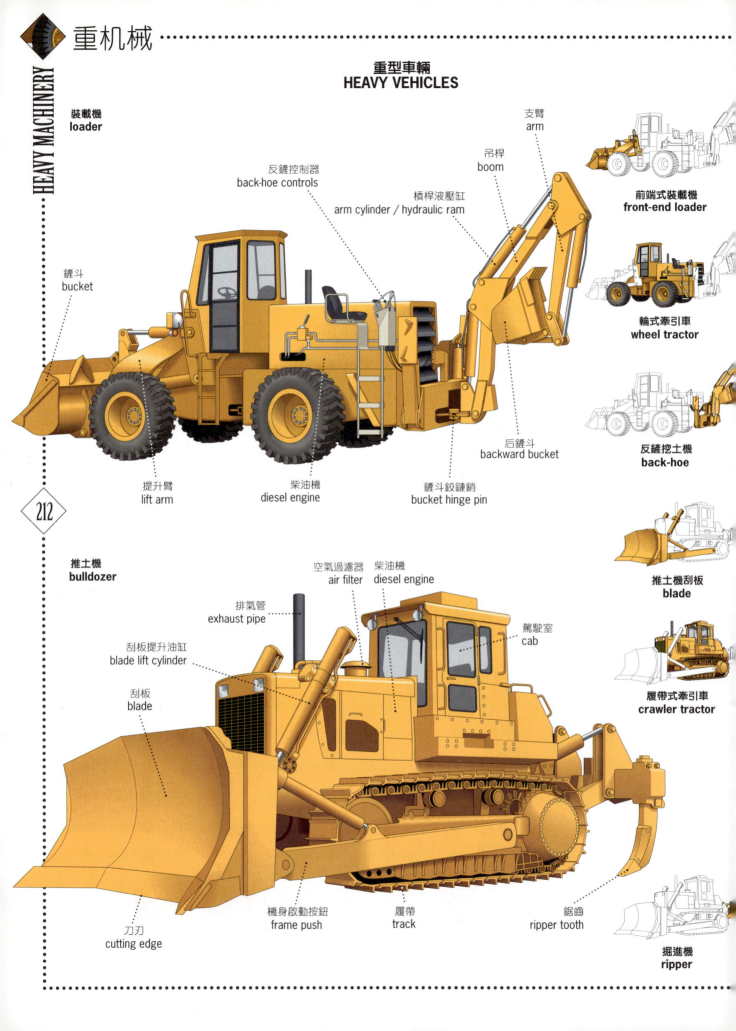

装載機
loader

反鏟控制器
back-hoe controls

槓桿液壓缸
arm cylinder / hydraulic ram

吊桿
boom

支臂
arm

鏟斗
bucket

提升臂
lift arm

柴油機
diesel engine

后鏟斗
backward bucket

鏟斗鉸鏈銷
bucket hinge pin

212

前端式裝載機
front-end loader

輪式牽引車
wheel tractor

反鏟挖土機
back-hoe

推土機
bulldozer

排氣管
exhaust pipe

刮板提升油缸
blade lift cylinder

刮板
blade

空氣過濾器
air filter

柴油機
diesel engine

駕駛室
cab

機身啟動按鈕
frame push

履帶
track

鋸齒
ripper tooth

刀刃
cutting edge

推土機刮板
blade

履帶式牽引車
crawler tractor

掘進機
ripper

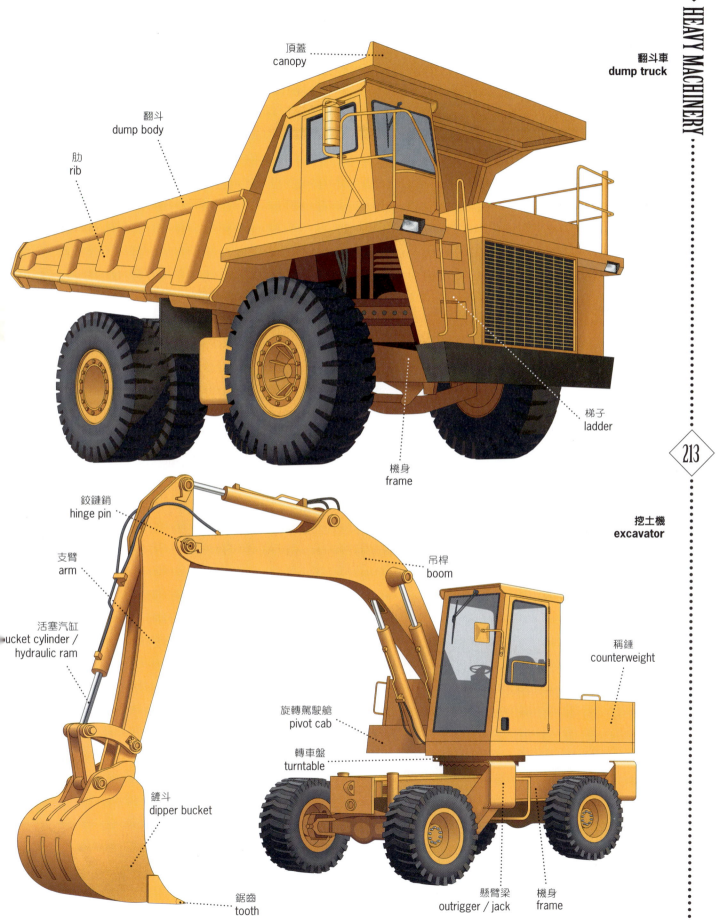

頂蓋
canopy

翻斗車
dump truck

翻斗
dump body

肋
rib

梯子
ladder

機身
frame

鉸鏈銷
hinge pin

挖土機
excavator

支臂
arm

吊桿
boom

活塞汽缸
ucket cylinder /
hydraulic ram

稱錘
counterweight

旋轉駕駛艙
pivot cab

鏟斗
dipper bucket

轉車盤
turntable

鋸齒
tooth

懸臂梁
outrigger / jack

機身
frame

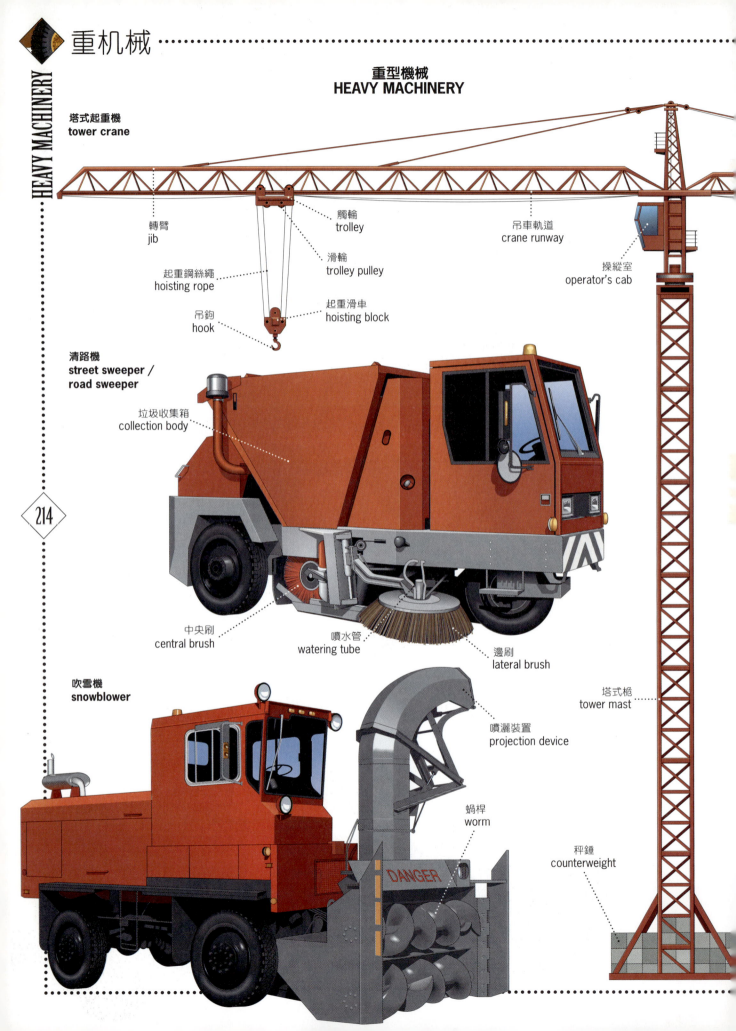

重型機械
HEAVY MACHINERY

塔式起重機
tower crane

轉臂
jib

觸輪
trolley

滑輪
trolley pulley

起重鋼絲繩
hoisting rope

吊車軌道
crane runway

操縱室
operator's cab

吊鉤
hook

起重滑車
hoisting block

清路機
**street sweeper /
road sweeper**

垃圾收集箱
collection body

中央刷
central brush

噴水管
watering tube

邊刷
lateral brush

塔式桅
tower mast

吹雪機
snowblower

噴灑裝置
projection device

蝸桿
worm

秤錘
counterweight

DANGER

上拉桿
jib tie

抗旋鎮重物
counterjib ballast

封隔器主體
packer body

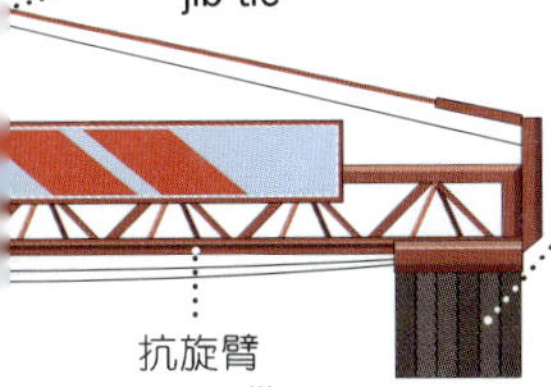

垃圾車
sanitation truck / refuse lorry

抗旋臂
counterjib

裝貨斗
loading hopper

伸縮式吊桿
telescopic boom

抬升液壓缸
elevating cylinder /
hydraulic ram

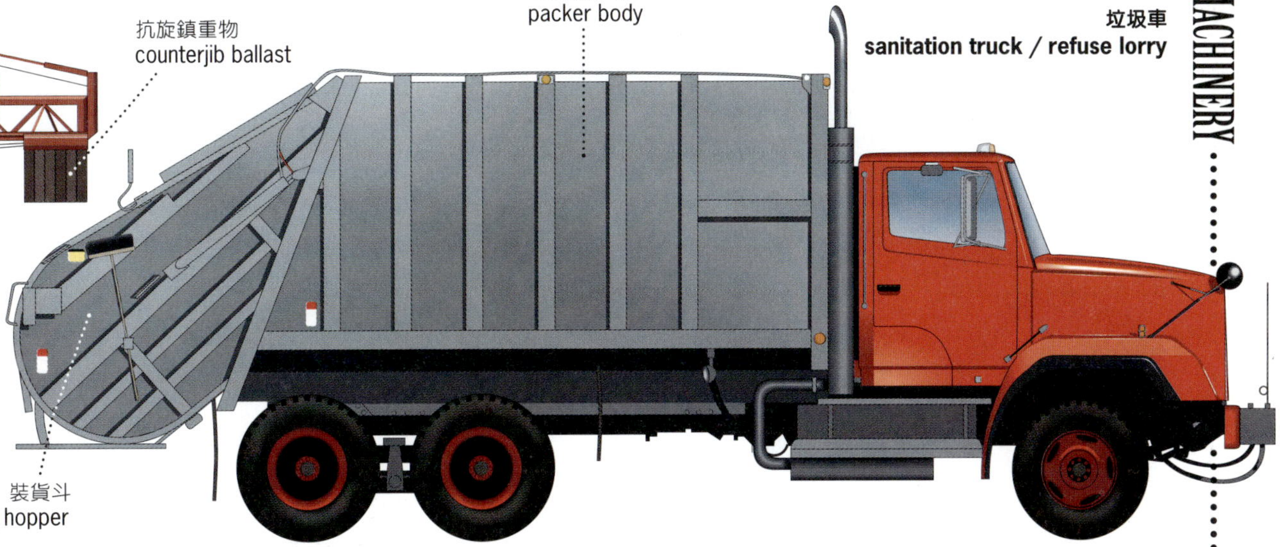

卡車起重機
truck crane / mobile crane

懸臂梁
outrigger / jack

215

吊桿；構架
boom

抬升液壓缸
elevating cylinder /
hydraulic ram

絞盤
winch

拖車
tow truck / recover lorry

纜繩
cable

吊鉤
hook

牽引裝置
towing device

絞盤控制器
winch controls

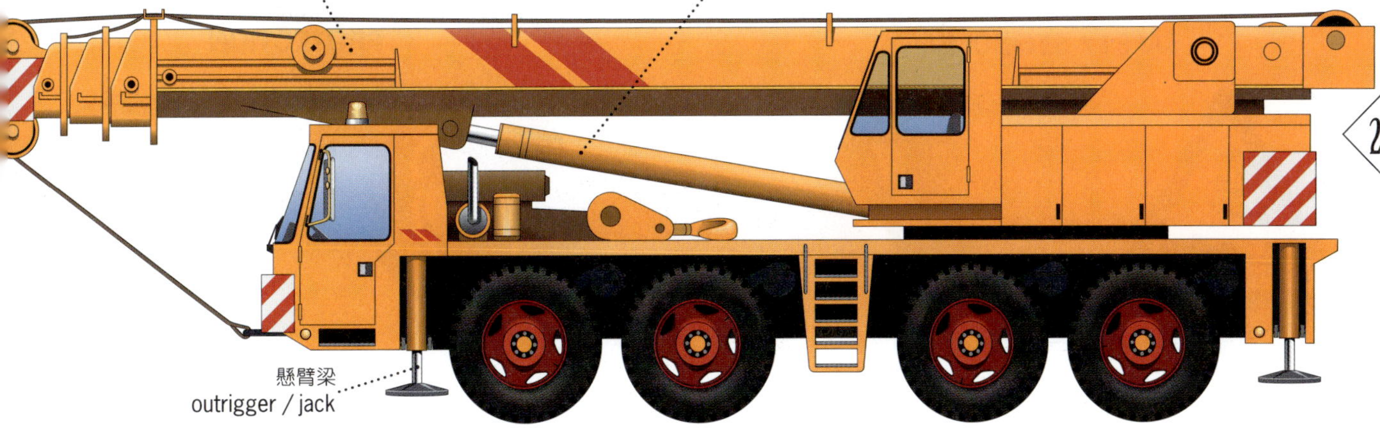

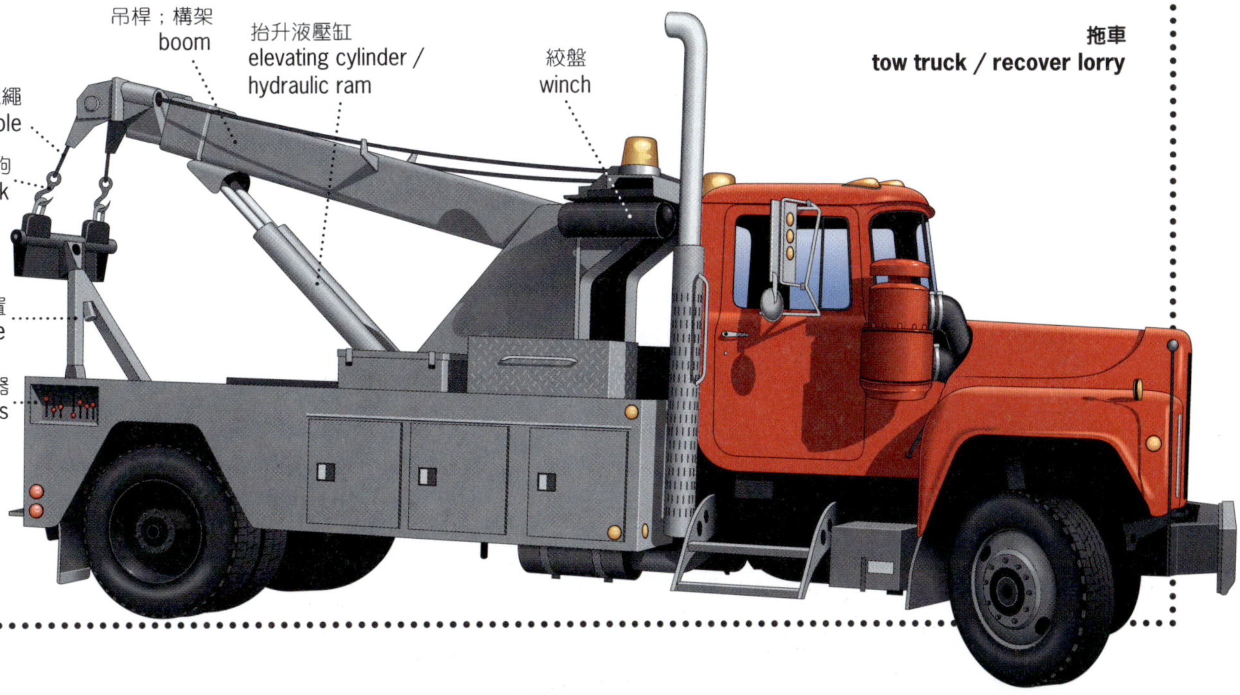

標識 ·

通用標識
COMMON SYMBOLS

女洗手間
women's rest room /
women's toilet

男洗手間
men's rest room /
men's toilet

輪椅通道
wheelchair access

醫院
hospital

電話
telephone

禁止吸煙
no smoking

露營地
camping (tent)

禁止露營
camping prohibited

交叉點停車
stop at intersection

安全標識
SAFETY SYMBOLS

保護標識
PROTECTION

腐蝕性
corrosive

高壓電
electrical hazard

護眼
eye protection

護耳
ear protection

易爆
explosive

易燃
flammable

護頭
head protection

護手
hand protection

輻射
radioactive

劇毒
poisonous

護足
foot protection

呼吸系統保護
respiratory system
protection

The terms in **bold type** correspond to an illustration; those in CAPITALS indicate a title.

The terms in **bold type** correspond to an illustration; those in CAPITALS indicate a title.

The terms in **bold type** correspond to an illustration; those in CAPITALS indicate a title.

INDEX

The terms in **bold type** correspond to an illustration; those in CAPITALS indicate a title.

220

221

222

The terms in **bold type** correspond to an illustration; those in CAPITALS indicate a title.

224

The terms in **bold type** correspond to an illustration; those in CAPITALS indicate a title.

The terms in **bold type** correspond to an illustration; those in CAPITALS indicate a title.

The terms in **bold type** correspond to an illustration; those in CAPITALS indicate a title.

226
O
P

227

228

The terms in **bold type** correspond to an illustration; those in CAPITALS indicate a title.

The terms in **bold type** correspond to an illustration; those in CAPITALS indicate a title.

229

The terms in **bold type** correspond to an illustration; those in CAPITALS indicate a title.

terms in **bold type** correspond to an illustration; those in CAPITALS indicate a title.

The terms in **bold type** correspond to an illustration; those in CAPITALS indicate a title.